Christ-F.I.T. for the Journey

Discover Your Freedom In Transformation

Lisa McConnell

Contents

Foreword

*I*t is a joy to write this foreword for my wife and for this wonderful project. I have watched Lisa go through so much of the transformation detailed in this book. As we both look back over the years of our marriage, we agree that this transformation, and the continual process thereof, have produced some great fruit and made us people who love Jesus more.

When we got married we were just like many other couples. We thought we would live the "happily-ever-after" kind of life, but shortly into our marriage, we discovered we were two different people. We both brought different strengths, weaknesses, and unwanted baggage from our pasts into our happy little home. These things led to many emotional highs and lows in the early years of our marriage.

Lisa started this transformation process by asking God, "Who am I, and who do You say that I am?" Lisa realized God wanted to change *her*—not just her circumstances. Through that process, she was renewed, discovering that in the eyes of the Lord she was beautifully and wonderfully made with many untapped gifts. It was a journey that caused her to look inward and to realize the importance of our upward relationship with a Holy God. This is a journey that is not always comfortable. As Lisa calls it, the process is like "becoming untangled," or "peeling back the layers." Looking back on this, I know that the Holy Spirit was at work transforming Lisa. She was a willing participant in the process, going back to the kitchen table each morning for more spiritual nourishment–as she continues to do to this day.

As you work through this book, be prepared to do a lot of introspective work on your own heart. It is worth the effort! At the other end, you will find peace and joy in your life and in your relationships. Truly, there is nothing more beautiful than a free woman who is living in God's will. Man or woman, this is where we want to be in every area of our lives—transformed, alive, and free! It is exciting for me to live with this beautiful, free woman. Lisa is my bride forever… and I look forward to all that God has for us in the future.

- Ray McConnell

INTRODUCTION

This book was born from a desire to have a deeper and more meaningful relationship with Jesus Christ. I was frustrated by "doing" church on Sundays before muddling through life the rest of the week. I was baffled by how I could be so nice to friends and so short with my own family. It didn't make any sense to me, and it did not line up with the character of Jesus Christ. I was tired of using others' behaviors to justify my own bad attitudes and out-of-control reactions. I knew it was not God's will for me, yet no matter how hard I tried, I could not change myself. I needed to incorporate the salvation and wholeness of Jesus Christ into every area of my life—every day of my life. Thankfully, as I have opened my heart to Him, He has taught me how to crucify the flesh, the carnal unspiritual man, and thus divide soul from spirit. As I learn to obey and abide in Him, He continues to change me from one level of His glory to another.

I have a passion and desire to see people become F.I.T. in Christ as they journey through life. There is *Freedom in Transformation!* God wants each one of us to come to faith in Him, to grow in that faith, to become free from the things that entangle us, and to begin bearing real kingdom fruit. This is the process of transformation. Freedom in Christ is a process that requires each of us to live in God's Word and be submitted to the leadership of the Holy Spirit.

How about you? Is there any area of your life that you would like to see changed? If so, there is hope! God beckons you closer to Him so that He can change you from the inside out. It all begins the moment we realize the state of our sinful hearts and jump into the arms of Christ. This is the point of salvation: repenting of your sins, while believing in your heart and confessing with your mouth that Jesus Christ is Lord. Unfortunately, many of us do not move beyond this starting point. Numerous Christians are freed from the penalty of sin but lack power over the temptation of it. The result is that their soul remains entangled with Satan. Christ died to give us power over sin on a daily basis. He does not want us to live in bondage to sin. Don't misunderstand—sin does not die when we accept Christ as our Savior; we must learn how to die to sin by surrendering our self-will. By faith, with our spirit connected to the Holy Spirit, God teaches and empowers us to live out the resurrected life of Jesus Christ through His grace and our obedience.

I have learned that the area most in need of help is our soul, which consists of our mind, will, emotions, and attitudes. Our souls tell us what we want, think, and feel. God wants us to forfeit our soul and our will to Him so that He can renew our mind, align our will with His, and heal all of our unhealthy and unbridled emotions. The Holy Spirit graciously uses the Word of God to untangle and free us from destructive and wrong thought patterns, from speech that does not glorify Him, from attitudes and actions that oppose His character, and from desires that do not agree with His own.

Christ has put His very nature inside of us. It cannot come out of us unless God Himself cleanses and purifies the soul realm of our lives. We need to move beyond the often prolonged stage of infancy in Christ, which Paul called carnal Christianity. It refers to people who are going to Heaven and maybe even "doing the work of God,"—yet something is missing. Sin, divisions, bitterness, and strife are still at work within them. The result is constant failure, condemnation, and hypocrisy. Why? This type of believer continues to live according to the flesh. He or she has not surrendered their soul and self-will to the Holy Spirit's leading, allowing Him to take over their entire being. Jesus wants all of us to take off the old, selfish nature and put on the new nature of Christ, wrapped in love, justice, and His righteousness.

To be sure, many Christians don't even recognize what Satan is trying to do. The Bible tells us that he comes to steal, kill, and destroy (see John 10:10). Most of all, he wants to do away with the life of Christ in us by whatever means that he can. Satan attacks our souls through deceit, desire, and disappointment with full force. Using wrong mindsets, destructive thought patterns, negative emotions, adverse circumstances, hardships, fame, and sometimes even seemingly "perfect lives," he constantly undermines the truth, attacking our new nature and the fruit of the Spirit which God places in us when we accept Him as our Savior. Satan's greatest fear is for a believer to really believe how much Jesus loves him and to accept the new identity and nature that He has given him. But this process can only happen as you partner with the Holy Spirit, thus allowing the new nature and the fruit of the Spirit to mature within your spirit, soul, and body.

Through this book, you will learn about the tactics of the enemy, how he constantly is trying to scheme and deceive us. But most importantly, you will learn the ways and the will of Christ. You will learn how to become undone from the skewed filtering system of your past and to become aligned to the mind and ways of Christ. You will learn to believe and say what the Bible says about you. God has a good plan for all of us, but we won't find it by merely wishing for it! We must make the decision to agree with Him in spirit, soul, and body.

The truth is that Jesus longs to possess our entire being, not just our spirits. He desires to uproot the old flesh-filled man while rooting and grounding us in love through the Holy Spirit's grace and power, coupled with our obedience. If we hunger and desire to see the resurrected power of Jesus Christ alive and working in our lives, we must live according to His Word and submit our self-will to His Holy Spirit daily. He is our teacher and our personal trainer. He will give us victory over sin and freedom from the past, from insecurities, and from all fears and doubts. Indeed, the Holy Spirit will teach us how to align our souls with God's heart.

As members of the body of Christ, we need to understand the New Covenant and what it means to be "in Christ." Each of us must learn to live our new life governed by the Holy Spirit not simply following a bunch of rules and laws. We can do nothing to earn God's love, but we do have a part to play in claiming His promises. We must learn to see ourselves as dead to our old nature, including; sin, selfishness, Satan, and the system of this world. We need to learn to be obedient and attentive to Christ and His system, which is based on His love, grace and truth. I aspire to see every person in the body of Christ embrace the love of Jesus, and thus affecting the world.

I suggest that you read the material in this book slowly without rushing through it. Let God use it to bring about change in your heart and deepen your personal relationship with Him. Perhaps you'd like to start in prayer, asking God's Spirit to guide and teach you as you proceed through the book. You might find it helpful to have a pen and journal close by. When you read something that speaks to your spirit, write it down and meditate on it. Then begin to put it into practice through obedience. Whether you use this book as a personal devotional or as a group study, make sure to allow ample time to process the information.

I pray that, with the help of this book, you become strong, bold, and confident in Christ. May you become a vessel F.I.T. for God's service. May you become a funnel through which the love, grace and truth of Jesus Christ flows freely. Jesus loves you! Begin by believing for yourself that He loves you right where you are. That includes every failure, imperfection, and insecurity that you think you may have. By remaining in His Word and obeying the leading of the Holy Spirit, you will see Him change you from one level of glory to another! Give Him your soul, self-will and desires and put on that robe of righteousness that He died to give you.

- Lisa McConnell

PART ONE:

Recognizing
The Work Of Satan
In Our Lives

Chapter 1

Sin:
A Force Emanating from Satan

———————————◆———————————

*S*in is an unwelcome word in our modern vocabulary, causing eyes to roll and people to claim innocence or become offended. Nevertheless, Romans 3:23 tells us that, "all have sinned and fallen short of the glory of God" (NIV). What, then, is this thing called sin, of which every person is guilty? According to the *World's Bible Dictionary,* to sin is to "miss the mark and to fall short of a divine standard. It is unbelief and rejects the truth God has revealed. It is ungodliness, and makes a person guilty before God."[1]

Sin occurs when:
1. You knowingly do what is wrong.
2. You knowingly don't do what is right.
3. You do wrong out of ignorance.
4. You disobey.

In order to recognize personal sin, there are two questions to ask yourself:
1. What mark did I miss?
2. How did I fall short?

To understand the desperate situation resulting from sin in our lives, we need to realize that God has set a standard for all of us through His Holy Law, as illustrated in the Ten Commandments.

The Ten Commandments were designed to awaken our consciousness of sin and to make it clear that we have all offended a Holy God by our inability to do what the Law says. Thus, we have all grossly violated God's standard, and we have all missed the mark. As a result, people are separated from God, deserving of eternal death, and in dire need of a Savior. Romans 6:23 states it like this, "For the wages which sin pays is death, but the [bountiful] free gift of God is eternal life through [in union with] Jesus Christ our Lord." This is the reality: Sin exists whether we acknowledge it or not. Failure to acknowledge this truth results in eternal damnation with Satan.

What remedy exists then for sin? Unfortunately, there is *nothing within us* and *nothing we can do* to conquer this sin. However, God has provided a way for our deliverance. The first step is to receive Christ as our personal Savior. If you have never prayed to receive the salvation Christ offers, please refer to the prayer in Appendix A in the back of this book for assistance in this important first step.

In Romans 7:24-25, Paul declares, "O unhappy and pitiable and wretched man that I am! Who will release and deliver me from [the shackles of] this body of death? Oh thank God! [He will!] Through Jesus Christ (the Anointed One) our Lord!"

Romans 7:7-8 says,

> . . . if it had not been for the Law, I should not have recognized sin or have known its meaning. [For instance] I would not have known about covetousness [would have had no consciousness of sin or sense of guilt] if the Law had not [repeatedly] said, you shall not covet and have an evil desire [for one thing and another]. But sin, finding opportunity in the commandment [to express itself], got a hold on me and aroused and stimulated all kinds of forbidden desires (lust, covetousness). For without the Law sin is dead [the sense of it is inactive and a lifeless thing].

Galatians 3:24 shows us the purpose of the Law: "So that the Law served [to us Jews] as our trainer [our guardian, our guide to Christ, to lead us] until Christ [came], that we might be justified (declared righteous, put in right standing with God) by and through faith." Please understand that the Law was never meant to give us "right-standing," (righteousness) with God. It is only as we place our faith in Christ and become partakers of what He accomplished for us on the cross that we are saved. The Law shows us our sin and our need for a Savior. God answered with loving grace that only comes from Jesus.

There are two distinct forces at work in this world, and both seek to rule our hearts. One is for evil, and the other is for good. They are:

1. Sin—the force that emanates from Satan and brings death.
2. Grace—the force that emanates from Christ and offers eternal life.

God had a plan for us from the beginning of time, and He revealed this plan in Genesis 1:26-31. He created men and women to reflect His glory. He entrusted mankind with the ability to display His character through our lives. God created the world for us to live in and He gave us dominion over it. However, we chose independence from God instead of dependence on Him and His Word. In the Garden of Eden, Satan tempted Eve to doubt God's goodness, and persuaded her to focus on what God had not given her as opposed to all He had given her. Satan implied that God selfishly did not want Adam and Eve to share in His knowledge of good and evil. Adam and Eve doubted God's love and care for them, which led to sin. God gives us the power of choice and calls it "free will." Men and women were created to be vessels through which God's Spirit might flow. Being made in God's image is the basis of our self-worth. But we often choose to depend on an ever-changing worldly standard for our self-worth instead. Satan wants to bring about death in every area of our lives—physically, mentally, spiritually, financially, relationally, and socially. Jesus, on the other hand, brings life to us in each of these areas.

Deuteronomy 30:19 says, "I call heaven and earth to witness this day against you that I have set before you life and death, the blessings, and the curses; therefore choose life that you and your descendants may live." God gives us the choice. He grants us the privilege of choosing which source of power we will allow to live through us. In order to understand that choice, we need to know the two paths before us. One leads to death. The other leads to eternal life and victory, starting now.

Who Is Satan and What Is His Purpose?

Satan wants to keep all people separated from God. He desires to steal, kill, devour, and destroy everything that God offers and desires for your life (John 10:10; 1 Peter 5:8). Satan is a master of deception. By cloaking lies as "suggestions" and falsehoods as "options," he wants you to entertain his ideas, so that he might begin to spin his web of bondage. By gaining a foothold in your mind, he will gain an entrance into your life. When you believe his lies, they become strongholds in your mind, intended to rob you of the fellowship and blessings of God in your life.

> **Satan is a master of deception by making**
> **"suggestions" in your mind.**
> **If these lies are entertained and**
> **believed, he begins to spin his web**
> **of bondage within your life.**

For example, Satan may suggest that you are worthless and no good. Situations and circumstances in your life might even seem to back that up. However, the Word of God says something altogether different. God says that you are fearfully and wonderfully made. He has a plan for your life—a plan for good and not evil, a plan to prosper you. He even calls you the righteousness of God in Christ! (See Psalm 139:14-15; Jeremiah 29:11; 2 Corinthians 5:21.)

Friends, it is a sin not to speak and think well of yourself in a balanced way! Most Christians struggle with the lies that Satan suggests regarding themselves. Remember: Satan is called the father of lies (John 8:44). Sin is intended to bring about destruction. It does this by shifting our focus, attention, and devotion from God and His Word to self, other people, drugs, food, money, sex, power, bad habits, wrong mindsets, negative attitudes, and so forth. These are all designed to keep you fixed on something other than God (see Romans 1:23).

Satan wants to steal the fruit of the Spirit that God has placed within you. This is love, joy, peace, patience, kindness, goodness, faithfulness, gentleness, and self-control (see Galatians 5:22-23). He also desires to keep you from following the Word and ways of God by keeping your focus on situations and circumstances. Satan wants to destroy the hope and the light of God in you. Finally, he wants to hold you in the grip of fear, while God desires for you to be alive in faith.

Questions for Study

1. What is the definition of sin and from whom does sin emanate?
2. What are the two questions you need to ask yourself regarding sin?
3. What is the purpose of the Law?
4. According to Romans 7:24-25, who is the only One able to rescue and deliver you from the sin you cannot conquer?

5. By nature, sin is designed to shift your focus, attention, and devotion from God to a vice or object of lust. What are the objects Satan uses? Which objects are personal struggles for you?

6. How does a stronghold develop in your mind and life? Ask the Lord to show you any strongholds that might be at work within you.

7. Satan wants you to believe lies about yourself to keep you in bondage to him. What lies have you believed? What does God's Word say about you? Start saying and believing the things that God Himself has declared regarding who you are in Him (see Psalm 139:14-15; Jeremiah 29:11; 2 Corinthians 5:21).

Personal Prayer

Lord, I know that I have fallen short of demonstrating the glory You have intended for me (Romans 3:23). Forgive me of my sins. I receive Your forgiveness. Thank You for rescuing me and for delivering me from a life of sin and eternal damnation. Help me now to live the life You intended for me to live. Sever my ties to sin, selfishness, and the system of the world. Help me to walk in Your ways. Lord, I know that I cannot overcome sin by being "good," but I can overcome sin with the help of Your Holy Spirit, teaching and leading me. Help me to submit my ways to Yours by declaring myself dead to sin and alive in Christ (Romans 6:8). Thank You for Your promise to complete the good work which You have started in me (Philippians 1:6).

Chapter 2

Sin:
Its Effect in the Believer's Life

———————◦———————

*S*atan uses sin like quicksand in a person's life. Though at first it may not feel like you are stepping in very deep, you can quickly find yourself in over your head. He is a masterful liar who will tempt you to believe something that deviates, *ever so slightly,* from the truth. The progression often looks something like this:

- Stage 1: You compromise the truth and believe a lie. Over time you become numb to it and no longer recognize or consider it a lie.
- Stage 2: Satan subjects you to another deviation from the truth, building on the previous lie. Again, over time you become numb to it. At this point, you are now "knee deep" in Satan's quicksand.
- Stage 3: You have turned this particular area of your mind over to Satan by believing his lies further. At this point you may totally abandon the truth and begin to pattern your actions and behaviors according to his lies, without even an alarm flashing in your conscience. You are bound by the quicksand and may feel unable or unwilling to escape its deadly grip.
- Stage 4: The stronghold of bondage has been fully developed, allowing Satan to pull you under and have complete control over you in this area of your life.

If you take a step back to see what sets this process in motion, you will find the root cause. It all starts with ignorance, or the compromising of God's truth, which is found in His Word. As a result, you give in to the temptation from Satan. This leads to *temporary* gratification but ultimately to slavery. Eventually, your life (what you think, speak, and believe) is patterned according to the lie Satan suggested to you.

There are two important things you need to remember regarding the schemes of Satan: First, he will never make it obvious to you that he is out to deceive you and steal the life God gave you. He will never ring your doorbell and say, "Hi, I'm Satan and I'm here to ruin your life, may I please come in? Second Corinthians 11:14 states that, "Satan masquerades as an angel of light." He is constantly working to entice and deceive. He is always seeking entry in areas of weakness and imbalance. Second, Satan never reveals the consequences of a person's wrong choices. Even in the Garden of Eden, he was quick to suggest, "You will not surely die!" (See Genesis 3:4.)

Consider the following story as an example:

Susan is married to John, but has been unhappy for some time because John is more interested in work and sports than he is in Susan. Mark and Susan work together and attend the same church, so they see each other every day and share a good friendship. Susan starts to flirt with Mark at work, thinking, *"It's not a big deal—we're just friends! Besides, it's nice to be noticed!"* Susan and Mark occasionally go to lunch together where they share their private lives with each other and seek the other's opinions about family, marriage, and so on. As he attempts to comfort Susan, Mark finds himself attracted to her. He realizes that he enjoys her company as well. Mark and Susan begin comforting each other in ways that God never intended for two already-married people. Over time, Mark and Susan find themselves in a serious relationship. They seek divorce from their respective spouses, and decide to marry each other.

Susan's downfall started innocently as she genuinely craved and needed her husband's love. But Susan's needs could only be truly fulfilled through her relationship with God first and foremost. She should have looked to Him and then to her marriage relationship with John to meet those needs. Both Susan and Mark chose to disobey God and let themselves become deceived and manipulated by Satan.

Satan's lies and manipulation result in stolen marriages, broken relationships, and destroyed lives. Indeed, the enemy comes to steal, kill, and destroy, and he is very patient in his effort to do so. Did Susan and Mark plan on this extramarital affair? No. One compromise and justification led to another, then another, which ultimately led to the death of two marriages and left only devastation and destruction in their wake.

**Satan's lies and manipulation result in stolen marriages,
broken relationships, and destroyed lives.**

This same scenario is true with anything you love more than God— your career, smoking, drinking, shopping, working, pornography, eating, or gossiping. The thing you yearn for may not even be considered a sin, but when you are controlled by the "thing," you become out of balance and now the "thing" owns you. Before you know it, Satan has developed a stronghold in your area of weakness and imbalance. We must to learn to recognize some of the lines that Satan uses to pull us into sin. They are:

- "This feels so good."
- "I've longed for this."
- "You're worthless and will never amount to anything."
- "Your circumstances will never change."
- "You can't even provide for your family."
- "Just a little won't hurt."
- "I've got to have more."

- "You deserve it . . . go ahead!"
- "If you could just get this one more thing you would have so much more power."
- "If you were just prettier, smarter, or not so heavy, you would get that promotion."
- "You aren't anything if you can't even keep up with your neighbors!"
- "You'd better have sex with him if you want to keep him."
- "Don't worry no one will get hurt; we're both adults."
- "This isn't fair; what about me?"
- "I'll get you back!"

But test and prove all things [until you can recognize] what is good; [to that] hold fast. Abstain from evil [shrink from it and keep aloof from it] *in whatever form or whatever kind it may be*. And may the God of peace Himself *sanctify you* through and through [separate you from profane things, make you pure and wholly consecrated to God]; and may your *spirit* and *soul* and *body* be preserved sound and complete [and found] blameless at the coming of our Lord Jesus Christ (the Messiah). (1 Thessalonians 5:21-23)

Questions for Study

1. Do you have a situation in your life where Satan's pull is like quicksand, attempting to bring about your destruction?
2. Ask the Holy Spirit to help you recognize any strongholds in your life.
3. Take a moment and ask the Holy Spirit to show you your weaknesses and any areas of compromise in your own life.
4. In your own words, what are the stages that follow when we compromise the truth?
5. What are some of Satan's favorite lines to use on people? Which have you fallen for?
6. In 1 Thessalonians 5:21-23, what are the three parts that make up each person? What does God hope to find in you at the return of Christ?
7. According to 1 John 1:9, what does God want you to do when you sin?

Personal Prayer

Lord, God of Peace, sanctify me through and through. Separate me from profane things; make me pure and wholly consecrated to You. May my spirit, soul, and body be healed and preserved. May I be found complete in You (1 Thessalonians 5:21-23). Help me to recognize the enemy's deceitful plots and plans that he uses to destroy me. Show me the areas in my life that need Your healing touch and divine guidance. Thank You for coming so that I may have life – You're Presence flowing through me – in abundance and to the full (John 10:10). Rid me of sin, Satan, sickness, selfishness, and the system of this world, making me a body wholly filled and flooded with You (Ephesians 3:19).

Chapter 3

Our Inner Lives–
Our Roots

s human beings we need to understand the way our bodies are made up. First Thessalonians 5:23 reveals human beings as tripartite: spirit, soul, and body. Trichotomy is the term describing this truth."[1]

First, we are a spirit. This is our innermost, eternal being that relates to God. It is sometimes referred to as our conscience, and it involves faith, hope, and love. Faith is assurance and stability and is fed by the Word of God. Hope is confidence and expectancy and is sustained by looking to Jesus. Love is communication and motivation and is nurtured by the flow of the Holy Spirit.[2]

The second part of our being is our soul. The soul tells us all about ourselves. This is our self-consciousness, made up of intellect, emotions, and will.[3]

We also live in a body. This is our world consciousness, which is made up of our senses, our well-being, and our appearance/actions. Our senses are what we see, touch, taste, smell, and hear. They may yield to indulgence and sensuality.[4]

At the point of salvation, the Spirit of God creates a new identity in us, and we become children of God (Romans 8:16). Instantly, the Spirit of God, His nature and all that He is, comes to live on the inside of us in the form of a seed (see 1 John 3:9). That is, God implants Himself and His nature—the fruit of His Spirit—inside of our spirits to be cultivated in our souls (mind, will, attitudes, and emotions). That seed then grows and blossoms out through our bodies through our actions and behaviors and into a lost world. Scripture states time and again that the things of this world are nothing in comparison to soul riches. Third John, verse two, says, "Beloved, I pray that you may prosper in every way and [that your body] may keep well, even as [I know] your soul keeps well and prospers." Similarly, Matthew 16:26 (NIV) asks, "What good will it be for a man if he gains the whole world, yet forfeits his soul? Or what can a man give in exchange for his soul?" In other words, riches, prestige, job promotions, big houses, and the like are worthless compared to the preservation of our souls. While you are here on this earth, the Lord God wants to redeem, renew, and restore you completely—spirit, soul, and body. Even after you are born again, with the seed of God living in your spirit, your soul needs healed, delivered and cleansed. It needs to be untangled from sin, selfishness, sickness, Satan, and the system of this world. Then God's presence, nature, and power will be manifested in our actions and behaviors. Until renewed, your soul and mine are rooted in sin.

Jesus said in Luke 6:44-45,

> For each tree is known and identified by its own fruit; for figs are not gathered from thorn bushes, nor is a cluster of grapes picked from a bramble bush. The upright (honorable, and intrinsically good) man out of the good treasure [stored] in his heart produces what is upright (honorable and intrinsically good), and the evil man out of the evil storehouse brings forth that which is depraved (wicked and intrinsically evil); for out of the abundance (overflow) of the heart his mouth speaks.

What is a root? A root is the base of something, or that which holds something in position. Think of a plant: the root secures the plant in the ground, draws water and nourishment from the soil, and also stores food. The type of plant is made clear by the fruit (or leaves) it produces. Compare this plant to a human being. A Christian's beliefs hold him secure. The soil of his soul nourishes him as his focus is on God and His Word. Thus, his actions and behaviors flow out of that soul-nourishment, revealing the type of new person he is. If someone's actions and behaviors are consistently negative and destructive, you can be sure that it is the roots that need to be dug up and planted in God's perspective and focus. The roots and the soil are the heart of the problem.

Our roots originate in four places.

1. Our upbringing.
2. The way we view ourselves.
3. The way we think others (i.e., our parents, siblings, peers, teachers, coaches) view us.
4. Our environment.

There are things about us that we have no power to change. We cannot change the events of our pasts, where we come from, or our upbringing. However, we can alter how we view these things, which can set the course for a healthy and balanced future! Once we are in Christ, we do not have to remain a product of our pasts.

Jesus makes it clear to His listeners that we cannot properly nurture and handle the new life that He puts in us while we hang on to our old lives. If we continue to fuel our hearts and souls with evil—our own way of thinking, speaking, and behaving, then our attitudes and behaviors will reflect these negative and destructive influences. Unless we change from the roots up, we will stunt the growth of the fruit of the Spirit and the presence of God in our lives.

> **Jesus makes it clear to His listeners that you cannot properly nurture and handle the new life He puts in you while hanging on to your old ways.**

Unfortunately, many Christians simply tack on proper "Christian" behavior instead of making their hearts pliable and ready for God's re-working.

> In Him also you were circumcised with circumcision not made with hands, but in a [spiritual] circumcision [performed by] Christ by stripping off the body of the flesh (the whole corrupt, carnal nature with its passions and lusts). [Thus you were circumcised when] you were buried with Him in [your] baptism, in which you were also raised with Him [to a new life] through [your] faith in the working of God [as was displayed] when He raised Him up from the dead. (Colossians 2:11-12)

Baptism parallels the death, burial, and resurrection of Christ, just as it does the death and burial of our old, sinful lives and resurrection into a new life with Christ. Jesus set us free from our evil desires through a spiritual operation performed on our hearts. He removed our old nature and gave us a new self. Sin did not die, but we must remain conscious of the fact that we are dead to sin and alive to Christ.

Questions for Study
1. What happens instantly at our spiritual rebirth?
2. What makes up your soul? From what must it be cleansed after rebirth?
3. According to Jesus, what ultimately dictates your words and actions?
4. What is a "root" in a human being? Where does it come from?
5. If the actions and behaviors of a person are consistently negative and destructive, what does this indicate?
6. If you are in Christ, you do not have to remain a _____ of your _____.
7. Rewrite Colossians 2:11-12 in your own words.

Personal Prayer
Lord, thank you, that I am dead to sin and alive to You. I realize that sin has not died, but that I have died to sin. I choose to live for You through the empowerment of Your Holy Spirit (Romans 6). I know that I cannot properly nurture and handle the new life that You put in me while I hang on to my old attitudes, mindsets, speech patterns, and behaviors (Colossians 2:11-12; Matthew 9:17). I do not want to hinder the work of the Holy Spirit within me. Therefore, as I have received Christ Jesus the Lord, establishing my faith, help me to be firmly rooted and built up in Him. I overflow with gratitude to You! Help me not to be taken captive through deception, empty philosophies, and the traditions of men (Colossians 2:6-8).

Chapter 4

The Soul Rooted in
Sin, Selfishness, and Disobedience

---

*I*n the last chapter we learned that we are made of spirit, soul, and body. Much of this book focuses on the soul of a person, (mind, will, emotions and attitudes), which must be renewed in order for us to be restored to God's original purpose. The soul part of man has been neglected and misunderstood for far too long.

God longs to redeem, renew, and regenerate *every* area of our lives so that His perfect will may be accomplished within us. He wants to untangle us from our previous ways of thinking, speaking, and acting and He desires for us to be aligned with His ways in our spirit. When we renew our minds with God's Word and cooperate with the Holy Spirit, the life and character of Jesus Christ is seen in us. If, however, we do not allow the Word of God and His Holy Spirit to renew us, we will yield to the world's ways and remain subject to the enemy's manipulation. The Holy Spirit's influence within our lives is then restricted and quenched.

Unconfessed and unrepented sin, along with a reluctance to conform to God's ways in a believer's life, closes the door to the blessings of God for His children. God calls this disobedience. When we choose disobedience, we forfeit His blessings: His Presence, wholeness, soundness, preservation, deliverance, ongoing forgiveness, healing, general well-being, and prosperity in spirit, soul, and body. If we remain disobedient, we live in sin and bondage. A willfully disobedient person looks no different than an unbeliever. People see us, this "Christian," handling our problems the same way they do—angry, frustrated, anxious, and joyless, with a tendency to gossip, and a slave-to-circumstances mentality.

Remember, we are partners with God Himself! Not only are we to cooperate with the Holy Spirit in the cleansing of our spirit, but we must also unite with Him for the cleansing of our soul and body. He desires to lead us into total sanctification and holiness.

**The Holy Spirit desires to
lead each of us into total
sanctification and holiness.**

It is important, then, to look at the person who continues to remain entangled in sin and selfishness. He or she is seemingly powerless against Satan's schemes. This is the result of a person not cooperating with the Holy Spirit and allowing the Word to transform his or her life. This is disobedience and the rejection of God's Word. Acts of injustice, moral wrongdoing, and iniquity come from continued entanglement with Satan. This is the very opposite of the new life that we received from Christ.

Before accepting Christ as Savior, you and I are naturally rooted in unrighteousness; for no good thing dwells inside of us apart from Jesus Christ (see Psalm 16:2; Romans 7:18). This leaves us helplessly under the influence of Satan. When we believe in Jesus Christ as our Savior, however, it all changes. The moment we are born again, we become new creatures in Christ (2 Corinthians 5:17). When God sees you and me, His new creation, He now sees us through Jesus. He now sees you and me as having right standing with Him. To be for certain, we don't automatically think, speak and act like Jesus would —just as a baby cannot do these things when he emerges from his mother's womb. However, we are no longer powerless! We now have the power of the Holy Spirit to engage in the ongoing process of "uprooting" our former ways of thinking, speaking, and being, so that we can become "re-rooted" in God's ways. This process gives us a whole new way of living—God's way! Righteousness is our new spiritual position in Christ and we must live from that vantage point.

The goal in a believer's life is to become like Jesus. Thus a vessel fit for God's service! This means that we come to faith, gradually becoming free and untangled from the enemy, and bearing fruit in this process of transformation.

The process looks like the shape of the cross:

1. His love coming down and being freely received into ourselves.
2. His love flowing freely from us back up to Him and then out to others.

Ongoing sin, disobedience and selfishness in a person's life, however, causes this flow to be blocked. A soul that continues to sin in thought, word, and deed is a soul that the enemy is able to keep entangled.

**A soul that continues to sin in thought, word, and deed
is a soul that the enemy is able to keep entangled.**

Many Christian people do not realize their need for detangling and for the healing of their own souls from their previous nature and way of living. We cannot obtain holiness without first receiving wholeness, which only comes as we spend time in Christ's presence, open to His Holy Spirit, asking for His help, and being obedient to the Word. This is how we are changed from the inside out. As we submit our self-will to Christ, He heals our wounds by leading us through them. Spending time with Jesus Christ allows Him to put us back together the way He desires, making us whole. Our newfound wholeness then displays His holiness as our thoughts, words, and actions reflect His own. This God-initiated transformation is often confused with our own desire to *apply external rules* to modify our behavior problems. However, trying to follow rules is simply self trying to change self from the outside in. No external rule will uproot the sin and selfishness rooted within. If we could keep all the rules, we wouldn't need a Savior.

Perhaps you've noticed how we often *see the need for others to change,* while ignoring our own need for it. For example, we might justify our negative thinking by blaming someone else. "If that person would just treat me better," we might say, "I wouldn't be so mean to him!" But this is evidence of selfishness.

1. The unrighteous thought is: *I'm waiting for the other person to treat me right first.* Jesus said, "Do unto others as you would have them do unto you" (Luke 6:31).
2. The unrighteous words are about: *justifying the mean words that are said about the person.* Yet, Jesus tells us to, "bless those who curse us and leave the vindication up to Him" (Matthew 5:44-45). Simply put, if we don't have something nice to say, then don't say it at all.
3. The unrighteous deed is: *seeking vengeance rather than trusting God to take care of it.* (See Hebrews 10:30).

The love of God does not flow through our sin and selfishness. Even though you may justify this behavior, God does not. I can think of a time when I would go to church and greet others with Christian phrases, smiles, and love, and then return home only to blow up at my family. Those types of behaviors are not consistent with Christ's character. Quite frankly, who you are behind closed doors is the true you. (Reread that statement and take a moment to view yourself in this light). When we give our lives over to God, we can no longer use the excuse, "This is just how I am," because it does not match the new nature (fruit of the Spirit; see Galatians 5:22-23) that has been placed on the inside of you. The standard is this: If it is not the nature and character emanating from Christ, it should not be the nature and character coming from you, and me either.

> **The standard is this: If it is not the nature**
> **and character emanating from Christ,**
> **it should not be the nature and character**
> **coming from you, and me either.**

Satan desperately wants to keep you under his control. If you allow your old nature to have its own way, your soul (mind, will, emotions and attitudes) will remain disconnected from God, and you will not experience all that God desires for you. Remaining in disobedience to God in thought, word, and deed breeds death to the soul and body of any believer.

Galatians 6:7-8 says,

> Do not be deceived and deluded and misled; God will not allow Himself to be sneered at (scorned, disdained, or mocked by mere pretensions or professions, *or by His precepts being set aside*). [He inevitably deludes himself who attempts to delude God]. For whatever a man sows that and that only is what he will reap. For he who sows to his own flesh (lower nature, sensuality) will from the flesh reap decay and ruin and destruction, but he who sows to the Spirit will from the Spirit reap eternal life.

Everything in God's Kingdom boils down to choosing whether we will follow the leading of the Holy Spirit and do things God's way in thought, attitude, word, and deed, or whether we will follow the leading of our flesh and physical senses. When we choose to do things God's way, we are choosing life for ourselves and our descendants. Likewise, when we choose

27

to do things our own way we are choosing death for ourselves and our descendants (See Deuteronomy 30:19).

Questions for Study
1. What is God's original intention for the soul of every believer?
2. How would you define sin and selfishness?
3. List the two main points that happen in a believer's life when his or her objective is to become vessels fit for God's service.
4. Most Christian people do not realize the need for the healing of their own soul and commonly confuse this with what?
5. What is wholeness and holiness, and how do we obtain it?
6. From the example in the text, "justifying negative thinking," list the unrighteous thought, word, and deed. Think of an example from your own life where you have struggled with this as well.
7. Does the behavior you manifest behind closed doors match that of Jesus Christ?
8. Do your thoughts and words reflect the heart and mind of Christ?
9. The work accomplished by the Holy Spirit's presence within a person is known as the fruit of the Spirit: According to Galatians 5:22-23, list the fruit of the Spirit (the characteristics of Christ). Is this the character that represents you?

Personal Prayer

Lord, help me not to harbor sin, selfishness, or disobedience in my soul. Be the Lord of my thoughts, attitudes, words, and deeds (Psalm 19:14). Untangle and heal my soul from any wrong thinking, speaking, and doing, which enables the enemy to further entangle me. I desire to live a God-centered life, not a self-centered life. Help me to spend time in Your presence, enabling You to create holiness and wholeness within my heart (Psalm 51). Help me to become the same person behind closed doors that I am in public or with church friends. Develop the fruit of the Spirit within me so that Your presence, nature, and character emanates from me (Galatians 5:16-26).

Chapter 5

The Soul Rooted in
the Sin of Pride

—————————•◦•—————————

*J*ust like the soul rooted in the sin of unrighteousness, the soul rooted in pride will also forfeit the blessings of God. The Bible has much to say about pride and its destruction that reaches to people, relationships, marriages, homes, businesses, churches, and nations.

Pride results when we follow the selfish impulses of our flesh rather than the Spirit of God. Proverbs 29:23 says, *"A man's pride will bring him low, but he who is of a humble spirit will obtain honor."* Pride is the reason that Satan lost his position in Heaven. It's why Adam and Eve had to leave the Garden of Eden. The flesh reaps death, but the Spirit brings forth life.

There are three distinguishing factors of pride in a person:

1. Placing a higher priority on self or anything we love over God and His ways.
2. Placing self over other people. This might include people of different race, gender, socioeconomic status, and so forth.
3. Claiming innocence and blaming others for problems rather than taking personal responsibility for our own behaviors.

**Satan wants to keep
every believer's soul strapped
in the bondage of pride.**

The soul rooted in pride stems from Satan himself. He wants to keep every believer's soul strapped in the bondage of pride. Pride is an overly high opinion of self and the devaluing of others. The essence of pride is self-centeredness, conceit, haughty behavior, and arrogance. Pride always elevates self, and in the process, deflates (and can destroy) the rights and hopes of others. The underlying tone of pride says, "I'm right and you're wrong and I'm better than you!"

Being right is overrated and proves itself to be very costly in the lives of many.

Pride always causes us to rely on our own way of doing things. It makes us depend on ourselves alone. Pride tells us to make "self" our god instead of surrendering our self-will to God. The Book of Proverbs repeatedly makes references to the "self-confident fool," which is someone who depends on self and human resources rather than on God and His ways. First John 2:16 says,

> For all that is in the world—the lust of the flesh [craving for sensual gratification] and the lust of the eyes [greedy longings of the mind] and the pride of life [assurance in one's own resources or in the stability of earthly things]— these do not come from the Father but are from the world [itself].

Here are some important things to remember regarding pride:

- Because it hides and always justifies the actions of self, pride is one of Satan's most effective lies.
- Pride always works together with unrighteousness.
- Pride is easy to detect in someone else and usually very difficult to find in ourselves.
- Pride judges and criticizes others with the hidden purpose of making self feel better and more important.
- Pride shows partiality.
- Pride loves self more than others.
- Pride always seeks to protect self.
- Pride seeks to make self look better than it truly is.
- Pride causes division.

Proverbs 24:23 says, "To discriminate and show partiality, having respect of persons in judgment is not good." Proverbs 28:21 says, "To have respect of persons and to show partiality is not good..." and in Acts 10:34 Peter says, "...God shows no partiality and is no respecter of persons." The promises of God are for "whosoever will obey His will." Sometimes it is amazing how easily we can develop an "I'm better than you" attitude when we compare ourselves to others.

Jesus said in Matthew 7:3-5,

> Why do you stare from without at the very small particle that is in your brother's eye but do not become aware of and consider the beam of timber that is in your own eye? Or how can you say to your brother, Let me get the tiny particle out from your eye, when there is a beam of timber in your own eye? You hypocrite, first get the beam of timber out of your own eye, and then you will clearly see to take the tiny particle out of your brother's eye!

Before we ridicule and try to correct the sinful and selfish tendencies in others, we must first look at our own sins and shortcomings. Perhaps that helps explain why the things that bother us about other people are usually the very things that we do and don't like about ourselves.

Consider these questions:

1. When does God ever ask us to compare ourselves with our neighbor?
2. Who does God say is to be our standard?

3. Who is the One with whom we should compare ourselves?

Pride is the exact opposite of humility, which is what God desires to see in our lives. Pride causes us to violate others with a self-righteous undercurrent that says, "I'm better than that" or "My way is better than that." This severs God's love from flowing into and out of us. Remember this; God resists the proud, but gives grace to the humble! (James 4:6). Proverbs 6:16-19 says,

> These six things the Lord hates, indeed, seven are an abomination to Him: a proud look [the spirit that makes one overestimate himself and underestimate others], a lying tongue, and hands that shed innocent blood. A heart that manufactures wicked thoughts and plans, feet that are swift in running to evil, a false witness who breathes out lies [even under oath], and he who sows discord among his brethren.

Pride causes prejudice and strife, which results in people made in God's image devouring other people made in God's image. If this is not brought under control in our lives, it will eventually consume and destroy us. (See Galatians 5:16.)

All of these abominations start with a spirit that overestimates or inflates self and underestimates or deflates others. That spirit is from Satan.

**Pride will always cause prejudice
and strife, which results in
people made in God's image devouring
other people made in God's image.**

Let's use the previous Scripture passages to look more closely at what happens when we regard ourselves as better than others:

1. A proud look. This comes when a person *thinks in his heart* that he is more superior to others, and he wears it on his face (a "snob").
2. A lying tongue. We must realize *we are lying to ourselves* when we think we are better than someone else.
3. A heart that manufactures wicked *thoughts and plans*. When we do this, what we think, say, and do does not agree with what God thinks, says, and does.
4. *Feet that are swift to run to evil*. When we are quick to tell an offense or wrong doing to someone else, our feet are swiftly running to evil.
5. A false witness who breathes out lies. A false witness *chooses* to say things about others that do not match God's way of speaking.
6. He who sows discord among his brothers. This discord happens when someone *chooses words and actions* that cause strife and disrupts unity and harmony, especially among God's people.

James 2:1-4 reveals much about the heart and soul that are rooted in pride.

> My brethren, pay no servile regard to people [show no prejudice, no partiality]. *Do not (attempt to) hold and practice the faith of our Lord Jesus Christ the Lord*

of glory [together with snobbery]! For if a person comes into your congregation whose hands are adorned with gold rings and who is wearing splendid apparel, and also a poor man in shabby clothes comes in, and you pay special attention to the one who wears the splendid clothes and say to him, 'sit here in this preferable seat!' While you tell the poor man 'stand there!' Or 'sit there on the floor at my feet!' *Are you not discriminating among your own and becoming critics and judges with wrong motives?* (emphasis added)

In contrast, verses in 1 Samuel and Galatians show us God's heart regarding the sin of pride:

1. 1 Samuel 16:7 says, "But the Lord said to Samuel, *Look not on his appearance* or at the height of his stature, for I have rejected him. For the Lord sees not as man sees; for man looks on the outward appearance, but *the Lord looks on the heart.*"
2. Galatians 3:28 tells us, "There is [now no distinction] neither Jew nor Greek, there is neither slave nor free, there is not male and female; for you are all *one* in Christ Jesus.

The flesh—the will of man—without the impact of the Holy Spirit will always see outward characteristics such as race, gender, bank accounts, social status, and so forth. In contrast, when the will of man is submitted to the Holy Spirit, it will always view others through God's eyes. This type of person will choose to see the need to encourage and uplift those around them.

Questions for Study
1. What are the three distinguishing factors of pride?
2. How would you define pride?
3. In the Book of Proverbs, what is a "self-confident fool"?
4. List the two reasons why pride is one of Satan's greatest deceptions to man.
5. Think of a person with whom you don't particularly see eye to eye. What characteristics in this person bother you? Are these characteristics present in your own life?
6. What does 1 Samuel 16:7 reveal to us about the heart of God toward people? Does this represent your heart attitude towards others?
7. In Galatians 3:28, what is the definition of *one?*

Personal Prayer
Lord, please remove the sins in my life that result in pride. You hate a proud look, a spirit that overestimates self and underestimates another, a lying tongue and hands that shed innocent blood. Release me from a heart that manufactures wicked thoughts and plans. Keep my feet from running to evil. May I not be someone who sows discord among brethren (Proverbs 6:16-19). Help me not to see others with my own eyes in accordance with my flesh—such things as race, gender, bank accounts, and social status. Rather, let me live submitted to the Holy Spirit, always seeing others in light of Your image. Help me to edify and encourage those around me to become all that You have intended for them (Galatians 3:28; James 2:1-4; Philippians 3:3). Thank You that You do not consider my outward appearances and personal achievements, but You look at the intentions of my heart (1 Samuel 16:7)!

Chapter 6

The Soul Rooted in
the Trap of Fear

*D*id you know that the words "fear not" appears 365 times in the Bible? Ironically, many people live each day in fear! God knows that if it remains unmanaged, fear will destroy us.

The Bible talks about two kinds of fear. The first is a healthy and appropriate honor for the Trinity: Father, Son, and Holy Spirit. It is a reverential fear that acts as a compass for life in moral and spiritual matters. This fear of God brings forth a sincere dread of displeasing God, and a speechless awe of who He is. This kind of fear will inspire within you a constant awareness and carefulness regarding Him, yourself, and how you view others.[1] It is a combination of fear and love which should constitute the attitude of man toward God and others. Proverbs 1:7 and 16:16 say, *"The fear of the Lord is the beginning of knowledge and wisdom!"* Healthy fear causes us to care more about what God thinks of us than what people think.

**Healthy fear causes us to care more about what
God thinks of us than what people think.**

The second type of fear, *unhealthy fear,* originates from Satan and describes who he is and what he does. Satan specifically launches attacks against our souls; (mind, will, attitudes, and emotions). He is particularly interested in killing, stealing, and destroying our healthy fear of God, along with the fruit of the Holy Spirit's presence in our lives: (Love, joy, peace, patience, kindness, goodness, faithfulness, gentleness, and self-control (see Galatians 5:22-23). If the enemy can cause us to live in fear of something or someone other than God, then he keeps us bound under his control. We will remain in agreement with Satan rather than with Christ.

Unhealthy fear causes us to value the opinions of others more than God's. Galatians 1:10 reminds us, "Now am I trying to win the favor or men, or God? Do I seek to please men? If I were still seeking popularity with men, I should not be a bond servant of Christ."

Let's take a look at a soul rooted in Satan's fear. This type of fear means to be scared, to cause flight, to run from, dread, and terror, caused by the intimidation of adversaries.[2] We will often *feel* fear, but what matters most is how we respond to it.

Fear causes us to do the following:

1. Act deceitfully.
2. Try to hide sin through lying.
3. Experience torment in our soul (1 John 4:18).
4. Experience paralyses in our soul.
5. Focus on self, in order to protect, hide, and vindicate ourselves.

Satan uses fear against us by planting thoughts in our minds intended to torment and punish us. If you focus on the thoughts Satan bombards your mind with, then your will, attitudes, and emotions will soon follow. Satan uses the force of fear to paralyze us, and his efforts are geared toward attacking our minds! If he can control your thoughts, he will control your life. The great revelation is that you *can choose what you think about!*

If you focus on the thoughts Satan bombards your mind with,
then your will, attitudes and emotions will soon follow.

Consider the process Satan uses. First, he places a thought in your mind, which you begin to dwell on. As you continue to dwell on the thought (or thoughts), it becomes bigger and bigger. Eventually, the mole hill has become a mountain. In time, that particular thought becomes a stronghold in your life which the enemy will use to torment and punish your soul. Does this sound familiar?

Fear is a great trap of deception that Satan uses in order to paralyze, control, and manipulate us through our thoughts and emotions. It becomes a stronghold which then acts as a barrier, intended to keep us believing wrong things about something or someone (including ourselves). In turn, this distorted belief causes us to give in to sinful behavior, which Satan intends to use to lead us further into bondage and paralysis. Satan uses strongholds in our minds to then manipulate and control us. This deceptive stronghold that Satan has been allowed to build will remain as long as you continue to cower in fear and run.

Some friends of ours lost their middle child at the age of two. Understandably, the wife fell into a pit of depression, unable to properly grieve and process the death of her child. She visited a spiritual leader who then wrongfully took advantage of her. Satan planted a lie in our friend's mind that sounded something like this: *"No one will believe you—not your husband, not the members of the congregation, or the community. The best thing you can do is to keep this to yourself or you will lose everything!"* Her belief of this lie became a stronghold in our friend's life. It caused her even more depression and despair. The enemy was undoubtedly out to destroy her through this stronghold of lies in her mind and emotions.

When our friend finally faced what she feared, God was able to deliver her little by little from Satan's stronghold. Jesus, our Redeemer, eventually led her back through her pain and healed her. As a result, she is now able to help other hurting people in similar situations. Indeed, if we stop running and allow God into our situation, He will take what the enemy has meant for harm and use it for good!

Look at what the Bible has to say in regard to the enemy. First Peter 5:8 says, "Be well balanced (temperate, sober of mind), be vigilant and cautious at all times; for that enemy of yours, the devil roams around *like* a lion roaring [in fierce hunger], seeking someone to seize upon and devour."

Fear can also be described by the acronym *False Evidence Appearing Real*.[3] Consider someone who is claustrophobic and experiences great fear when enclosed in small places. To this claustrophobic person, very real evidence exists that there is reason to fear. Satan has distorted the truth for this person by simply placing a thought in his mind: "*I can't breathe and I'm going to die!*" If he believes the lie, a stronghold takes root in his mind and causes him to be in bondage whenever he is enclosed in small spaces. As long as he continues to believe the enemy, this *False Evidence* (that he can't breathe and is going to die on an elevator) *Appears very Real*. This person will remain under the control of the enemy in this area of his mind until he decides to "fear not."

This is how you "fear not":

1. Partner with the Holy Spirit.
2. Allow the Word of God to renew your mind daily.
3. Recognize Satan's attacks.
4. Use God's Word to ward off the constant fear that the enemy tosses your way.

Second Corinthians 10:4-5 says

> For the weapons of our warfare are not physical [weapons of flesh and blood], but they are mighty before God *for the overthrow and destruction of strongholds,* [inasmuch as we] refute arguments and theories and reasonings and every proud and lofty thing (or word)* that sets itself up against the [true] knowledge of God; and we lead every *thought* and *purpose* (motive)* away captive into the obedience of Christ (the Messiah, the Anointed One).

Remember:

1. Prayer is our greatest weapon.
2. Practice living and remaining in God's presence.
3. People are not the enemy, Satan is!

Second Timothy 1:7 says, "For God did not give us a spirit of timidity (of cowardice, of craven and cringing and fawning fear), but [He has given us a spirit] of power and of love and of calm and well-balanced mind and discipline and self-control." In this passage, God tells us that He gave us power over the enemy. He has given us the ability to love along with the right to a calm and well-balanced mind. These things are manifested in our lives when we believe that we possess them and begin to exercise discipline and self-control continuously.

Questions for Study
1. What do healthy fears cause us to be concerned about? What do unhealthy fears cause us to be concerned about?
2. List the five things that fear from Satan causes in our lives.

3. List the things that Satan does in order to cause us to fear.
4. Finish this sentence. Fear is a great trap of deception that Satan uses in order to:
5. What does 1 Peter 5:8 tell us to do? What does this verse say about the enemy?
6. A person will remain in the control of the enemy until he decides to do what?
7. What is God telling us in 2 Corinthians 10:4-5 and 2 Timothy 1:7?
8. What are some fears you experience in your own life, and how might you apply the previous verses to your life?

Personal Prayer

Lord, help me to recognize any fears that Satan throws my way in an attempt to keep me in bondage. I recognize that the fear of what others think of me is a trap to keep me more concerned about pleasing others then I am with pleasing You (Galatians 1:10). Forgive this sin, Lord. I know it is wrong. Help me to focus on what you Word says about me. Thank You that You did not give me a spirit of fear, but of power, love, and a sound mind (2 Timothy 1:7). Help me to develop the mind of Christ that You have placed in me (1 Corinthians 2:16). I choose to partner with and surrender my mind and will to the Holy Spirit as my teacher in this area. I need Him to help me take every thought captive and line it up with Your Word in order to determine where the thought is coming from (2 Corinthians 10:3-5). Thank You for the power of Your Word and the Holy Spirit working together inside of me to bring me freedom. Help me now to make it a habit to think about those things that are pure, lovely, noble, true, right, admirable, praiseworthy, and of good report (Philippians 4:8). Help me to keep my mind fixed on You, and thank You for promising to keep me in perfect peace as I do this. (See Isaiah 26:3).

Chapter 7

The Fruit of a Soul
Rooted in Sin, Pride, and Fear

God longs for His followers to live in victory. However, if our souls remain rooted in sin, pride, and fear, then we will not experience the victory which God desires for us to have in this life. Even though we are saved and headed to Heaven, if our minds, wills, attitudes, and emotions remain in agreement with the enemy, our lives will lack the abundance that Christ came to give. Our relationship with the Lord and with others will lack depth and immaturity will rule our lives. When we leave our souls rooted in these things, we find our lives to be based on "what I want, what I think, and what I feel." We live selfish, self-centered lives instead of Christ-centered lives. This is disobedience. Romans 8:8 says, "So then those who are living the life of the flesh [catering to the appetites and impulses of their carnal nature] cannot please or satisfy God, or be acceptable to Him."

Let's recap the meaning of a soul rooted in sin, pride, and fear:

1. Sin, selfishness, and disobedience describe many Christians whose souls continues to be in agreement with the enemy. This person insists on doing things his or her own way as opposed to God's. Most people do not understand that God sees this opposition to His will as wickedness. Lots of Christians choose to remain stubborn in their own ways, trapped in bondage, and not in agreement with God in thought, word, attitude, and deed.

2. Pride hides and justifies our actions. It keeps our focus on the shortcomings and problems of other's. Pride causes us to blame everyone else for our circumstances and emotional responses. It never takes responsibility. It causes us to look down on others, to be self-focused, and to think we are always right.

3. Unhealthy fear causes paralyses, especially in our thought lives. It keeps us running from something or someone, unable and unwilling to face truth. Fear keeps us from placing our full trust in God.

The fruit produced by someone whose roots are buried in sin, pride, and fear, will always result in "rotten" thoughts, attitudes, actions and behaviors. For example; picture the trunk of a tree. The base of this tree trunk reveals three main roots which have the words, "sin, pride, and fear," written on them. These roots hold this big tree in place. Now picture the rest of the tree: the strong branches, the green leaves, and the fruit hanging from the limbs. Let's go one step further and pick each piece of fruit on that tree so we can get a *good* look at it. Clearly, the fruit from the tree is unhealthy because its roots are unhealthy.

Even though the fruit looks all right from the outside, you can be assured that there are unwholesome spots under the surface. Matthew 7:18-20 says,

> A good (healthy) tree cannot bear bad (worthless) fruit, nor can a bad (diseased) tree bear excellent fruit [worthy of admiration]. Every tree that does not bear good fruit is cut down and cast into the fire. Therefore, you will fully know them by their fruits.

Whether we like it or not, we are known by our fruit—our attitudes, actions and behaviors.

**Whether we like it or not, we are known by our fruit–
our attitudes, actions, and behaviors.**

Some of the fruit that we might find growing on a tree suffering from the unhealthy roots of sin, pride, and fear are included in the following list:

- Envy—General negativity—Easily offended
- Extreme guilt—Hostility, especially toward family—Easily depressed
- Jealous of others—Self-pity—Controlled by circumstances
- Self-condemnation—Comparing yourself with others—Easily upset
- Worry about yourself—Competing with others—Dejected easily
- Relational strife—Frustration—Filled with shame
- Manipulation—Bitterness—Doubt
- Judgmental attitudes—Resentment—Attempt to control others with impatience
- Low self-esteem—Irritability—Critical of yourself and others
- Lack of confidence, insecurity—Bad attitudes—Use words that wound
- Angry undercurrent—Chip on shoulder—Discouraged

Do you recognize yourself in this list? If so, why not circle those things? Circle the things on this list that describe you. Circle the attitudes, actions and behaviors that describe who you are toward your spouse and children on a regular basis.

I must admit that I thought I was "fine," and it was the people around me who "pulled my chain" that had the problem. I was oblivious to the fact that God was using the people in my life who "pulled my chain" to help change me, by digging up my roots and replacing them with His. Yes, there were annoying people with bad behaviors and rotten attitudes in my life. Yes, they did need to change. However, I found myself focused on them rather than on God's desire for my own soul. I wanted to help God change them because pride had caused me to see the need for others to change while remaining oblivious to my own actions, attitudes, and reactions. With God's help, I finally realized that I cannot change or control anyone, but I can seek Him to change my attitudes, actions, and reactions!

God wants to teach each of us a new way to react to situations, circumstances, and our environments. While many of us want our lives to change, we need to realize instead that God is using our lives to change us. This is where Christianity gets hard. If you want to be delivered from these immature actions and behaviors that are governing your life, you must come face-to-face with what is going on *inside of you*. If you truly want to change, you must grasp this truth and recognize that you have been held captive by the enemy through sin, selfishness, disobedience, pride, and fear. Do you want to be released from these behaviors? Are you realizing that trying harder will not take away these behaviors permanently? God wants to heal your wounded heart, which causes your actions, attitudes, and reactions. Most people want to perfect their behavior without healing the wound or taking the time to come untangled. Sometimes people will choose to wait a lifetime hoping for someone else to change first. It doesn't work that way.

> **Most people want to perfect their behavior
> without healing the wound or taking the time to
> come untangled. Sometimes people will choose to
> wait a lifetime hoping for someone else to change first.
> It doesn't work that way.**

God wants to uproot these actions, attitudes, behaviors, and mindsets. He wants to replace them with His roots of righteousness, humility, and faith. God desires for the fruit of His Spirit (love, joy, peace, patience, kindness, goodness, faithfulness, gentleness, and self-control) to truly become your new, habitual nature. He will not force you, nor will He overwhelm you. He invites you to take His hand, allowing His Holy Spirit to walk with you through this uprooting and untangling process of your soul. This is how He provides healing in the areas where you have been bound by wounds, deception and captivity.

John 8:31-32 tells us how to have this victory: "If you abide in My Word [hold fast to My teachings and live in accordance with them], you are truly My disciples. And you will know the Truth and the Truth will set you free." If you struggle with sin, selfishness, disobedience, pride, or fear, why not find verses in the Bible that deal with that particular topic? Then begin to think about the verses. Write them down. Roll them over in your mind. Practice saying them out loud. In the process, God will show you the truth and He will free you from the enemy!

We accomplish victory by living in God's Word, not by visiting it occasionally. *God's Word combined with our submission to His Holy Spirit brings about a change from the inside out!* Slowly but surely, as we replace these old habits and mindsets with the truth of God's Word, they start to die and lose their power in our lives. Then we start to resemble Jesus and become true witnesses of His character to a dying world. This is God's resurrected power working in us and untangling us from Satan.

> **We accomplish victory by living in God's Word,
> not by visiting it occasionally.**

God designed us to have dominion over Satan while on this earth and in this present body. Victory over sin, selfishness, disobedience, pride, and fear, requires that we *continuously* and *consistently* face every area of our lives that produces negative, death-giving thoughts, actions, attitudes, words, and behaviors. When we partner with the Holy Spirit, He will walk us through to freedom. Just as God brought the Israelites up out of Egypt, He brings us up out of sin. We enter the wilderness (sometimes a dark and lonely place) and *walk through it* to the Promised Land of Victory!

Romans 6:11 says, "Even so consider yourselves also dead to sin and your relation to it broken, but alive to God [living in unbroken fellowship with Him] in Christ Jesus." Sin does not die when we become a Christian, *instead we consider ourselves dead to sin and alive to Christ*. Think of yourself in this way. We cannot go deeper in our relationship with God without facing who we are and where we are right now. He longs for us to know Him and to receive His love into our hearts so we will know our true identity. Remember that we receive something from God by believing it in our hearts and confessing it with our mouths, just as we did when we received salvation. For example, "God, I believe that You love me and I receive Your love into my heart right now, by faith, through Your empowering grace."

Waiting for people to change, serving more in the church, saying all the right Christian phrases, continual busyness, and exhaustion will not deepen someone's relationship with Jesus. Rather, learning to require Him as our vital necessity in every area of our lives is the key to a deeper walk with Christ. Our one desperate need is an unbroken relationship with Him.

Questions for Study
1.   Why won't the person whose soul is rooted in sin, pride, and fear experience much victory in Christ?
2.   List any unhealthy fruits that describe you.
3.   Do you want to change the fruit on your "tree" so it matches the fruit of Christ?
4.   What two things work together inside of us to change us into His image and witnesses of His character?
5.   Do you want to know God more? Ask Him to help you. Then give Him the time to do so.
6.   How do we receive anything from God?
7.   Write out Romans 8:8 and 6:11 and meditate on those verses. Do you see yourself as dead to sin and alive to Christ? Ask the Holy Spirit to help you die to sin and become alive to Him. Confess with your mouth, "I am dead to sin and alive to Christ."
8.   Romans 8:9 says, "But you are not living the life of the flesh, you are living the life of the Spirit, if the [Holy] Spirit of God [really] dwells within you [directs and controls you]." Are you living your life according to the Spirit or to the dictates of the flesh?

Personal Prayer
Lord, please remove the roots that produce the negative fruit that has developed in my life. I realize that these actions, attitudes, and behaviors are sin because they are not in agreement with Your character (Galatians 5:19-21). Please heal any wounds in my heart that would cause me to sin in this manner. Please teach me how to react to situations and circumstances in a way that is worthy of the Gospel (Romans 8). Help me to continuously and consistently live, dwell, and remain in You and Your Word. Thank You for the promise that if I live in Your Word, I will know the truth and the truth about me shall set me free (John 8:31-32). I ask You, Holy Spirit, to teach, lead, and guide me into all truth (John 16:13-15).

PART TWO:

*Understanding
the Life Christ Desires
for His Children*

Chapter 8

Salvation:
The Life Christ Desires for Us

*W*ithout a doubt, God's greatest gift to mankind is salvation. He does not want even one of us to perish. Rather, He deeply desires for all to turn to His Son in faith and repentance. He wants each of us to receive His salvation and to grow in the knowledge of His truth. First Timothy 2:4-6 says that God our Savior,

> . . . who wishes all men to be saved and [increasingly] to *perceive* and *recognize* and *discern* and *know* precisely and correctly the [divine] Truth. For there [is only] one God and [only] one Mediator between God and men, the Man Christ Jesus, Who gave Himself as a ransom for all [people, a fact that was] attested to at the right and proper time.

God designed salvation to affect and impact every dimension of our lives. When we understand God's objective for salvation, we will grow and become more of the person God intends us to be. The purpose of salvation includes the following:

1. God uses salvation to *redeem* a person (spirit, soul, and body) from a past that was characterized by sin. He releases that person from the control and bondage of Satan and self (Romans 3:23-23).
2. Through salvation, God offers total *renewal* for a person (spirit, soul, and body). This means a new nature, new direction, and new precedence for the mind, will, attitudes, and emotions (see Romans 12:1-2).
3. When we accept God's great gift of salvation, we are *regenerated* from spiritual death to life as God intended it (see Ephesians 2:1-5). He wants to untangle people from sin and restore them to His original plan.

Let's camp on these three purposes so that we can understand them better:

Redeem: means "To buy out," especially of purchasing a slave with a view to his freedom; to release by paying a ransom price.[1]

Before giving your life to Christ, whether you knew it or not, you were a slave. I was, too, enslaved and bound by sin. The enemy had a certain amount of control over your life. But God, in the person of His Son Jesus, died on the cross in order to buy us out of that life of bondage. He leaves it up to us then, to come into agreement with His plan for living – *spirit, soul, and body*. He does this through His Word, His Holy Spirit within us, and His empowering grace. These three things work together to enable us to live our lives the way He wants us to.

Romans 3:23-24 says,

> Since all have sinned and are falling short of the honor and glory which God bestows and receives. [All] are justified and made upright and in right standing with God, freely and gratuitously by His grace (His unmerited favor and mercy, and empowerment*), through the redemption which is [provided] in Christ Jesus.

Amos 3:3 says, "Do two walk together except they make an appointment and have agreed?" Many Christians understand their need for salvation from sin, yet fail to truly and fully place their inner selves (mind, will, attitudes, and emotions) in agreement with and under the authority of the Word of God. Sadly, these individuals don't recognize the power they would have if they lived everyday obediently submitted to God's Word and Holy Spirit.

**Many Christians understand their need for salvation from sin,
yet fail to truly and fully place their inner selves
in agreement with and under the authority of the Word of God.**

Ephesians 2:1-3 tells us,

> And you [He made alive], when you were dead (slain) by your trespasses and sins, in which at one time you walked [habitually]. You were following the course and fashion of this world [were under the sway of the tendency of this present age], following the prince of the power of the air. [You were obedient to and under the control of] the [demon] spirit that still constantly works in the sons of disobedience [the careless, the rebellious, and the unbelieving, who go against the purposes of God]. Among these, we as well as you once lived and conducted ourselves in the passions of our flesh [our behavior governed by our corrupt and sensual nature], obeying the impulses of the flesh and the thoughts of the mind [our cravings dictated by our senses and our dark imaginings]. We were then by nature children of [God's] wrath and heirs of [His] indignation, like the rest of mankind.

Titus 3:3-8 says;

> It wasn't so long ago that we ourselves were stupid and stubborn, dupes of sin, ordered every which way by our glands, going around with a chip on

our shoulder, hated and hating back. But when God, our kind and loving Savior God, stepped in, He saved us from all that. It was all his doing; we had nothing to do with it. He gave us a good bath, and we came out of it new people, washed inside and out by the Holy Spirit. Our Savior Jesus poured out new life so generously. God's gift has restored our relationship with him and given us back our lives. And there's more life to come—an eternity of life! You can count on this (MSG).

God's love has rescued us from His wrath. This very love led to Jesus' death and shed blood on the cross. Because we cannot keep the Ten Commandments through our own self effort, Jesus willingly took the punishment of our sins for us. In doing so, He bridged the gap between mankind and God.

Renew means to "make new," especially the inward man. This renewal involves both immediate and progressive dimensions. At rebirth, the Spirit of God bears witness with the core of man and enters into his spirit immediately. The progressive dimension of the Christian life occurs in the soul (mind, will, attitudes, and emotions). The Word of God renews the mind (see Romans 12:2; Ephesians 4:23). Furthermore, the will needs to be conformed to God's (see Amos 3:3), and the attitudes and emotions need to be healed and balanced (1 Peter 5:8). James 1:21 promises that the Word implanted (rooted) in a person has the power to save their soul.

In John 8:31-32, Jesus is saying these five things:

1. Remain in my Word
2. Hold fast to my teachings
3. Live according to them
4. Then you will know the truth (about you)
5. This truth will set you free

Are you willing to partner with the Holy Spirit to take responsibility for your part of this process? If so, you will begin to see great change within yourself, your circumstances, and your relationships.

Regeneration means to restore to life and return it to the original design God had for you. Regeneration "takes place when a person humbly submits himself to Jesus Christ and trusts Him for forgiveness, salvation and life."[2]

What have we been restored to? Because of His great love for us, God restores sinners to unbroken fellowship and union with Him; the same kind of fellowship that Adam and Eve had with God before they sinned in the Garden of Eden. Think about life in the Garden of Eden before sin. Adam and Eve's constant communion with God was fulfilling, freeing, rich, prosperous, joyous, and peaceful—a most blessed life! That is what God wants to restore to us! Life! "The regenerated person is a new person. He has a new life inwardly, characterized by a renewed mind that governs all his thinking, attitudes and actions. He also has a new life outwardly, characterized by loving behavior toward others, hatred of sin and victory over the world's temptations."[3]

Ephesians 2:4-5 says

> But God—so rich is He in mercy! Because of and in order to satisfy the
> great and wonderful and intense love with which He loved us, even when
> we were dead (slain) by [our own] shortcomings and trespasses, He made
> us alive together in fellowship and union with Christ; [He gave us the very
> life of Christ Himself, the same new life with which He quickened Him, for]
> it is by grace (His favor and mercy which you did not deserve) that you are
> saved (delivered from judgment and made partakers of Christ's salvation).

God's plan in redeeming, renewing, and regenerating is to take us from spiritual death—no communication with God—to a life of personal relationship and unbroken fellowship with Him.

Luke 4:18 paraphrased says that Jesus came to preach the good news of salvation to the poor (the humble/those who realize they need a Savior). It says He came to announce the captives release (those being controlled by Satan) (see 2 Timothy 2:26). Jesus came to give sight to the blind, for Satan has blinded them to the light of the gospel (see 2 Corinthians 4:4). He came for those who are oppressed and harassed by the power of the enemy and for the broken-hearted—those who have been bruised, crushed, and broken down by calamity and sin from Satan (see Acts 10:38).

When we accept Christ as our Savior, we enter into a great exchange: God takes us in our spiritually dead state and gives us all that He is and has (life). He seats us in Heavenly places with Him, that we might live connected to Him (Ephesians 2:1-7). Salvation is Christ Himself rescuing us and giving us forgiveness, deliverance, righteousness, preservation, soundness, wholeness, and prosperity. He provides us with the opportunity to grow spiritually, mentally, physically, and emotionally, crossing all realms of life! It is all-encompassing! Who wouldn't want these blessings?

Isaiah 61:3, 7-8, 10, says that Christ will come,

> To grant [consolation and joy] to those who mourn in Zion—to give them
> an ornament (a garland or diadem) of beauty instead of ashes, the oil of joy
> instead of mourning, the garment [expressive] of praise instead of a heavy,
> burdened, and failing spirit—that they may be called oaks of righteousness
> [lofty, strong, and magnificent, distinguished for uprightness, justice, and
> right standing with God], the planting of the Lord, that He may be glori-
> fied. Instead of your [former] shame you shall have a twofold recompense;
> instead of dishonor and reproach [your people] shall rejoice in their portion.
> Therefore in their lands they shall possess double [what they had forfeited];
> everlasting joy shall be theirs. For I the Lord love justice; I hate robbery and
> wrong with violence or a burnt offering. And I will faithfully give them their
> recompense in truth, and I will make an everlasting covenant or league with
> them. I will greatly rejoice in the Lord, my soul will exult in my God; for
> He has clothed me with the garments of salvation, He has covered me with
> the robe of righteousness, as a bridegroom decks himself with garland, and
> as a bride adorns herself with jewels.

Ephesians 2:6 states, "He raised us up together with Him and made us sit down together [giving us joint seating with Him] in the Heavenly sphere [*by virtue of our being*] in Christ Jesus (the Messiah, the Anointed One)." Why did He do this?

1.   John 3:16; "For God so greatly loved and dearly prized the world that He [even] gave up His only begotten (unique) Son, so that whoever believes in (trusts in, clings to, relies on) Him shall not perish (come to destruction, be lost) but have eternal (everlasting) life."
2.   Ephesians 2:7; "He did this that He might clearly demonstrate through the ages to come the immeasurable (limitless, surpassing) riches of His free grace (His unmerited favor) in [His] Kindness and goodness of heart toward us in Christ Jesus."
3.   John 10:10; "I came that they may have and enjoy life, and have it in abundance (to the full, till it overflows)." Note: this does not mean that you will have a life without trials! It is very clear in His Word that in this life we will have troubles (John 16:33), but He will teach you how to live above your problems and keep them from controlling you.
4.   1 John 3:8; "The reason the Son of God was made manifest (visible) was to undo (destroy, loosen, and dissolve) the works the devil [has done]."

Therefore, through the extending of God's love to us through Christ, you and I can confidently claim that we will be viewed as innocent before God on the Final Day of Judgment. We can also know that we have been:

1.   Delivered from the control of the enemy—dead to sin in spirit, soul, and body.
2.   Given the life of Christ living on the inside of us
3.   Free to serve Him as He wants us to.

Questions for Study
1.   List and explain the three main aspects of salvation.
2.   What is God's plan in redeeming, renewing, and regenerating us?
3.   What occurs between God and man because of the great exchange?
4.   Define the word "Life."
5.   Give one reason why Christ came to earth.
6.   List the four things that are yours and mine because God extended His love to us through Christ.

Personal Prayer
Lord, even when I was dead in my own shortcomings and sins, You made me alive for fellowship and union with You. Thank You for giving me the very life of Christ Himself. Thank You for Your grace and unmerited favor, mercy, and power, which I do not deserve but choose to receive gratefully. Thank You for delivering me from judgment and making me a partaker of Your salvation (Ephesians 2). Lord, I give You all of my ashes in exchange for all of Your beauty. I receive this blessed salvation which You died to give me: forgiveness, rescue, deliverance, righteousness, preservation, soundness, wholeness, prosperity, and the opportunity to grow in spiritual, mental, physical, and emotional well-being (Isaiah chapter 61). To You be the glory for my new life. I submit to and partner with Your Holy Spirit to untangle me from the effects of sin in my life and to empower, teach, lead, and guide me into all of your ways (1 John 3:8-9).

Chapter 9

The New Covenant and You

❧

When we accept Christ as our Savior we enter into a covenant agreement—a partnership. God has already provided all of the promises within the agreement, along with the empowerment to see them at work in our lives. As believers, it is our responsibility to order our lives according to the ways of God's Kingdom. Partnered with God, we are called to find out exactly how His Kingdom operates. We do this with the help of the Holy Spirit and by studying His Word. Unfortunately, many Christians want to claim the promises of God without taking on the responsibility and partnering with His Holy Spirit to work out those promises within their lives. It is impossible to live as God has called us to live if we are not willing to work within the partnership.

Think of a business partnership or marriage. If you were to open a business with a partner or get married and only spend two hours each week developing the relationship with your partner or spouse, the partnership or marriage would not be successful at all. The same is true of our partnership with God. Spending two hours a week in a church will not develop the *relationship* or *partnership* we need if we are to live our lives in accordance with God's decrees and receive His blessings. The Bible tells us in Hosea 4:6 that we perish for lack of knowledge. Satan wants to keep all of us ignorant of this fact. If we are deceived, we are not free and cannot possibly work out our salvation as God intended.

Let's look at the definition of covenant. In Bible times, a *covenant* was "an agreement between two parties that laid down conditions and guaranteed benefits, depending upon a person's keeping or breaking the covenant and it was sealed by some form of witness."[1]

The covenant between God and man, however, involves an agreement between unequal individuals. As human beings, we can do nothing to deserve God's favor or His promises. Such gifts and promises are based on who He is and what He has done for us. This is His part of the covenant.

Jesus Christ is the *mediator* of the new covenant between God and man (See Hebrews 12:23-24). A *mediator* is someone responsible for both parties to fulfill the obligations of the covenant or promise."[2] This means that Jesus is responsible for both God's part of the covenant and ours. He is our guarantee that God will fulfill His promises. The Holy Spirit, then, enables us to fulfill our part of the covenant, the *commitment* to live according to His ways. He empowers us with His grace to obey and keep the commandments of God, just as Jesus told His disciples in John 14:16 when He said, "I will ask the Father, and He will give you another Counselor to be with you forever." The Holy Spirit is the enabler for us to obey and keep the commandments of God.

Old Covenant:

In the Old Testament, God's relationship with His people was based on the old covenant. The Mosaic Law, or the Ten Commandments, was designed to lead the nation of Israel to a life of practical holiness. Within the Ten Commandments, the people could see God's nature, His character and His moral standards. The Ten Commandments were not only guidelines for living, but were also used to direct the Israelites to meet the needs of the people in a responsible and loving manner. Remember, God is love and love does what is best for the person being loved. God's heart is all about developing relationships.

However, the old covenant was based on God's people following external rules in order to remain "clean" before Him. The priests used animals as sacrifices to atone for the sins of the people because imperfect people cannot perfectly keep the Law (the Ten Commandments). These sacrifices stood as symbols of the perfect and complete sacrifice that was to come: Jesus Christ, the perfect Lamb of God and the new covenant.

The old covenant was incomplete because the people could not continuously obey the law and because Christ had not yet shed His blood. Hebrews 9:9 tells us that in the old covenant, ". . . gifts and sacrifices are offered, and yet are incapable of perfecting the conscience or of cleansing and renewing the inner man of the worshiper." Following rules does not and cannot change us from the inside out, nor can it give us right standing or a right relationship with God.

The old covenant consists of God *demanding* His people to obey His laws knowing full well that they could not do this. Therefore the Law was designed to bring people to the end of their "self-efforts" of trying to "please" God. The new covenant, found in Jesus Christ, contains the *supernatural supply of grace* and the empowerment of the Holy Spirit to obey God's commands. This includes all people, not just one certain person or nation.

The New Covenant:

The New Covenant does not demand obedience to a set of laws. Rather, the Holy Spirit circumcises hearts, putting God's laws in them, along with the supply of grace for the empowerment needed to obey.

Ezekiel 36:27 gives witness to this when it states, "And I will put My Spirit within you and cause you to walk in My statutes, and you shall heed My ordinances and do them." Hebrews 8:10 says, "For this is the covenant that I will make with the house of Israel after those days, says the Lord: I will imprint My laws upon their minds, even upon their innermost thoughts and understanding, and engrave them upon their hearts; and I will be their God, and they shall be My people."

When we accept and put our faith in the work that Jesus Christ did on the cross, trusting His death, burial and resurrection for our salvation, God automatically grafts us into His family.

This is new birth. Now we must see ourselves as God does. We have exited from the system of the world that is governed by Satan and have entered into God's system that is governed by His Holy Spirit, alive and living in us. Because the cross is all inclusive, we too have been crucified with Christ and have been resurrected to a new life in Him. We must now consider ourselves a new creation (See 2 Corinthians 5:21). Christ in me! I in Him and Him in me!

Jesus Christ's perfect sacrifice provided us a new covenant with God the Father. Now we have access to His benefits because we have entered into a relationship with Him. As we partner with the Holy Spirit, God justifies us. This means that *all* of our sins have been washed away (See Romans 6:23). As the Holy Spirit continues His work, and we continue in *faith* and *obedience*, the promises of our new inheritance are made certain and will eventually manifest in the physical realm.

When we accept Christ as our Savior, we enter into a great exchange. We are in an active and ongoing partnership with Jesus Christ *through the Holy Spirit*. We give Him all that we are and have—the good, the bad, and the ugly and in return, He gives us all that He is and has! We are to become a living sacrifice to Him which is our reasonable act of service. (See Romans 12:1.) We are not our own but have been bought with a price (the blood of Christ), and we are to honor Him with our lives through our choices. Therefore, what we think, say, and do must now be in agreement with His Word. The best thing that we can "offer" to God each day is our love, heart, mind, self-will, devotion and complete obedience.

The Difference Between the Two Covenants:

- Romans 6:14 says, "For sin shall not [any longer] exert dominion over you, since now you are not under Law [as slaves], but under grace [as subjects of God's favor and mercy].

- The law shows us what we ought to do, but gives no strength to enable us to do it. This leads us to the never ending roller coaster ride of condemnation and failure.

- The law is a set of commands etched in stone. Grace and truth comes in a living Person; Jesus Christ. He gives us His presence and His power.

- The law promises life if we obey through self-effort and determination.

- Grace and truth gives life through the Holy Spirit, assuring and empowering us to obey through God's supernatural strength and surrender of our self-will. In other words, grace points to what we cannot do, and offers to do it for us and in us through the power of the Holy Spirit.

Unfortunately, many Christians are living under the law rather than under grace. It takes a long time to come untangled and switch our focus from trying to "get" God to be pleased with us rather than receiving, by faith, His acceptance of us because we believe in Jesus and all the benefits that He has already provided for us.

Romans 6:16 says, "Do you not know that if you continually surrender yourselves to anyone to do his will, you are the slaves of him whom you obey, whether that be to sin, which leads to death, or to obedience which leads to righteousness (right doing and right standing with God)?"

Through our partnering with the Holy Spirit, the New Covenant provides us three crucial things:

1. A way to God through Jesus Christ.
2. Hearts that rejoice to follow the leading of the Holy Spirit and obeying God.
3. New hearts that have been freed from the power of sin, selfishness, Satan, and the system of this world.

Our part in the new covenant involves:

1. Believing.
2. Submitting to the ways of God – being obedient.
3. Asking the Holy Spirit to counsel and empower us.
4. Cooperating with the Holy Spirit to crucify our old nature and selfishness.

As we do these things we find the promises and blessings of God in our lives.

Having received Christ as your Savior, and making Him the Lord of your everyday life, are two very different things. Both are necessary in order to receive and enjoy the promises of God. If He is not the Lord of your everyday life, then you will be unable to conform to His ways. Please understand that choosing to do things your own way will stunt your growth. In all honesty, we don't really know God in the truest sense if we have not yet allowed Him the place of Lordship in every area of our lives, including the attitudes of our hearts. I know this because I lived like this for years—*doing* "good" things, but never really spending the time getting to *know* Him. Only as we partner with the Holy Spirit, surrender our self-will, and submit to His guidance can we come to know Him as He desires.

> **Only as we partner with the Holy Spirit,**
> **surrender our self-will, and submit to His guidance,**
> **can we come to know Him as He desires.**

Bible teacher Joyce Meyer has said, "I can sit in a garage all day, but that doesn't make me a car; just like I can go to church every week, and that doesn't make me a Christian."

Questions for Study
1. What is a covenant?
2. What is the responsibility of the believer in covenant relationship with God?
3. How often do you spend time getting to know Jesus in a deeper, more intimate way?
4. What is a mediator?
5. What role does the Holy Spirit play within our covenant relationship with God? Have you asked for His help?
6. According to Hebrews 9:9, what makes the old covenant inadequate?
7. According to Hebrews 8:10 and Ezekiel 36:27, what happens to a person as he or she partners with the Holy Spirit?
8. What's the difference between the two covenants?
9. What must we do in order for the promises and the blessings of God to come about in our lives?

Personal Prayer

Lord, I know that I cannot find favor with You by keeping a list of rules. Forgive me for trying to reach You according to my own methods. Thank You for providing a new agreement, a new covenant, for me to enter into. I desire to partner with You! Your Word says that You will put Your Spirit within me and cause me to walk in Your ways, and I shall heed Your commands and do them (Ezekiel 36:27). Lord, by Your grace, help me to do this. Thank You for the covenant that You have made with me, putting Your ways upon my mind and upon my innermost thoughts and understanding. Engrave them upon my heart, and be my God! (Hebrews 8:10). Lord, thank You for blessing me with every spiritual blessing given by the Holy Spirit (Ephesians 1:3). Now help me to honor You with my entire being, and thank You for not withholding any good thing from me as long as I continue to walk in Your ways (Psalm 84:11).

Chapter 10

Who Is He?

One of the main things that the Holy Spirit wants to reveal to every believer is the true identity of God. When we come to Christ, we have our own ideas about who we think God is. Unfortunately, many times our perception of God, and the reality of who He really is, are two very different things. We oftentimes see God as we see authority figures in our lives. If our parents, pastors, teachers, or coaches did not represent God well to us, then our view of Him is probably skewed. That's why we must take the time to talk to God, to listen to Him, to read and study His Word, to think about His character, and to consider how He handled Himself in every situation. The interweaving of the Word and the Spirit within us will gradually transform us into the image of Jesus Christ as we grow in our belief and understanding of God's true character.

It is the interweaving of the Word and the Spirit within each of us that will gradually transform us into the image of Jesus Christ as we grow in our belief and understanding of God's true character.

God the Father, Jesus the Son, and God the Holy Spirit together make up the Three-in-One God. God the Father reigns in heaven. Jesus the Son sits at the right hand of the Father. God the Holy Spirit abides here on earth, representing and imparting the fruit of the Spirit within us. In other words, the Triune God loves, He is joyful, peaceful, patient, kind, good, gentle, faithful, and self-controlled. He is polite, always acts like a gentleman, and always has our best interests at heart. He is faithful, steadfast, and enduring. He loves to bless, reward, and heal those who diligently seek Him. He is not biased, racist, or sexist. He loves all and desires to be the lifter of our heads. He is forgiving, full of wisdom, grace, mercy, and truth. He is compassionate and full of knowledge; He never holds a grudge or lies. He will never leave us nor will He ever forsake us. He cares enough to discipline, correct, and even punish us if necessary, and always with our good in mind! The Triune God has a great plan for our lives; He will never quit or give up on us! He is the strong, sovereign Creator of the universe and of all things. And He is crazy about you! God the Father, God the Son and God the Holy Spirit has called you into relationship with Himself, to partner with Him so that you can represent Him here on earth!

I believe the words Paul wrote to the Philippians about his own purpose. I believe it should be our focal point as well. Philippians 3:10-12 says,

> *[For my determined purpose is] that I may know Him* [that I may progressively become more deeply and intimately acquainted with Him, perceiving and recognizing and understanding the wonders of His Person more strongly and more clearly], and that I may in that same way come to know the power out-flowing from His resurrection [which it exerts over believers], and that I may so share His sufferings as to be continually transformed [in spirit into His likeness even] to His death, [in the hope] that if possible I may attain to the [spiritual and moral] resurrection [that lifts me] out from among the dead [even while in the body]. Not that I have attained [this ideal], or have already been made perfect, but I press on to lay hold (grasp) and make my own, that for which Christ Jesus (the Messiah) has laid hold of me and made me His own.

These verses pack a powerful punch. So let's dissect them here.

1. Paul wanted to *know* Jesus the Person, not just *know about* Him. To *know* someone means to develop a deep and intimate relationship with him or her. It is to see, recognize and understand what a person is about; their character, actions, and reactions; the way they live life.[1] To *know about* someone is to simply have an acquaintance, not an intimate relationship, with that person.

2. Paul wanted to *know* through personal experience the out-flowing power of Christ's resurrection. That is, Paul wanted to know how to live above the circumstances of life just as Jesus did. Jesus's strong connection to God kept Him from being intimidated by His enemies. He knew who He was, where He had come from, and why He was here. Therefore, He was untainted by other people's thoughts and words about him. Paul wanted to become like that. We should, too!

3. Paul wanted to share in His *sufferings:* A study of Paul's life reveals great suffering on his part in order that he would be like Christ and spread the Word about Him. Paul was beaten, abandoned by friends, shipwrecked, put in prison, and executed. Although most of us are not likely to be shipwrecked or beaten for what we believe, we are called to the same daily-dying-to-ourselves that Paul was called to. We must die to sin, our self-will, and the selfish desires that dictate our flesh. Without a doubt, we will all face some kind of suffering in this life. Yet the greatest suffering we must undertake is to "die daily" to self, just as Paul did.

4. This "suffering" of dying daily transforms us to His likeness. As believers, we need to be willing to die to our own self-centeredness and become alive to Christ-likeness. The only way to achieve this is by receiving God's grace, renewing our minds with the Word, and allowing the Holy Spirit to empower us.

Philippians 3:11 talks about "being lifted out from among the dead even while in the body." It pictures the overcoming of selfishness and negativity and the refusal to wallow in sinful practices that keep someone "dead" to Christ. It means not allowing the muck and mire to keep you bound while you're still in the body, just like Jesus! Paul determined to not allow his circumstances to dictate his level of joy or how he felt about himself. He was intent on not allowing his circumstances to alter who he was. We see him live this out when he and Silas were thrown into prison for setting a girl free from an evil spirit. (See Acts 16:16-26.) Seriously, do you think for one minute that Paul felt like singing when he was imprisoned? Would you have felt like singing in such circumstances? Probably not. Clearly, the resurrection power was at work in Paul, even while he remained in the body! From what he could see, his circumstances were obviously dark, but something happened when he began to sing!

1. His spirit was lifted.
2. His belief became grounded.
3. His circumstances changed!
4. The chains that bound him fell off, and the doors flew open!

Do you find yourself in dead circumstances that need to be changed? Are you willing to allow the Holy Spirit to change you, even in your attitude?

In verse twelve of Philippians 3, Paul writes that he has not yet been made perfect. He says that he keeps "pressing on" to lay hold of this every time he finds himself in a situation full of dead circumstances. Paul wanted to understand and claim the character and power that Christ made available to him when He chose the cross. By choosing the cross and sending the Holy Spirit, Christ gave us the power to live a life that represents His character and resurrection power, even while in our earthly bodies! Our part is to believe in God's grace, be willing to take hold of this power by dying to ourselves and surrendering to the Holy Spirit.

Do you realize that the Creator of the universe lives inside of you and has made His power available to you? *Everything* that God is and has, He has made available to you and me through the cross that leads to salvation, healing, and provision.

We have a right to the benefits and inheritance of salvation if we are willing to do these things:

1. Partner with His Spirit.
2. Separate ourselves from the ways of the world.
3. Place our faith in His power, ability, efficiency, and might.
4. Praise Him.

**Do you realize that the
Creator of the universe lives inside of you
and has made His power available to you?**

Look at the names of God that describe who He is to us:

1. *Elohim:* God Almighty!
2. *Jehovah:* Lord!
3. *Adonai:* Master and owner of all people!
4. *El-Shaddai:* God almighty, all powerful and able!
5. *Jehovah-Jireh:* The God who foresees and provides!

6. *Jehovah-Rophe:* The God who heals and sweetens!
7. *Jehovah-Nissi:* My banner and protector!
8. *Jehovah-M'Kaddesh:* The God who sanctifies and sets apart!
9. *Jehovah-Shalom:* The God of peace!
10. *Jehovah-Tsidkenu:* The God of righteousness!
11. *Jehovah-Rohi:* My Shepherd!
12. *Jehovah-Shammah:* The God who is always there!

Ask yourself these questions: Do I *know* God personally in accordance to the meaning of His names? Am I determined in my purpose to know Him as Paul knew Him? Paul tells us in Philippians 3:9 that he wants to be known as "in Him," a person without any self-achieved righteousness that can be called his own. This includes his obedience to all the laws, demands, or ritualistic uprightness and supposed right-standing before God that *he* acquired. Instead, he wanted to own for himself the genuine righteousness that comes through faith. Thus he considered all of his own achievements as rubbish. Paul could only do this by placing confidence in what Christ has done for him on the cross. Only then could he be considered as having right-standing before God . . . a saving faith in what Jesus had made available to him.

Questions for Study:
1. How has God been misrepresented to you?
2. What are some of the characteristics of the Trinity (God the Father, Jesus the Son, and the Holy Spirit) that you would like to know more intimately?
3. What does it mean to "know" Him?
4. What does it mean to know the power out-flowing from Christ's resurrection? Why was Jesus so strong?
5. What does it mean to suffer? How can suffering be used for our good?
6. What happened to Paul when he began to sing in prison?
7. Look at the list of the names of God listed above. Which names do you personally "know" Him to be to you and which ones would you like to "know" more intimately?
8. In Philippians 3:9, Paul wants no self-achieved righteousness that can be called his own. List anything in your life that would be considered self-achieved righteousness.

Personal Prayer
Lord, my determined purpose is to know You so that I may progressively become more deeply and intimately acquainted with You, perceiving, recognizing, and understanding the wonders of Your Person more strongly and clearly. May I know the power out-flowing from Your resurrection that is exerted over believers. Help me when I suffer in the flesh to realize that as I suffer, I am continually being transformed into Your likeness, and I am putting to death the deeds of the flesh. Help me attain to the spiritual and moral resurrection that lifts me out from among the dead. Help me, Lord, to continuously press on and make my own, that for which Christ Jesus took hold of me (Philippians 3:10-12). Lord, because You chose the cross and sent Your Holy Spirit to me, I can live a life that represents Your character while I live in this body here on earth! Help me to "die daily" and surrender my will to Yours (1 Corinthians 15:31). I choose to partner with Your Holy Spirit; separated from the ways of the world, and to become a holy and fit vessel used for your service (2 Timothy 2:21).

Chapter 11

Who Am I "in Christ"?

This chapter is dedicated to helping you understand the authority you have in Christ and who you are *in partnership* with Him. John 15:5 tells us that "apart from Him we can do nothing," but with Him all things are possible (see Matthew 19:26). Proverbs 23:7 tells us, "For as a man thinks in his heart, so is he." In order to receive anything from God, we must partner with Him and believe in our hearts what He says about us in His Word! You and I have the right to receive all that Christ is so that we might become like Him. When we accept Christ as our Savior, the devil knows that we belong to Him. God has put His seal upon us by giving us His Holy Spirit to live in our hearts. This is our security deposit and guarantee that God will fulfill His promise (2 Corinthians 1:22). Thus, in the spiritual realm of life,—the part of life that is very real but that we cannot see with our physical eyes—we are covered with a robe of righteousness (See Isaiah 61:10; 2 Corinthians 5:21). God is on our side and has already defeated and overcome the world. He who lives in us is greater and mightier than he who is in the world (See 1 John 4:4).

Our partnership with Jesus is like no other. Our responsibility in the partnership is to believe, cooperate, and submit ourselves to Him. Completely. In proportion, as we yield ourselves to Christ, His character permeates our lives *because the Holy Spirit has empowered us to believe, cooperate and submit ourselves to His Word*. When we truly cooperate with God's Word and what it says about who we are as His partners, we become more like Him! We understand how to walk in love, grace, faith and truth, just as Jesus did. We hunger for the anointing and empowerment of the Holy Spirit. We become totally determined to do the will of the Father.

When we truly cooperate with God's Word
and what it says about who we are as His partners,
we become more like Him!

Let's start by confessing with our mouths and believing in our hearts these truths about who God says we are in partnership with Him.

- I am a child of God (John 1:12).
- I am the salt of the earth (Matthew 5:13).
- I am the light of the world (Matthew 5:14).
- I am Christ's friend (John 15:15).
- I am a slave of righteousness (Romans 6:18).
- I am a joint heir with Christ, and I share His inheritance with Him (Romans 8:17).
- I am a temple—a dwelling place of God. His Spirit and His life dwell in me (1 Corinthians 3:16; 6:19).
- I am a new creation (2 Corinthians 5:17).
- I am reconciled to God, and I am a minister of reconciliation (2 Corinthians 5:18-19).
- I am Christ's ambassador; God is making His appeal through me (2 Corinthians 5:20).
- I am the righteousness of God in Christ Jesus (2 Corinthians 5:21).
- I am a saint (Ephesians 1:1; 1 Corinthians 1:2; Philippians 1:1; Colossians 1:12).
- I am God's workmanship, His handiwork, born anew in Christ to do the work that He chooses for me (Ephesians 2:10).
- I am a fellow citizen with the rest of God's family (Ephesians 2:19).
- I am righteous and holy (Ephesians 4:24).
- I am a citizen of heaven, (positionally by virtue of being "in Christ"), seated in heaven right now (Philippians 3:20; Ephesians 2:6).
- I am hidden with Christ in God (Colossians 3:3).
- I am chosen by God, holy and dearly loved (Colossians 3:12; 1 Thessalonians 1:4).
- I am a partaker of Christ; I share in His life (Hebrews 3:14).
- I am one of God's living stones, being built up in Christ as a spiritual house (1 Peter 2:5).
- I am a member of a chosen race, a royal priesthood, a holy nation a person for God's own possession (1 Peter 2:9-10).
- I am an alien and stranger to this world in which I temporarily live (1 Peter 2:11).
- I am an enemy of the devil (1 Peter 5:8).
- I am born of God, and the evil one cannot touch me (1 John 5:18).
- I have been justified—completely forgiven and made righteous (Romans 5:1).
- I died with Christ and died to the power of sin's rule over my life (Romans 6:1-6).
- I am free forever from guilt and condemnation (Romans 8:1).
- I am free from the law of sin and death (Romans 8:2).
- I have received the Spirit of God into my life that I might know the things freely given to me by God (1 Corinthians 2:12).
- I have been given the mind of Christ (1 Corinthians 2:16).
- I have been bought with a price, I am not my own, I belong to God (1 Corinthians 6:19-20).
- Since I have died, I no longer live for myself, but for Christ (2 Corinthians 5:14-15).
- I have been crucified with Christ and it is no longer I who live, but Christ lives in me. The life I am now living is Christ's life (Galatians 2:20).
- I have been blessed with every spiritual blessing . . . all that belongs to Christ belongs to me and all that I am and have belongs to Him (Ephesians 1:3).

- I was chosen in Christ before the foundation of the world to be holy, and I am without blame before Him (Ephesians 1:4).
- I was predestined—determined by God to be adopted as His son/daughter (Ephesians 1:5).
- I have been redeemed and forgiven, and I am a recipient of His lavish grace (Ephesians 2:5).
- I have been raised up and seated with Christ in heavenly places (Ephesians 2:6).
- I have direct access to God through the Spirit (Ephesians 2:18).
- I have been secured from the domain of Satan's rule and transferred to the Kingdom of Christ (Colossians 1:13).
- I have been redeemed and forgiven of all my sins. The debt against me has been cancelled (Colossians 1:14).
- Christ Himself is in me (Colossians 1:27).
- I have been made complete in Christ (Colossians 2:10).
- I have been given the spirit of power, love, and a sound mind (2 Timothy 1:7).
- I have been saved and set apart according to God's doing, not of my own righteousness or good deeds (2 Timothy 1:9; Titus 3:5).
- I have a right to come boldly before the throne of God to find mercy and grace in time of need (Hebrews 4:16).
- I have been given exceedingly great and precious promises by God, by which I am a partaker of His divine nature (2 Peter 1:4).
- I have a right to be protected by the armor of God in order to stand firm against the schemes of the enemy (Ephesians 6:10-18).
- The Lord has made me the head and not the tail, above and not beneath. He has opened His good storehouse for me, to bless all the work of my hands. I lend to many, but never have to borrow—I listen to the commandments of the Lord and observe them carefully (Deuteronomy 28:12-13).
- Like Abraham, I am blessed to be a blessing (Genesis 12:2).
- I have been made by Him to be but a little lower than angels (or heavenly beings), and He has crowned me (given me favor) with glory and honor (Psalm 8:5).
- I have been given dominion over the works of God's hands (Psalm 8:6).
- I was destined from the beginning to be molded into the image of His Son and share His likeness (Romans 8:29).
- As I stare into the Word of God like a mirror, I am constantly being transformed into His very own image, from one degree of glory to another (2 Corinthians 3:18).
- The Father has given me the gift of the Holy Spirit because I ask Him and continue to ask Him for His help (Luke 11:13).
- The Holy Spirit has come upon me, and I am filled—receiving power, ability, efficiency, and might in order to be His witness (Acts 1:8).
- I am strong in the Lord, and I am empowered through my union and communion with Him, drawing my strength from Him (Ephesians 6:10).
- I have been given authority and power (physical and mental strength and ability) over Satan. Nothing shall in any way harm me (Luke 10:19).
- I have strength for all things in Christ who empowers me (Philippians 4:13).

First and foremost, God has called you into a relationship with Himself (see 1 Thessalonians 5:24). If you believe these things and act on them, God will transform you and complete this work He has begun inside of you. It is right and appropriate for you to have this confidence and feel this way about yourself and all other believers. The transformation happens because we become partakers and sharers of grace: God's unmerited favor, empowerment, and spiritual blessings. This is our starting point!

We have the strength for all things because we partner with Christ who empowers us. We must continually cooperate with His Holy Spirit to work the character of Christ in us. When we do so, we are ready for and can handle anything He assigns us to do through Him. He infuses us with His inner strength, through the power of the Holy Spirit (See Philippians 1:6-7; 4:13). By submitting to the Holy Spirit, we have right-standing with God and we desire to do things His way in thought, word, attitude, and deed. Thus, we will flourish like the palm tree, and we will grow like a cedar in Lebanon. We are planted in the house of the Lord, and we will flourish in the courts of our God. We will still yield fruit in old age. We will be full of the life-giving sap of the Holy Spirit emanating out from us and drawing others to Him. We will forever declare that the Lord is upright. He is our Rock, and there is no unrighteousness in Him! (See Psalm 92:12-15).

Questions for Study
1. Go through all the verses and highlight or rewrite the verses the Holy Spirit uses to speak to you. Make it a daily practice to confess the Word of God regarding who He says you are, and how He sees you.
2. Do you really believe who God says you are in partnership with Him, or are you more concerned with who people say you are?
3. Do you believe that nothing is impossible with Him and that He can accomplish anything within you and through you if you partner with Him?
4. Are you cooperating with His Holy Spirit and submitting yourself to Him every day?

Personal Prayer
Lord, I realize that apart from you I can do nothing, but with you all things are possible! (John 15:5; Matthew 19:26). Help me to understand who I am in Christ. Your Word says that Your people perish for lack of knowledge (Hosea 4:6). Thank You for showing me my authority as a believer and help me to walk in that. I want to start seeing myself as You see me and align my thoughts, words, attitudes, and deeds with Yours. Your Word says that "I am the righteousness of God in Christ." I believe Your Word that says I can become more like You (2 Corinthians 5:21; Isaiah 61:10). I am Your temple, and Your Spirit lives in me (1 Corinthians 3:16; 6:19). Make me Your servant, Lord. Thank You for making me complete in You (Colossians 2:10). Thank You for choosing, appointing, and approving me so that I may go and bear much fruit through the power of Your Holy Spirit. Cause this fruit to remain and bring glory to Your Name. I know that as I live a life completely dedicated to you, I can ask of the Father in Your Name and He will give it to me (John 15:16). I am consecrated, holy, and set apart for Your service! Thank You that I am a member of a chosen race, a royal priesthood, a holy nation, in Your possession so that I may proclaim your praises—You who called me out of darkness into your marvelous light (1 Peter 2:9).

Chapter 12

The Soul
Rooted in Righteousness

s God's Word, His love, and His Spirit become rooted inside of us, we learn to detect sin in various areas of our lives more easily. Suddenly we become uncomfortable with wrong thought patterns, bad attitudes, misdeeds, hurtful words, and so forth, and we want them out of our lives.

Second Corinthians 5:21 informs us that we are the righteousness of God in Christ Jesus. At rebirth our spirit is cleaned up instantly. The Spirit of God cannot dwell where sin remains. Because the Holy Spirit is living in our spirit, He desires to cleanse and penetrate our souls (mind, will, attitudes, and emotions), and to radiate His love through us in our thoughts, word, attitudes, and actions toward others. The soul of man must be totally surrendered to the Holy Spirit in order to be cleaned up, renewed, and made whole. Remember, the soul is the part of us that is always in contact with what we want, think, and feel.

Only the Word of God can divide soul from spirit (see Hebrews 4:12). This can only be accomplished as we submit to and partner with the Holy Spirit. As we cooperate, He conforms our ways to His, bringing healing, wholeness, and restoration. James 1:21 tells us that the Word implanted in our hearts has the power to save our souls. Jesus intends to teach us how to live with our spirit connected to His Spirit, penetrating our souls and manifesting through our behavior. This is known as dying to self and walking in the Spirit. In other words, God synchronizes our spirits, souls, and bodies to be in agreement and harmony with His. He makes us vessels, pouring Himself into us and flowing freely out from us.

Matthew 6:33 says, "But seek (aim at and strive after) first of all His kingdom and His righteousness (His way of doing and being right), and then all these things taken together will be given you besides." Let's look more in depth at the key words of this Scripture. What does it mean to seek God? To *seek* means to desire, require, crave or to go after; pursue.[1] What is the Kingdom of God? Romans 14:17 says, "[after all] the kingdom of God is not a matter of [getting the] food and drink [one likes], but instead it is righteousness (that state which makes a person acceptable to God) and [heart] peace and joy in the Holy Spirit."

God does not want us to chase after the "things" of the world (promotions, cars, vacations, power, bigger houses, etc.). Rather, He wants us to seek Him and the way He does things first. We think that the "things" of the world will bring us joy and peace, but we are sadly mistaken. Righteousness, right-standing with God by faith in Jesus Christ, must first be established in our lives. Peace and joy will follow as we walk with the Holy Spirit (see Romans 14:17). When the proper order is established in our lives, then, "all these things," shall be added unto us because "things" do not own us.

Righteousness is having right standing with God. It means to have moral and spiritual rectitude in every area of our lives and every relationship we are in. "It is one who is right, just clear, clean, righteous; a person who is characterized by fairness, integrity, and justice in his dealings. It conveys justice and integrity in one's lifestyle."[2] Righteousness cannot be obtained by earning or working for it. We can only receive it as a gift from God because of what Jesus did for us.

Proverbs 15:9 says, "The way of the wicked (those who follow their own ways)* is an abomination, extremely disgusting and shamefully vile to the Lord, but He loves him who *pursues* righteousness (moral and spiritual *rectitude* in every area and relation)."

Pursue means to "run after, chase, put to flight, follow after,"[3] and *rectitude* means "to conduct according to moral principles; strict honesty; uprightness of character, correctness of judgment or method, straightness."[4]

If we want lives that are rooted in righteousness, we must do the following three things:

1. Receive Christ's work on the cross for ourselves.
2. Be determined to see ourselves as already having right standing with God.
3. Partner with the Holy Spirit.

Please understand that becoming holy, pure, and blameless in the sight of God costs the believer something. It is misleading to simply speak of the rewards of following Christ without mentioning the cost. There is a price tag attached. As we hand ourselves over to Jesus, He will walk us through the valleys and will use everything for our good, even what the devil intends for our harm!

Look at the cross of Christ and what it cost Jesus. Now "pick up your cross," and take on the pain of:

- Dying to self—giving up your way of thinking and being.
- Suffering the cost of denying your fleshly desires.
- Nailing your old ways to the cross.
- Continuously and consistently choosing the reactions of Christ.

Depriving the flesh of the things it desires will cause great pain. I know this to be true in my own life when I am tempted to spout off with my mouth without thinking first. God uses His Word and His Holy Spirit to remind me of the character of Christ and to help me live according to it. James 1:19 says that we should be quick to listen and slow to speak, which means anything at odds with this behavior does not match the character of Christ and must go. Therefore, whenever I am in a situation where I want to spout off first, I pray for the Holy Spirit to help me and I thank Him for His grace. I often quote James 1:19, stating that, "I am quick to listen and slow to speak!" I also claim the truth of Proverbs 17:27 which says, "I have knowledge and understanding therefore I use my words sparingly and my spirit remains cool."

This enables the course of my direction to be changed. I make the decision not to spout off, and I set my mind to think before I speak. (On a side note, I have failed at this a lot, but I'm a constant work in progress).

When I do not give in to my natural way of doing things, I pay the cost:

1. I die to self (what I wanted to do—spout off).
2. My flesh takes the beating (I suffer to keep quiet).
3. I nail the old behavior to the cross (my natural reaction without Christ).
4. I determine to submit my natural way of being to the Holy Spirit's leading.

The rewards of following righteousness are plentiful. The enemy is defeated. His stronghold in this area is weakening and the resurrection of the new nature is working in me! This is the picture of Philippians 1:6 and 2:12

> And I am convinced and sure of this very thing, that He Who began a good work in you will continue until the day of Jesus Christ [right up to the time of His return], developing [that good work] and perfecting and bringing it to full completion in you. And: . . ." work out (cultivate, carry out to the goal, and fully complete) your own salvation with reverence and awe and trembling (self-distrust, with serious caution, tenderness of conscience, watchfulness against temptation, shrinking from whatever might offend God and discredit the name of Christ).

Consider the words of our Lord in the Garden of Gethsemane when He prayed to God to "take this cup (what He was about to endure) away from Him . . ." before stating, "But not My will be done, but Your will." Jesus desired to remain in right standing with God at all costs. Every temptation of the flesh that the enemy uses to keep you in bondage and out of right standing with God can be broken and defeated. When we continuously submit to the Holy Spirit and request His help while remaining in God's Word, He is able and willing. He will lead you out of the old habits, temptations, and mindsets that previously brought about death to your situations. He will untangle you and lead you into life. The flesh is weak and wants no part of suffering, but the spirit is willing.

What we think and what we say are greatly correlated to the state of righteousness within our souls. Alluding to that fact is:

> The mouths of the righteous (those harmonious with God) bring forth skillful and godly Wisdom, but the perverse tongue shall be cut down [like a barren and rotten tree]. (Proverbs 10:31] And:..." The thoughts and purposes of the [consistently] righteous are honest and reliable, but the counsels and designs of the wicked are treacherous." Remember the saying: "Rotten roots, rotten fruit; healthy roots, healthy fruit. (Proverbs 12:5)

These proverbs are saying just that. Literally, we need to push away unholy thoughts, words, attitudes, and deeds, along with any and all impurities. For this is the will of God. Our level of spiritual growth is revealed in how we react to God, self, and others when we don't get our way.

**Our level of spiritual growth is revealed in how we react to
God, self, and others when we don't get our way.**

Meditate on the following verses regarding righteousness or right standing with God in every area of your live.

Matthew 5:6 says, "Blessed and fortunate and happy and spiritually prosperous (in that state in which the born-again child of God enjoys His favor and salvation) are those who hunger and thirst for righteousness (uprightness and right standing with God), for they shall be *completely* satisfied!" (That is: despite our current conditions or circumstances).

Proverb 12:3 says, "A man shall not be established by wickedness *(doing things his own way), but *the root* of the [uncompromisingly] righteous shall never be moved." (Remember one of the tactics of the enemy is to get us to compromise slightly in order to trap us. Don't fall for this! No compromising of the Truth!).

Proverbs 12:12, 21, 26, and 28 say, " . . . but the root of the (uncompromisingly) righteous yields (richer fruitage). No [actual] evil, misfortune, or calamity shall come upon the righteous." (Please note, this does not mean you will live a trouble-free life). It does mean that you will know how to deal with your troubles when they come. With God's enabling grace and your mind set on remaining in right standing with Him, is a power that no foe can defeat). . . . The [consistently] righteous man is a guide to his neighbor, but the way of the wicked causes others to go astray. . . . Life is in the way of righteousness (moral and spiritual rectitude in every area and relation), and in its pathway there is no death but immortality (perpetual eternal life)."

Proverbs 13:6: "Righteousness (rightness and justice in every area and relations) guards him who is upright in the way, but wickedness plunges into sin and overthrows the sinner."

I pray we will always choose to put on righteousness, and to disregard the cost as we focus on the gain!

Questions for Study
1. What is righteousness?
2. If you want your life to be rooted in "right standing" with God, what three things must you do?
3. List the four costs for establishing righteousness within your soul.
4. What are the rewards for following after righteousness?
5. What must you do in order to escape the bondage of Satan and the dictates of the flesh so that the Spirit can lead you into life in all your circumstances?
6. Consider three very important areas of your life—home, work (or school), and your friends. Do you have right standing with God in all three areas and in all of your relationships?
7. Ask the Holy Spirit to reveal to you any areas or relationships in your life that are displeasing to Him, and then repent of them.

Personal Prayer

Lord, thank You that I am the righteousness of God in partnership with Christ Jesus (2 Corinthians 5:17-20). I realize that the enemy desires for me to see myself as a sinner, so that I will never rise above that capacity. Forgive me for viewing myself in that manner and help me to see myself as You do. Teach me, Lord, to live according to Your Spirit. Impart Your grace to me now which empowers me to do so (Romans 8:14). Help me to pursue and desire the kingdom of Heaven and Your righteousness all the days of my life (Matthew 6:33; Romans 14:17). Please align my mind, will, attitudes, and emotions to Yours so that I may live an honest and reliable life (Proverbs 10:31; 12:5). Lord, I do consider myself blessed, fortunate, and happy because I hunger and thirst for Your righteousness. I am completely satisfied in You (Matthew 5:6).

Chapter 13

The Soul
Rooted in Humility

The personal, "hands on" experience of spending time in God's presence enables us to grasp the love He has for us. The Word of God, Christ's cleansing blood, and the Holy Spirit work together within us. When we spend time in His presence, He gives us glimpses of His heart, of who He is, and how He works to make us like Himself. He uses this ongoing process to show us attitudes in our lives that need to be adjusted or completely removed. God wants our every attitude to agree with Him, carrying His precious fragrance of love. The attitudes we hold about ourselves and others make up the aromas of our hearts.

These fragrances express themselves through our words, the looks on our faces, our attitudes, and body languages. Thus, a heart rooted in sin, selfishness, pride, and fear carries the fragrances of rot and decay. These roots are the cause of spiritual blindness, which stunts our growth. On the other hand, a heart that is rooted in righteousness, humility, and faith naturally displays God and His love. Our attitudes reveal our roots, leading us to either spiritual blindness or to real life. It is safe to say that humility is an attitude and a mind-set, just as pride is. Our level of humility, or spiritual maturity, is revealed through our attitudes and manifested in how we treat others.

As followers of Christ, it is important to understand the role our attitudes play in our lives. The outcome of our lives is directly connected to the attitudes of our heart and soul. Not only do our attitudes display the fragrances of our hearts, but they do for our spirits what our arteries do for our bodies. These thick-walled tubes carry blood directly from our hearts to the principle parts of our bodies.[1] If a tube is unobstructed, then blood flows smoothly and is able to carry life to the rest of the body. If the arteries are clogged with the sludge of an improper diet, the blood cannot flow properly throughout. This leads to serious breakdowns within the entire body.

In the same manner, our attitudes carry life or death to our souls, our circumstances, and our relationships.

Our attitudes carry life or death to our souls, our circumstances, and our relationships.

Roots of humility grow life-giving attitudes, but roots of pride grow death-giving attitudes. If we allow ourselves to feast on the sludge of pride (what we want, think, and feel), then our souls become clogged, dramatically hindering the Spirit of God from working in our lives. This causes breakdown not only for us, but for those around us as well.

Remember, God's character is the standard. If our attitudes agree with the character and nature of Christ, His Spirit is able to flow freely.

Let's look at what humility means. *Humility,* by definition, is the exact opposite of pride. It is modesty, lowliness, *an attitude* or mindset of unselfish concern regarding the welfare of others. It is a total absence of arrogance, conceit, and haughtiness. It means to be meek and mild tempered.[2]

Humility and meekness go hand in hand. *Meekness* is an attitude of *humility* toward God and gentleness toward people. Meekness is a result of a person's conscious choice. *It is strength and courage under control, coupled with kindness.*[3]

Humility and meekness of heart should always distinctly characterize a follower of Christ. Pride and arrogance, on the other hand, are two very distinct characteristics that identify the nature of those who live in agreement with Satan.

The Apostle Paul wrote about Jesus' life of humility in Philippians 2:2-8. He wrote,

> Fill up and complete my joy by living in harmony and being of the same mind and one in purpose, having the same love, being in full accord and of *one harmonious mind and intention.* Do nothing from factional motives [through contentiousness, strife, selfishness, or for unworthy ends] or prompted by conceit and empty arrogance. Instead, in the true spirit of humility (lowliness of mind) *let each regard the others as better than and superior to himself* [thinking more highly of one another than you do yourselves]. Let each of you cstccm and look upon and be concerned for not (merely) his own interests, but also each for the interests of others. *Let this same attitude and purpose and [humble] mind be in you which was in Christ Jesus;* [let Him be your example in humility]. Who although being essentially one with God and in the form of God [possessing the fullness of the attributes which make God God], did not think this equality with God was a thing to be eagerly grasped or retained, *but stripped Himself [of all privileges and rightful dignity] so as to assume the guise of a servant (slave),* in that He became like men and was born a human being. And after He had appeared in human form, He abased and *humbled* Himself [still further] and carried His *obedience* to the extreme of death, even the death of the cross!

These verses clearly depict the fragrance of the heart of Christ. He set His mind and determined that His purpose was to become a slave! Christ's attitude *purposefully* placed Himself beneath that of another. By choosing to do this, Jesus lifted us up closer to God. Jesus humbled Himself and gave up the comforts of Heaven, taking on the abuse so readily given by mankind so that we might have a relationship with God. Consider what it cost Jesus for us to have a relationship with Him! How many people are willing to do the same thing for someone else? Am I? Are you?

By choosing to place Himself under another,
Jesus lifted us up closer to God.

It is important to note that humility and obedience always work together in a person's life. Please realize that when we choose to place ourselves under another we are lifting that individual up closer to God. Jesus' life truly portrays a story of "riches to rags" for the sake of another. Our level of humility will always be revealed through our attitudes and manifested in how we treat others.

Choosing humility, through God's empowering grace, will enable us to:

- Set aside ourselves and our will;
- Set aside our feelings;
- Set aside unfair treatment;
- Set aside our circumstances;
- Set aside what others think of us;
- Set aside our excuses;
- Set aside wrong mindsets and attitudes;
- Set aside our rights;
- Set aside our efforts toward self-vindication.

God requires these things for those of us who claim to be His disciples. It is our portion! It is our cup, just as it was that of Christ's. Humility is the attitude and decision to continuously place another above self. Pride, on the other hand, is the attitude and decision to place self over another. Notice the way that God cares for the humble. Don't miss the truth that, as you release the care of yourself to God and become a doer of His Word, He will care for you! We see it at the end of the passage in Philippians 2:9 which says, "Therefore, [because He stooped so low] God has highly exalted Him and has freely bestowed on Him the name above every name!" Most definitely, in the Kingdom of God, the last shall be first (see Matthew 19:30).

I'd also like to point out that an attitude of humility does not mean remaining in an abusive relationship. By all means, if you or your children are in danger of being harmed, humility does not enable you to stay. In fact, it is humility that will enable you to leave. God never designed for anyone to become the "punching bag," or doormat of another.

Humility produces a peaceful quiet and enables you to hear God speak and reveal His ways directly into your heart. By submitting your will to the Holy Spirit, you will be refined and empowered with grace to walk out the humility of Jesus Christ in your own life. This is the result of spending time in *quiet* before God. John 3:30 says, "He must increase, but I must decrease. [He must grow more prominent; I must grow less so]." First Peter 3:4 says, "A gentle and peaceful spirit is very precious in the sight of God." By abiding in Him, you can exhibit this gentle and peaceful spirit in your life and the joy of the Lord will be your strength.

Conversely, those who choose not to spend time with God consistently will not have this inner quiet. Instead, their inner selves, their souls, will be tuned in to the noise of the world. They will find confusion within them about which voice is God's, the enemy's, others, or their own. Oftentimes, these people will confuse polished and perfected behavior with real humility.

True humility, however, always shows up in how we treat others, and especially behind closed doors. Consider this—can you hear someone whispering during a loud storm? Neither can you hear the still small voice of God inside of you if there is a storm raging in you.

These three things are sure to occur during quiet time with God:

1. Minds will be renewed and empowered by the Word and the Spirit to think like God thinks.
2. Self-will will be surrendered and broken to the point where the only concern is pleasing Christ.
3. Emotions and attitudes will be healed, bridled, or removed, no longer able to control you.

Questions for Study

1. Attitudes that come from within us are literally the _____ of our hearts.
2. How is our level of humility revealed and manifested?
3. The outcome of our lives is directly connected to _____ ?
4. Write out the definitions of humility and meekness.
5. Pride and arrogance are two distinct characteristics that identify a person in agreement with Satan. What are two characteristics that should identify those of us who claim to be identified with Christ?
6. What is the attitude and fragrance that emanates from Christ and out to others?
7. What three things happen to you personally by spending quiet time with God?
8. Ask the Holy Spirit to reveal any hidden attitudes in your heart that may be displeasing to Him. Then, confess, repent, receive His grace and empowerment—and move on.

Personal Prayer

Lord, forgive me for not always choosing to display Your humility and grace to others as You have so graciously shown me. I confess it as sin and place myself in Your hands, and I ask You to work humility into my soul. May that humility then bear witness to the truth of Your character. Help me to do nothing from selfish ambition, arrogance, or conceit. Help me not to exclude others because they are different from me or do not think as I do. Help me, instead, to show humility, which is rooted in love. Help me to consider others as better than myself. Help me to be concerned with the interests of others and not merely my own interests. May I display the same attitude that Christ Jesus displayed (Philippians 2:2-8). Help me to remember that when I choose to place myself under another, as opposed to arguing with them, I am choosing to lift that individual up closer to You. Help me to have a healthy balance in this area of my life. Help me to decrease so that You may increase (John 3:30). Thank You that the last shall be first. Thank You that You exalt those who will humble themselves before You. Help me to be humble (Philippians 2:9; Matthew 19:30). Cause me to partner with Your Holy Spirit as He works Your humility within me.

Chapter 14

Humility Is
Virtue and Power

———◦———

Humility and meekness are two characteristics that Jesus lived out despite His circumstances or situations. What we must understand as believers is that humility and meekness equal virtue and power. Neither can be obtained by simply trying harder. But, we can obtain them by *cooperating* with and *surrendering* to the Holy Spirit and the Word of God. He uses these things to untangle us from our natural reactions, old habits, and wrong mindsets and to train us in the ways of God according to His nature and character. Humility will cause us to run to Jesus, especially when we've blown it.

Humility enables us to draw near to God and His throne of grace for help in our time of need (see Hebrews 4:16). Ultimately, a truly humble person lives revering God and His Word and refuses to live life according to his or her own ideas, reasoning, judgments, and thinking. (See Proverbs 3:5-6; Matthew 19:26.) Acts 1:8 and Luke 11:13 assure us of His power, ability, efficiency and might, which comes from the Holy Spirit as we ask for help and surrender to Him and His Word.

Let's take a look at the definitions of virtue and power:

1. Virtue: Moral excellence; intrinsic value; goodness.[1]
2. Power: Generally the word means "capacity" or "ability," whether physical, mental, or spiritual. If power suggests physical strength, authority suggests a moral right or privilege. Wealth, means, or substance.[2]

God has made it possible for us to be like Christ by giving us every quality that Jesus has. 2 Peter 1:3 says, "For His divine power has bestowed upon us all things that] are requisite and suited] to life and godliness, through the [full personal] knowledge of Him Who called us by and to His own glory and excellence (virtue)." Our responsibility is choosing to believe that His nature and character resides within us and allowing Him to live through us. We do this by choosing the ways of the Spirit over the ways of the flesh and our carnal thinking. We choose to focus our attention on Christ and not on our behavior alone. As we spend time in His presence, God will reveal to us the root cause of any undesirable, attitudes, thoughts, words and behaviors and heal our wounds.

It is important to focus our attention
on Christ and not on our behavior alone.

Think about the relationship between Jesus and Judas. You might remember that Judas was the disciple who betrayed Jesus by turning Him over to be killed. As His disciple, Judas spent a lot of time with Jesus. They had fellowship together, ate together, ministered together, and went to various towns doing good and preaching the Gospel. They were friends! What's amazing to me is how Jesus *chose* to treat Judas, even while knowing all along that Judas would one day betray Him. This is the picture of humility, virtue, and power at work in Jesus. Despite everything, Jesus loved Judas up to the very end. Look at Matthew 26:49-50, which describes the scene when Judas betrays Jesus. "And he (Judas)* came up to Jesus at once and said, Hail (greetings, good health and long life to you), Master! And he embraced Him and kissed Him with (pretended) warmth and devotion. Jesus said to him, *"Friend . . ."*

It's hard to miss Jesus' attitude of humility toward Judas. We see it in His mindset and His response toward Judas from start to finish. Despite what He knew about Judas, Jesus displayed virtue toward him by choosing to treat him with goodness and respect. Jesus displayed power in this situation by loving Judas, no matter what. That is power over the enemy! We too can demonstrate that same moral excellence by treating someone with goodness and respect despite how they treat us, or have treated us in the past.

Perhaps you are thinking, *"Well that was Jesus, but I just can't love people who have hurt me like that."* Yes, you can and I can too, but only by the grace of God! It starts with a choice to do so because the greater One lives in us. God asks us to live this way. Therefore, through His grace, He will provide us with His supernatural empowerment and strength. Simply ask Him for it. This is what Christianity is all about: partnering with Christ and living out the rest of our lives by witnessing His nature and character to the rest of the world. This, in turn, makes the dying world thirsty for what we have. We only need to be willing to crucify our old nature, habits, and natural responses and take on the new nature and empowerment of Christ.

Having said all this, I imagine there are still those who would look at the words meekness and humility and think, "Well, I certainly don't think I'm supposed to be a doormat!" In our own sense and reasoning, however, we often mistake meekness for weakness, but nothing could be further from the truth. Jesus is called both the meek Lamb and the bold Lion. We must become partakers of both. Joseph was a man who lived out this truth. We read his story in Genesis chapters 37-50. This man endured unfair treatment for the sake of others . . . but then came honor.

The words of 2 Chronicles 7:14 tell us how to live as God wants us to, humbly and yet boldly in His grace and mercy. "If My people, who are called by My name, shall humble themselves, pray, seek, crave, and require of necessity My face and turn from their wicked ways, then will I hear from heaven, forgive their sin, and heal their land." According to this verse, this is how you humble yourself before God:

1. Pray. Talk to God and ask Him to enable you to face where you are right now. Confess and repent of your sins, admitting that you need His help so that He can heal your wounds and impart His grace.

2. Seek His face. Desire a vital relationship with Him because of who He is, not just what He can do for you. (No offense intended, but wanting God's benefits without wanting the relationship is wrong heart motives).
3. Crave time with Him. Make it your priority every day.
4. Turn from your wicked ways; from your way of doing things, thinking, speaking, and being.

According to His promise, He will hear from heaven and heal you and your land. Look at the words of 1 Peter 5:6-10,

> Therefore, humble yourselves [demote, lower yourselves in your own estimation] under the mighty hand of God, that in due time He may exalt you. Casting the whole of your care [all your anxieties, all your worries, all your concerns, once and for all] on Him, for He cares for you affectionately and cares about you watchfully. Be well balanced (temperate, sober of mind), be vigilant and cautious at all times; for the enemy of yours, the devil, roams around like a lion roaring [in fierce hunger], seeking someone to seize upon and devour. Withstand him; be firm in faith [against his onset—rooted, established, strong, immovable, and determined], knowing that the same (identical) sufferings are appointed to your brotherhood (the whole body of Christians) throughout the world. And after you have suffered a little while, the God of all grace [Who imparts all blessing and favor], Who has called you to His [own] eternal glory in Christ Jesus, will Himself complete and make you what you ought to be, establish and ground you securely, and strengthen, and settle you.

Take a look at the conditions and promises in these verses.

Condition: If I choose to humble myself under the mighty hand of God, by asking for His help and discipline myself to do things His way . . .

Promise: Then He will exalt me in due time. "Due time" means God's timing, not ours. In the midst of this process, I must remain patient and keep a good attitude. God will teach me to do the right things consistently, long before I'll see any changes.

Condition: Cast all of my cares (everything that concerns me) into His hands. Become well balanced. Withstand the enemy and be firm in God's ability to take care of me.

Promise: He will care for me affectionately and watchfully; He will bestow on me blessings and favor. He will complete me. He will make me what I ought to be. He will establish and ground me securely in Him. He will strengthen and settle me.

Notice the pattern. I obey… God works in me.

Examine for yourself the pathway of humility, which always leads to the glory of God— His virtue and power! Christ is our perfect example at every crossroad of His life:

1. In Gethsemane. He had a choice to make. Am I going to choose my way or God's way?
2. At the Cross. We see the pain and suffering of identifying with Christ.
3. In His Death. We see the pain of setting self aside and crucifying our own ways.
4. At the Grave. We bury that old crucified nature that is unpleasing to Christ.

Then comes the promise of Resurrection bringing with it the glory of God—His virtue and power growing up in us, healing our spirits, souls, bodies, and exhibited through our attitudes, actions and behaviors towards God, others and ourselves.

In all of this, look at what happens to Satan.

1. He has no power over us despite our circumstances.
2. We are free from his grasp.
3. He is defeated.

Questions for Study
1. What do humility and meekness equal and how do we obtain them?
2. Think about the example of Jesus and Judas. Do you have any "Judases" in your life? How are you choosing to treat them despite what they have done to you?
3. How did Jesus display His humility, virtue, and power towards Judas?
4. How can you treat the people who have hurt you the same way that Jesus chose to treat Judas?
5. What is Christianity all about?
6. According to 2 Chronicles 7:14, how do you humble yourself?
7. Christ was the perfect example of humility. Write out the pathway He took. Is this the path you are choosing?
8. What cares, concerns, anxieties, fears, attitudes, old mindsets, habits, and so on, do you need to cast upon the Lord?

Personal Prayer
Lord, forgive me for "trying harder" in order to obtain humility. I confess that as sin, and I know that a change in me occurs because of your Spirit working in me, not because of my power or might (Zechariah 4:6). Thank You for providing a way for me to become like You and for bestowing upon me all things that are requisite and suited to life and godliness (2 Peter 1:3). Thank You that nothing is impossible with You! I ask You for the power and help of Your Holy Spirit, whom You willingly give to all of those who ask (Acts1:8; Luke 11:13). I ask You to show me the root cause of my thoughts, words, and actions that are not in agreement with Your character. Please heal any wounds in me that are causing me to hinder the work of the Holy Spirit. Thank You for desiring to heal and deliver me so that I can display Your true character, which is virtue and power (2 Chronicles 7:14). Lord, I am choosing to cast all of my cares, anxieties, and worries on You because You care affectionately for me. Help me to become well-balanced in my soul in order to withstand the attacks of the enemy. Complete and make me what I ought to be; establish, ground, and strengthen me in You (1 Peter 5:6-10). In everything, help me to treat others as I wish they would treat me (Matthew 7:12).

Chapter 15

The Soul
Rooted in Faith

———————◦———————

The soul rooted in righteousness and humility also exercises a great amount of trust and faith in God. Righteousness, humility, and faith work together to build in you an indestructible foundation and to breathe life into you, into your circumstances, and into your relationships. On the other hand, sin, selfishness, pride, and fear work together to bring about destruction and death in you, in your circumstances, and in your relationships. We cannot dabble in both of these worlds and please God, expecting His promises of blessings. How can we live by faith if we are fearful of man? How can we claim righteousness, right standing with God, and continue to be alive to sin? How can we humble ourselves for the sake and betterment of another, yet carry prejudice in our hearts? We cannot. This double-mindedness causes instability and strife. It also keeps us from the promises of God. This kind of life does not portray partnership with the Holy Spirit. Instead, this is a life that continues to be more self-centered rather than Christ centered.

To live by faith, we must set our minds, surrender our wills, and our emotions to follow God as His Spirit directs our hearts through His Word. To the unrenewed mind, this does not make sense. But to those of us desiring to be led by the Spirit of God, it is a necessity. We must take that leap of faith and jump wholly into the arms of Jesus.

The person with a faith-rooted soul has a distinct disposition. He is a person who places his entire trust, the entire leaning of his human personality, confidence, and assurance in Someone Greater than himself. He releases *all* cares, concerns, and vindication to God, *knowing* that He is at work and is fitting things together for good into a plan *for those who love and obey Him*. This individual no longer follows the physical senses and desires of his flesh (what he wants, thinks, and feels) or the circumstances in his life. Rather, his life is based on what Christ has accomplished for Him through the finished work of the cross and the Word of God. Together, the finished work of Christ, the Word, and the Holy Spirit govern his spirit, soul, and body. This is the faith-filled life!

Philemon 1:6 (paraphrased) tells us to recognize, appreciate and acknowledge every good thing that is ours in our identification with Christ. Perhaps you're wondering what exactly did Jesus accomplish for me when He went to the cross? Great question!

Isaiah 53:4-6 says,

> Surely He has borne our griefs, (sicknesses, weaknesses, and distresses) and carried our sorrows and pains [of punishment], yet we [ignorantly] considered Him stricken, smitten, and afflicted by God [as if with leprosy]. But He was wounded for our transgressions, He was bruised for our guilt and iniquities; the chastisement [needful to obtain] peace and well-being for us was upon Him, and with the stripes [that wounded] Him we are healed and made whole. All we like sheep have gone astray, we have turned every one to his own way; and the Lord has made to light upon Him the guilt and iniquity of us all.

More simply stated:

- Jesus was wounded so that my sins can be forgiven.
- Jesus was bruised so that I can be declared not guilty of sin and freed from eternal damnation.
- Jesus was chastised so that I can receive peace and well-being.
- Jesus was beaten so that I can be healed and made whole.
- Jesus bore my sins, iniquities, and guilt so that I can have His righteousness (right-standing) with God who now sees me as holy and pure.

Our minds must be renewed every day to what Christ has already accomplished for us or our souls will fall back into the temptation of being led by our physical senses and the carnal desires of our bodies (what we see, hear, touch, etc.). Oftentimes many Christians are content to simply snack on God's Word. However, we will never be totally satisfied or live a life that is full of God and His constant blessings.

Romans 1:17 says: "For the just shall live by faith." Paraphrased, this says, "For the justified—just as if we never sinned—and those who understand their position of righteousness—right standing with God—will live by believing and declaring what Christ has already done for them." Indeed, faith is the first and most essential element in a believer's life. As believers we must believe that God is able to make something good come about for His glory because of what Jesus did for us!

Let's look at the definition of faith as described in Hebrews 11:1-2: "Now faith is the assurance (the confirmation, the title deed) of the things [we] hope for, being the proof of things [we] do not see and the conviction of their reality [faith perceiving as real fact what is not revealed to the (physical) senses]."

Let me share with you a vital Kingdom Principle: In God's economy, or the way He does things, *we must believe first. Then we'll see the results second.*

In God's economy, we must believe first.
Then we'll see the results second.

What's more, when we become totally devoted to God, our requests match His will. The desires of our hearts will change until all we want is to know Him and to become more like Him. We will even stop trying to change ourselves and allow Him to transform us into His image. There will be no room in our requests to God for our self-centeredness. Second Corinthians 5:7 tells us to walk by faith, placing our confidence in God. It instructs us *to regulate our lives and to conduct ourselves according to our convictions or beliefs . . . with trust and holy fervor, not by sight or by how things appear.* Walking by faith requires us to regulate our lives and conduct ourselves according to Christ's finished work on the cross and to God's Word. Authentic faith cooperates with God's Holy Spirit to work out His Word from our spirits into our souls and out of our bodies.

Let's look at the definitions of trust, holiness, and fervor, for they give us even more insight as to how we are to work out this life of faith:

1. Trust—A firm belief or confidence in the honesty, integrity, reliability, justice, etc. of another person or thing; faith; reliance.[1]
2. Holiness—Godly, pure, clean in all areas and relationships. People who are removed from secular life and consecrated to the service of God. Moral perfection.[2] (This is a life emptied of selfishness and filled with the desires and ways of God).
3. Fervor—Intensity, strenuously, earnestly.[3]

I encourage you to ask yourself these three questions:

1. Am I placing my trust in God? (Remember, when you trust you are at rest, and your focus is on Jesus and what He has done for you, not on your problems or circumstances. See Hebrews 4:3).
2. Do I live a holy life? Am I pure, clean, and godly in every area and relationship? Have I decreased so He can increase? Is my thought life pure?
3. Am I intent about seeking God and about trusting Him and remaining pure before Him regarding all of my choices?

Please don't misunderstand; I'm not asking if you go to church every week or if you are signed up for spiritual and ministry related activities. I'm asking if you spend time every morning seeking God and thanking Him for Who He is and then inviting Him with you everywhere you go. This is how the Holy Spirit builds and imparts increasing faith. As we get to know Jesus more and more intimately, we will trust Him more and more completely.

**As we get to know Jesus more and more intimately,
we will trust Him more and more completely.**

If you are having trouble in these areas, I would bet that there is sin and turmoil in your life. Why not take a moment to allow the Holy Spirit to expose any area of concern in your life that is keeping you from faith—from fully trusting in God.

As believers we have all been given a measure of faith from God (see Romans 12:3). The working of our faith is like the working of our muscles. If we exercise the muscle, it will grow. Similarly, if we exercise our faith, our faith will grow. In the same way, if we don't exercise our muscles or the faith that we have been given, both will atrophy with inactivity. John 6:28-29 says,

> What are we to do, that we may [habitually] be working the works of God? [What are we to do to carry out what God requires?] Jesus replied, this is the work (service) that God asks of you: that you *believe in the One Whom He has sent [that you cleave to, trust, rely on, and have faith in His Messenger]*.

It seems that most professing Christians want to walk in faith, but admittedly we simply don't understand how to appropriate the faith that God has given to us. Perhaps some of us are refusing to give up living according to our physical senses, natural reactions, old habits, and wrong mindsets. Indeed, the old nature longs to dominate and rule us. More than likely, it is the combination of all these things. Instead, as followers of Christ we must be determined to spend time enjoying Jesus and allowing Him to nourish our souls. Studying and declaring the Word, as well as praying and meditating on Christ's finished work on the cross will also help us. In doing these things, we are being built up by the Holy Spirit; becoming rooted and grounded in love, changing from one level of glory to another, and growing and exercising our faith muscles.

Confessing and declaring the Word helps us to believe what it says, hence making it more natural for us to replace old habits and wrong mindsets in our lives through the choices we make. This is the ideal spiritual diet. If we want our faith to be strong, then we must learn to be determined to create these habits and separate ourselves from the world's "diet." Everything we think, say and do, watch on TV, or listen to, needs to honor God.

Confessing and declaring the Word
helps us to believe what it says.

Christ set a perfect example for us in maintaining faith. Acts 10:38 says, "How God anointed and consecrated Jesus of Nazareth with the [Holy] Spirit and with strength and ability and power; how He went about doing good and, in particular, curing all who were harassed and oppressed by [the power of] the devil, for God was with Him." Jesus set aside specific time to spend with God every day before He went out and started His day. At times He spent all night with God. Other times He would slip away from the crowds to regroup. If Jesus found this necessary, we should too.

Isaiah 40:31 says: "But those who *wait* for the Lord [who expect, look for, and hope in Him] shall change and renew their strength and power; they shall lift their wings and mount up [close to God] as eagles [mount up close to the sun]; they shall run and not be weary, they shall walk and not faint or become tired." The word, "wait" means: "To bind together (by twisting); to be gathered together, be joined; to meet; to lie in wait for someone; to expect, await, look for patiently, hope; to be confident, trust; to be enduring."[4]

If we are to carry the presence of God with us all day long wherever we go, we must spend time with Him dedicating our spirits, souls, and bodies to Him. As we do this, we become ready to obey His voice. Remember the words of Paul in Galatians 2:20:

> I have been crucified with Christ [in Him I have shared His crucifixion]; it is no longer I who live, but Christ (the Messiah) lives in me; and the life I now

live in the body I live by faith in (by adherence to and reliance on and complete trust in) the Son of God, Who loved me and gave Himself up for me.

Like Paul, we too must view ourselves as having been crucified with Christ. If we have accepted Christ as our Savior, God sees us as if we had died with His Son. We are no longer condemned. Our sins died with Christ, and we are now one with Him. His experiences are to become our experiences. Literally, Christ came to earth to die on the cross in order to abolish the sin nature from ruling in our physical bodies.

In like manner, we are called to "die" to our old nature on a daily basis. We must regularly "crucify" our sinful desires, bad attitudes, wrong mindsets, bitterness, resentment, unforgiveness, impatience, irritability, and anything operating within us that does not represent or line up with the Word, character, and nature of Christ. These sins come from selfishness, Satan, and the system of the world, which hinder us from following Him. We have been set free from sin's strong grip that reigned over us. We have been empowered to grow into Christ's likeness through our partnership with the Holy Spirit in order to fight the good fight of faith. We are no longer alone in fighting sin, sickness, or poverty on our own, for Christ lives in us—He is our Source of power for living.

Questions for Study
1. What is the key to living by faith?
2. What is the revealed "Kingdom Principle" in this chapter?
3. When we truly devote ourselves to God, what do our requests become?
4. According to John 6:28-29, what must we habitually do in every situation to work out the works of God?
5. According to Acts 10:38 and Isaiah 40:31, how does your life compare to that of Christ's? Where do you need to make improvements?
6. What must you do to carry the anointing or power of God in your life throughout your day?

Personal Prayer
Lord, uproot any selfishness, pride, and fear that is operating within me. I want righteousness, humility, and faith to take root in me in order to build an indestructible foundation in You. Help me to regulate my life and conduct according to your Word, rather than what I see or how things appear to my physical senses (2 Corinthians 5:7). These things are hard for me to do, but I surrender all of my self-effort. I place my entire trust in You. Empower me now to believe that Your Word is true and that You desire for me to experience it personally in my life. Your Word says that the just shall live by faith. Please forgive my unbelief and help me to believe! (Mark 9:24). Teach me how to exercise the measure of faith that You have placed within me so that it may grow stronger every day (Romans 12:3). Thank You, Lord, that as I look, wait, and hope in You, I shall be changed, and my strength shall be renewed! (Isaiah 40:31).

Chapter 16

Faith in Action

———————————❖———————————

Faith believes that God is able to do what He needs to do in you and through you with your cooperation, but without your help! This is why He is called, "I Am." Ephesians 3:20 gives a great definition of what "I Am" is capable of doing. It says,

> Now *to Him,* Who, by (in consequence of) the [action of His] power that is at work within us, is able to [carry out His purpose and] to do superabundantly, far over and above all that we [dare] ask or think [infinitely beyond our highest prayers, desires, thoughts, hopes, or dreams.

The power that is at work within us comes from receiving God's love and living in right standing and humility with God, ourselves, and others. This power becomes real to us when we have a clear conscience before Him. We are each responsible before God regarding our own hearts, regardless of what others have said or done to us. When we live by faith, we entrust ourselves to Him while we go about humbly doing what is right to and for others with an attitude of humility. Being rooted and grounded in God's love strengthens our faith. This enables God to tend to our circumstances while we confidently rest in His ability, efficiency, and might to work things out for our good. (See Ephesians 3:16-20).

**Being rooted and grounded
in God's love strengthens our faith.**

Luke 6:31 says, "And as you would like and desire that men would do to you, do exactly so to them." Romans 12:21 tells us, "Do not let yourself be overcome by evil, but overcome (master) evil with good." Friends, only the people who totally entrust themselves to God can truly go about doing this God-kind of good toward others as loving acts of faith. If you live in strife and do not have right standing with God, yourself, and others, you cannot expect the blessings of God to flow into and out of your life. Just as clean water cannot flow from a muddied well; neither can the Holy Spirit flow from a life filled with the clutter of sin, selfishness, and unforgiveness.

The faith-filled life is willing to become a living sacrifice, which pleases God. This should be our reasonable response for all that He has done for us (see Romans 12:1). We are to become individuals who are willing to dedicate all of ourselves for the purpose of becoming totally F.I.T. vessels for God's service. He calls us to dedicate our minds, mouths, hands, feet, wills, emotions, feelings, attitudes, money, desires, dreams, and hopes. In short, God wants us to give our entire inner beings, all of our belongings, gifts, and talents to the Lord Jesus as an offering. In return, all that He is will flow through us without measure.

Romans 6:19 tells us, " . . . For as you yielded your bodily members [and faculties] as servants to impurity and ever increasing lawlessness, so now yield your bodily members [and faculties] once and for all as servants to righteousness (right being and doing) [which leads] to sanctification." God desires holiness in every area and relationship in our lives. He calls us to be severed from impurities and become servants of righteousness.

As we faithfully partner with His Holy Spirit, in full confidence in God's ability, and as we entrust ourselves to Him by believing and obeying His Word, He is faithful to do His part. He cares for us in ways that are above and beyond what we could dare ask, think, or imagine!

Hebrews 11:6 explains that faith in God must become the foundation with which we are rooted and grounded. "But without faith it is impossible to please and be satisfactory to Him. For whoever would come near to God must [necessarily] believe that God exists and that he is the rewarder of those who earnestly and diligently seek Him [out]." The Holy Spirit will impart more faith to believers as we *earnestly* and *diligently* seek God. This happens as we become more interested in the heart of God than we are in God's pleasing us. We must become "God-absorbed" instead of self-absorbed. We need to set self aside and desire His ways of thinking, speaking, being, and doing.

As we *delight* ourselves in Him in this manner, He will give to us the desires and secret petitions of our heart (see Psalm 37:4). To delight means "To take pleasure in (His ways); to be bent or inclined toward; to cherish; to be favorably disposed toward someone; to love and desire."[1] This depicts an individual whose top priority is pleasing God in every manner of his or her life. It takes great belief in Christ to obtain such faith as to delight ourselves in Someone we cannot see with our physical eyes. Yet, when He is given first priority in our lives, this Someone, Jesus Christ, becomes just as real to us as the things we can see. Make no mistake about it, as believers our greatest challenge is to love, believe, and trust in the One we cannot see.

The tragedy of unbelief often occurs because of four main reasons:

1. We are not becoming rooted and grounded in love-union with Christ and the Word of God. Therefore, we are not exercising the measure of faith that God gave us.
2. We seek Him only for what He can give us.
3. We make our own plans, and then ask Him to bless them.
4. We speak something different than what we say we believe.

Clearly, becoming rooted in Someone and something that we cannot see requires our *attention* and *time*. Building up our faith requires four things of us:

1. We must spend time in the Word; studying it, as well as getting to know Jesus personally for ourselves.
2. We must confess what the Word says instead of how we feel.
3. We must ask for faith to believe the Word.
4. We must practice what we learn as the Holy Spirit directs us.

Mark 9:24 encourages us to express our belief in Christ as well as to ask God for help in our areas of weakness, even when that weakness is faith. "At once the father of the boy gave [an eager piercing inarticulate] a cry with tears, and he said, Lord, I believe! *[Constantly] help my weakness of faith!*"

In our Christian walk, which is a walk of constant belief and confidence in God, we must wholeheartedly take God at His Word, believing that He will never leave us nor will He ever forsake us. He will not leave you alone to deal with this life, and He will not abandon or give up on you. Most likely, He is waiting for you to totally hand over all of yourself and every detail of your life to His care once and for all, so that He can move on your behalf. Romans 14:23 reminds us that whatever is not of faith (confidence in God) is sin. We must learn to stop placing our trust in our education, finances, positions, job, charisma, wit, physical appearances, body structure, color, gender, and so on, and place our trust and confidence in Christ alone.

We must learn to stop placing our trust in our education, finances, positions, jobs, charisma, wit, physical appearances, body structure, color, gender, and so on, and place our trust and confidence in Christ alone.

Philippians 3:3 tells us,

> For we [Christians] are the true circumcision, who worship God in spirit and by the Spirit of God and exult and glory and pride ourselves in Jesus Christ, and *put no confidence or dependence [on what we are] in the flesh and on outward privileges and physical advantages and external appearances.*(emphasis added)

God despises independence, because He knows that our lives apart from Him will be disastrous. He desires for us to be totally dependent upon Him alone. Our enemy, Satan, is out to kill, steal, and destroy us. The main thing he wants to kill, steal, and destroy is our God-given faith. If he can succeed at that, he will continue to control us. However, despite our individual pasts, despite our circumstances, despite any situation we are in, faith steps in as *"the assurance of the things we hope for, the proof of the things we cannot see"* (see Hebrews 11:1). Nothing is ever too difficult or impossible with God. If in faith you will give Him your ashes, from your messes to your accomplishments, He will give you His beauty. God will make your life a living epistle, worthy to be read of all men in honor and glory of Him.

Hebrews 12:1-2 sums this chapter up nicely. It says,

> Therefore then, since we are surrounded by so great a cloud of witnesses [who have borne testimony to the Truth]; (this is referring to the faith-filled people who stuck with God despite their circumstances, in Hebrews chapter 11),* let us strip off and throw aside every encumbrance (unnecessary weight) and that sin which so readily (deftly and cleverly) clings to and entangles us, and let us run with patient endurance and steady and active persistence the appointed course of the race that is set before us. Looking away [from all that will distract] to Jesus, Who is the Leader and the Source of our faith [giving the first incentive for our belief] and is also Finisher [bringing it to

81

maturity and perfection]. He for the joy [of obtaining the prize] that was set before Him, endured the cross, despising and ignoring the shame, and is now seated at the right hand of the throne of God.

Did you catch that? Death to self must come before we can obtain the fullness of Christ. When we humble ourselves under the mighty hand of God, picking up our cross and denying ourselves, God will fill us with Himself and exalt us. I believe that "every encumbrance and unnecessary weight" develops from our lack of trust in Christ. This, in my opinion, is the sin that entangles us and keeps us ineffective. We are to focus our attention instead on Jesus who will mature and bring to perfection that which He started in us through faith. The focus of Jesus was not on the reality of His circumstances, which included the Cross. Rather, He focused on the glory of doing His Father's will by entrusting Himself totally to God.

**The focus of Jesus was not on the Cross,
but on the glory of doing His Father's will
by entrusting Himself totally to God.**

Questions for Study
1. Finish this sentence: Faith believes that God is _____ .
2. Where does the power come from that is at work within us? Read Ephesians 3:16-20. Write it out, meditate on it, and pray it over yourself and others.
3. Describe the type of people who can go about doing Luke 6:31 and Romans 12:21 to others, especially those who are undeserving.
4. In the previous question, does this type of person describe you? Why or why not?
5. As described in Hebrews 11:6, what is required for one to come near to God?
6. How might you delight yourself in God?
7. As believers, what is our greatest challenge?
8. What four things are required of each of us in order to help build our faith in Christ?
9. List the things that are keeping you from growing in your faith.

Personal Prayer
Lord, I know that without faith, it is impossible to please You. Help me to come near to You by believing that You exist and that You reward those who seek You out (Hebrews 11:6). Lord, help me to seek You out in all things. Forgive me for the many times that I do not consult with You first. I know that whatever is not simple faith and confidence in You is considered sin (Romans 14:23). Help me to believe that You are able to do in me, and through me, that which You desire as I delight myself in You (Psalm 37:4). Help me to stop placing my faith in education, finances, position, job status, charm, appearance, color, and gender. May my confidence be in You and You alone (Philippians 3:3). Forgive me of my independence, and teach me how to lean on You totally. Help me to become a faith-filled person who sticks with You despite my circumstances. I strip off and lay aside all of the things which cling to me and entangle me from believing in You (Hebrews 12:1-2). Doubt and unbelief are two of those things that entangle me. I renounce them as sin and confess to You, Lord, that I am a believer—not a doubter!

Chapter 17

The Fruit of a Soul
Rooted in Righteousness,
Humility, and Faith

———————————◆———————————

*H*person whose soul is rooted in righteousness, humility, and faith will become a person who experiences much victory and joy in life regardless of their circumstances. Righteousness, humility, and faith are rooted in the soil of love, with God's love as the anchor of these roots. This person's every desire is to please Jesus Christ and to do things His way in every situation. Just as sin, selfishness, pride, and fear wreak havoc on families, businesses, churches, and relationships, so righteousness, humility, and faith activates the power of God on behalf of those involved. This power is made available to us as we choose to obey God and react as He would.

Romans 5:19 tells us that,

> For just as by one man's disobedience (failing to hear, heedlessness, and carelessness) the many were constituted sinners, so by one Man's obedience the many will be constituted righteous (made acceptable to God, brought into right standing with Him).

Our choices matter. When we make good choices, we and the people around us will benefit. Similarly, when we make bad choices, we and those around us will be affected for the negative. Jesus is our perfect example in righteousness, humility, and faith. When we choose these as Jesus did, the gates of hell close and the gates of Heaven open in our lives. We, too, have the choice.

Let's review the meanings of righteousness, humility, and faith cited in earlier chapters.

1. *Righteousness* is justice, rightness; having right standing with God and having moral and spiritual rectitude in every area and relationship.

2. *Humility* is the total absence of arrogance, conceit, and haughtiness. It means to be meek and mild-tempered. It is modesty, lowliness, an attitude and mindset of unselfishness and regard for the welfare of others over self. Humility, or lack of it, is observed in us by how we treat others.

3. *Faith* is the assurance of the things we hope for and being sure of the things that we do not see. In God's economy, we believe first; then we see the manifestation of that belief in due season (God's timing). Our position in faith is to believe that He is able, while we wait patiently for Christ to bring the desired thing to pass. Just as Peter got out of the boat and placed his trust in Christ in order to walk on the water, we are called to do the same thing (Matthew 14:28-30). Faith encourages us to step out and dare to believe. Faith believes in what Christ has already accomplished for each of us on the cross claiming it as our own.

Let's face it, only healthy trees produce healthy fruit. In like manner, when a person is rooted in righteousness, humility, and faith, he or she exhibits healthy fruit. Psalm 1:3 describes the kind of people who are rooted in God's ways, His Word, and His Spirit. It says, "And he shall be like a tree firmly planted (and tended) by the streams of water, ready to bring forth its fruit in its season; its leaf also shall not fade or wither; and everything he does shall prosper (and come to maturity)." We must remember that as we walk in the ways of God, everything we experience brings recompense (reward or payback) and blessings if we don't give up or quit believing.

> **We must remember that as we walk in the ways of God,**
> **everything we experience brings recompense**
> **and blessings if we don't give up or quit believing.**

The verses in Psalm 18:19-30 verify this truth. They say,

> He brought me forth also into a large place; He was delivering me because He was pleased with me and delighted in me. The Lord rewarded me according to my righteousness (my conscious integrity and sincerity with Him); according to the cleanness of my hands has He recompensed me. For I have kept the ways of the Lord and have not wickedly departed from my God. For all His ordinances were before me, and I put not away His statutes from me. I was upright before Him and blameless with Him, even (on guard) to keep myself free from my sin and guilt. Therefore has the Lord recompensed me according to my righteousness (my uprightness and right standing with Him) according to the cleanness of my hands in His sight. With the kind and merciful you will show yourself kind and merciful, with an upright man you will show yourself upright. With the pure you will show yourself pure, and with the perverse you will show yourself contrary. For you cause my lamp to be lighted and to shine; the Lord my God illumines my darkness. For by you I can run through a troop, and by my God I can leap over a wall. As for God, His way is perfect! The Word of the Lord is tested and tried; He is a shield to all those who take refuge and put their trust in Him.

Indeed, following the ways of the Lord will bring forth His blessings and benefits to our lives and those around us.

Picture a tree. The fruit hanging from this tree is born from the roots of righteousness, humility, and faith. First and foremost is the fruit of the Holy Spirit mentioned in Galatians 5:22-23. This is the fruit of love, joy, peace, patience, kindness, goodness, faithfulness, gentleness and self-control. Verses 18 and 23 of Galatians chapter 5 say, "But if you are led by the Holy Spirit, you are not subject to the Law," and "against such things there is no law." This means that when we display the fruit of the Spirit consistently, no one can bring a charge against anything in our behavior. This is what a mature Christian looks like! This person will be used by God to break down walls of division, tear down strongholds, and establish peace and unity among believers.

The soul rooted in righteousness, humility, and faith continues to produce fruit. These people:

- Are content with what they have and are relaxed about everything.
- Love self and others and are positive in thought, word, attitude, and deed.
- Enjoy healthy relationships. They give freedom to others by allowing them to be themselves.
- Are not critical or judgmental; rather, they are compassionate and caring.
- Meditate on God's Word and are grateful and thankful.
- Have a peaceful undercurrent, rarely being depressed or upset.
- Are concerned for others and have an overall good attitude.
- Are radical in giving and are not easily rattled or shaken.
- Believe the best in others, speaking words of life.
- Compare themselves only to Jesus.
- Are sweet-spirited.
- Are full of confidence in Christ and enjoy life.

God desires to grow the fruit of His Spirit up within us, so that the rest of the world becomes thirsty for what we have. When we are able to consistently show these qualities at home, work, school, in our relationships, and at church, God is living powerfully through us. At this stage of the Christian walk, we are filled with and led by the Spirit of God on a continual basis. He is the only one who can impart and display these qualities within us, and only He can work them out in us as we submit our ways to His and cooperate with His Spirit.

The rooting and grounding of righteousness, humility, and faith established in our lives will bring great honor to God and us, and we will be rewarded both now and for eternity. These roots will cause us to work "good" into every area and relationship in our lives.

First Peter 2:15 and 1 Peter 3:11-12 say this:

> For it is God's will and intention that by doing right (consistently)* [your good and honest lives] should silence (muzzle gag) the ignorant charges and ill-informed criticisms of foolish persons . . . turn away from wickedness (doing things your own way)* and shun it, and let him do right. Let him search for peace (harmony; undisturbedness from fears, agitating passions, and moral conflicts) and seek it eagerly. [Do not merely desire peaceful relations with God, with your fellowmen and with yourself, but pursue, go after them].

The growing of these roots exhibited in the fruit of the Spirit allows just that! We need to be willing to die to self and say "Yes" to God, rooted in righteousness, humility, and faith anchored by God's love for each of us.

Questions for Study

1. People who are rooted in righteousness, humility, and faith are people who have come into agreement with Christ. What is their desire?
2. What does Romans 5:19 teach us?
3. Write out Psalm 1:3. Does this describe you?
4. Even though salvation is a free gift, it costs us something to continuously walk in the ways of God. What is God's purpose for this?
5. Look through Psalm 18:19-30. Highlight those things that grab your attention. Briefly write out those things that you want to see in your life.
6. List the fruit of the Spirit. Ask the Holy Spirit to help you be committed to developing this fruit in and through your life.
7. How will a mature Christian, who displays the fruit of the Spirit consistently, be used by God?
8. According to 1 Peter 2:15, God's will and intention by our doing right is to silence the ignorant charges of foolish persons. According to 1 Peter 3:11-12, what must we do to help this process?

Personal Prayer

Lord, Your Word says that through one man's disobedience the many were counted sinners, and by one Man's obedience the many will be counted righteous (Romans 5:19). Forgive me for all of the times that I have made wrong choices and have perhaps led others astray because of it. From this day forth help me to make choices that will affect others for good and lead them to You. Thank You that as I become rooted and grounded in righteousness, humility, and faith, I will be like a tree firmly planted by the streams of water, ready to bring forth fruit in due season, and that everything I put my hand to shall be prosperous and come to maturity (Psalm 1:3). Thank You that my life exhibits the fruit of the Spirit. Please continue to grow that up in me, so that the world will become thirsty for You. Anoint me, Lord, to go about doing good to others, and overcoming evil in the process (Acts 10:38; Romans 12:21). Help me to live an honest life, turning away and shunning all wickedness. Let me search for peace and pursue it eagerly (1 Peter 2:15; 3:11-12).

PART THREE:

*Recognizing the Work
of the Holy Spirit
within Our Lives*

Chapter 18

The Holy Spirit:
Our Partner

---

he Holy Spirit is the third person of the Trinity, the one imparted to us by Christ after His ascension. In the Holy Spirit, God and Jesus literally live inside of the believer. Not simply a principle or influence coming from God, He is as much an individual as God the Father and Jesus the Son. The Holy Spirit is full of the intelligence of God. He causes people to turn to Christ and to become like Him. As one of His main functions, the Holy Spirit is continuously pointing people to Jesus and working His character in the lives of believers. In turn, His works uses this changed character to show others about the life of Jesus Christ.

Each person of the Godhead—Father, Son, and Spirit—serves the other, constantly pointing to and exalting each other. They are in a never-ending, forever committed relationship with each other. There is no hierarchy and no lines of superiority between the three. Because love is their foundation, they all share mutual authority, willingly submitting to each other as they edify and build each other up. They serve as an example for the Church, modeling how brothers and sisters in Christ ought to treat each other.

In John 14:16-17, Jesus described the Holy Spirit's job in the believer's life. He said,

> I will ask the Father, and He will give you another Comforter (Counselor, Helper, Intercessor, Advocate, Strengthener, and Standby), that He may remain with you forever—the Spirit of Truth, Whom the world cannot receive (welcome, take to its heart) because it does not see Him or know and recognize Him. But you know and recognize Him, for He lives with you [constantly] and will be in you.

Take note of the words that the Amplified Bible uses to describe the functions of the Holy Spirit in our lives:

1. *Comforter*—a calling of Him to our side; either as an exhortation (encouragement or the alleviation of grief). Consolation, comfort, tenderness, soothing; suggesting the capability or adaptability for giving aid.[1]
2. *Counselor*—one who consults with us or another in order to give advice or counsel.[2]
3. *Helper*—a fellow worker, to help, render assistance and minister to the weak or needy.[3]
4. *Intercessor*—one who falls in with us, and meets with us in order to converse. One who makes petition on our behalf.[4]
5. *Advocate*—denotes legal assistance; one who pleads another's cause.[5] (The Holy Spirit will always agree with God, Jesus, and the Word).
6. *Strengthener*—one who gives power, ability, efficiency, might, and dominion.[6]
7. *Standby*—one who supports, makes good a promise, maintains, remains near or is present; remains tuned in.[7]

The Holy Spirit is waiting to act on our behalf! However, we must be willing to become a partner with Him. We must believe that He loves us. We must believe that He has our best interest at heart. We must ask Him for His help. We must submit our ways to His. We must obey His commands. We must cooperate with Him at all times.

As believers, the only way to accomplish anything that God has intended for us to live out is to partner with the Holy Spirit. Just as Paul said to the Galatians in Chapter 3:3; "Are you so foolish and so senseless and so silly? Having begun [your new life spiritually] with the [Holy] Spirit, are you now reaching perfection [by dependence] on the flesh?"

As believers, the only way to accomplish
anything that God has intended for us to live out
is to partner with the Holy Spirit.

God used our faith and His grace to give us our spiritual lives. He uses our continued partnership with the Holy Spirit to make us like Christ and to enable us to accomplish the tasks that He has for us. The Holy Spirit's greatest task is to help believers remain in vital union with Jesus Christ. In Chapter 15 of his gospel, John describes the Holy Spirit as our lifeline connector to Christ. He says Christ is the vine and believers are the branches of that vine. The branches of a tree can produce fruit only when they are attached to the vine from which they come. The same is true in our lives. We cannot produce the fruit of the Spirit without continuously and consistently being connected to the Holy Spirit.

Consider a pregnant woman and her child. The child needs the umbilical cord, the lifeline between him and his mother, in order to survive. In like manner, the Holy Spirit functions as the "umbilical cord" between Jesus and a believer.

How do we partner with the Holy Spirit? We ask God the Father to give Him. Luke 11:13 says; "how much more will your Heavenly Father give the Holy Spirit to those that ask and *continue* to ask Him?

Luke 11:13 says; "How much more will you Heavenly Father
give the Holy Spirit to those that ask and continue to ask Him?"

There is much confusion about how or when we receive the Holy Spirit. When we are born again, God *seals* us with the Holy Spirit (see 2 Corinthians 1:22; Ephesians 1:13, 4:30).

This *seal* is an emblem of ownership or authenticity designated by the sealer (God) on behalf of believers, as they are open to receive and believe that Christ died for their sins, sicknesses, weaknesses, distresses, guilt, shame, peace, well-being, provisions, and blessings and is the giver of eternal life.[8] (See Isaiah 53:4-5.)

This means that at the moment of rebirth, the Spirit of God comes to live inside of us. The remainder of our Christian life, then, is to be spent learning how to listen, surrender, and receive. We are to spend the remainder of our lives letting the Holy Spirit lead and empower us, in particular our minds, wills, attitudes, emotions, decisions, and behaviors. The Spirit of God lives in the spirit of every believer. Indeed, when a person receives Christ as his or her Savior, their spirit is instantly made right with God. Now, as we live from this position of "right-standing" with God, He wants to train each of our souls to conform and adapt to His ways. Then the life of Christ can be manifested out through our bodies as His fruit shows itself in our words, actions, and deeds. God Himself enters our lives and changes us from the inside out making us like Him! The Holy Spirit serves as our teacher throughout this process.

Second Corinthians 3:4-6, 8 and Romans 8:14 verify this:

> Such is the reliance and confidence that we have through Christ toward and with reference to God. Not that we are fit (qualified and sufficient in ability) of ourselves to form personal judgments or claims or count anything as coming from us, but our power and ability and sufficiency are from God. [It is He] Who has qualified us [making us to be fit and worthy and sufficient] as ministers and dispensers of a *new covenant* [of salvation through Christ], not [ministers], of the letter (of legally written code) (following of external rules),* but of the Spirit (grace)*; for the code (of the Law) kills, but the [Holy] Spirit makes alive! Why should not the dispensation of the Spirit [this spiritual ministry *whose task is to cause men to obtain and be governed by the Holy Spirit*] be attended with much greater and more splendid glory? . . . For all who are led by the Spirit of God are the sons of God!

How can people be led by God if they are not emptied of their own power, efficiency, ability, and might and are filled with that of God's Holy Spirit? There is a big difference between fleshly zeal and the Holy Spirit's leading. God seals every believer with the Holy Spirit, but not every believer finds himself to be *led* or continually *filled* by the Spirit's empowerment.

Several reasons for this are:

1. Ignorance. Perhaps we do not understand the difference between being sealed with the Spirit and being led by or filled with the Spirit.
2. In order to receive His help and guidance, we need to invite the Holy Spirit into our *lives daily*. His are gentlemanly, full of ease and grace. He's ever ready, on "standby," waiting to help!
3. We think that we can empower ourselves to become like Christ and do the work that He desires for us to do. But we cannot. We have to receive His grace and let Him empower us with His ability, efficiency, and might.
4. The Holy Spirit will lead and guide, but we must be willing to leave and forsake what we want, think, feel, and do. We must be willing to replace these things with what He

wants, thinks, and would have us do. This is how we die to self, cooperate with Him, and follow His lead.

John 12: 24-26 attests to this fact. The Message Version of this Scripture says it like this:

> Listen carefully: Unless a grain of wheat is buried in the ground, dead to the world, it is never any more than a grain of wheat. But if it is buried it sprouts and reproduces itself many times over. In the same way, anyone who holds on to life just as it is (through submission to the ways of the world and personal desires),* reckless in your life (for Jesus),* you'll have it forever, real and eternal. If any of you wants to serve Me, then follow Me. Then you'll be where I am, ready to serve at a moment's notice. The Father will honor and reward anyone who serves Me.

We cannot serve and follow God if we are still filled with our carnal ways rather than filled with His ways. The Holy Spirit speaks through our spirits to enlighten our minds, and to tell us what He wants us to do. Remember—His will is His Word, the Bible.

In Acts 1:8, we see the role of the Holy Spirit spelled out for us. It says, "But you *shall receive power* (ability, efficiency and might) *when the Holy Spirit has come upon you,* and you *shall be My witnesses . . ."* This verse tells us that:

1. We will receive *power* that is supernaturally inherent to His witnesses and ambassadors, like the working of dynamite![9] In other words, we will become capable of doing whatever the Spirit directs us to do. That might mean performing signs, or great, glorious, strange, marvelous, or miraculous works, prophesying, or preaching (see Acts 2:14-18). *Remember, we receive things from God by believing in our hearts and confessing with our mouths. This habit should not stop after we have accepted Christ into our hearts.
2. *When the Spirit has come upon us*—"Come upon" means to arrive, supervene, occur, impend, influence; the superimposition of time, place, and order; *to rest upon, have charge of, to work through.*[10]
3. Then *you shall be My witnesses*. We will show, as well as tell, the world of the nature, character, and resurrected power of Christ.

Furthermore, Acts 1:8 tells us that we will receive God's dynamic, supernatural power when the Holy Spirit has the freedom to work through us. He will do so according to His time, place, and order so that we can show and tell this dark and dying world who Jesus Christ really is. Our need for the continuous and ongoing "filling" of the Holy Spirit in our lives is repeated throughout the Bible. Yes, we are sealed with the Holy Spirit once, but in order for the Holy Spirit to lead us, we must constantly empty ourselves and allow Him to fill us through the Word. We must ask in prayer, wait on His directions, and surrender our ways for His.

In essence, we must:

- Shut the noise of the world out.
- Clear our minds of our own human reasoning.
- Seek Christ through His Word.

- Learn to hear the voice of the Spirit in our spirits.

When driving a car, you wouldn't fill the tank one time and then expect it to last for the entire life of the car! You need to keep returning to the gas station. The same is true with believers. If we intend to live in accordance with Christ we must keep going back to the Word and the Holy Spirit's "empowerment station." (See the following verses that testify to this fact: Ephesians 3:19; 5:18; Acts 2:4; 4:8; 4:31; 9:17.)

> **If we intend to live in accordance with Christ**
> **we must keep going back to the Word and**
> **the Holy Spirit's "empowerment station."**

Jesus Himself was filled with the Holy Spirit. Now He imparts, infuses, and baptizes us with His Holy Spirit (see Mark 1:10; John 1:32; Mark 1:8).

Paul said to some disciples in Acts 19:2, "Did you receive the Holy Spirit when you believed [on Jesus as the Christ]? And they said, No, we have not even heard that there is a Holy Spirit." In this particular case, they were baptized in the Holy Spirit by the laying on of Paul's hands. Then these people went out boldly persuading, arguing, and pleading the cause of the Kingdom of God, speaking in foreign languages, prophesying, and preaching the Lord Jesus Christ (Acts 19:2-8).

The only way we can move from bondage to freedom is through the working of the Holy Spirit within our lives. This working is the only way we will ever move from religion to relationship, from law to grace, from legalism to love, from wounded to healed, from insecure to confident, from fear to faith, from patronizing one another to really loving one another, and from doubter to believer.

Questions for Study

1. Who is the Third Person of the Trinity?
2. How does each Person of the Godhead, (Father, Son, and Spirit) serve each other? Are you doing this with the Christians God has placed around you?
3. What are the seven names given in the Amplified Bible for the Holy Spirit? Do you know and recognize Him in your life according to these names?
4. How do we partner with the Holy Spirit? (See Luke 11:13).
5. Why are some people sealed with God's Spirit, but not led or filled with God's Spirit?
6. What is the difference between being sealed with, being led by, or being filled with His Spirit?
7. How is the Holy Spirit's empowerment similar to putting gas in your car?
8. According to Ephesians 3:19; 5:18 and Acts 2:4; 4:8; 4:31; and 9:17, is it evident to you that the same people were filled with God's Spirit over and over? Why were they "ever-filled?"
9. According to Mark 1:8, with what does Jesus baptize?
10. Have you asked Jesus to baptize you with His Spirit?

Personal Prayer

Lord, thank You for Your Holy Spirit! Help me to come to know Him as a Comforter, Counselor, Helper, Intercessor, Advocate, Strengthener, and Supporter (John 14:16-17). I desire to partner with Him, to submit my will to His, and to be obtained and governed by Him (2 Corinthians 3:4-6, 8). Your Word says that I will receive power when the Holy Spirit comes upon me (Acts 1:8; Luke 11:13). Lord, I desire and receive that power now by faith. I realize that I need to be continuously filled and led by the Holy Spirit (Ephesians 5:18). Help me not to hang on to the ways of this world or allow my personal desires to quench the work of the Holy Spirit. Your Word says that the true sons of God are those who are led by the Spirit of God (Romans 8:14). Lord, I choose to let go of my life and serve You. Help me now, by the power of Your Spirit, to follow You (John 12:24-26). I want to be Your witness to a dying world. I realized that John the Baptist baptized with water as a sign of the forgiveness of my sins and that You baptize with the Holy Spirit so that I may be empowered to live my life for You (Mark 1:8; John 1:32; Luke 3:16). Because of the blood You shed on the cross and the Holy Spirit's empowerment, I am dead to sin and alive to Christ! (Romans 6:11). Thank You, God, for Your amazing grace!

Chapter 19

The Work of the Holy Spirit
within the Believer

———————•———————

*G*od promises His followers that He will complete the work that He has started in them. He does this through the work of the Holy Spirit. When the Holy Spirit comes to live inside of us, He opens our ears to hear Him through His Word. Passages that we read before begin to "jump off the page at us," ready for us to believe and apply to our circumstances and relationships. The Holy Spirit causes us to see differently. That is, He opens the eyes of our hearts, our spiritual eyes, and causes us to see with the eyes of God. He causes us to hear His voice with spiritually sensitive ears. He causes us to think and speak His will. The Holy Spirit will change our thoughts, attitudes, and behaviors and will ultimately cause us to want to live in total agreement with Him. The Holy Spirit truly transforms us from the inside out—if we allow Him into every area of our lives. In all honesty, there is no need to run or hide from Him! He already knows everything about us and He still loves and accepts us and wants to work in us and through us (Jeremiah 1:5). We are that valuable to Him!

**The Holy Spirit will change our thoughts, attitudes,
and behaviors and will ultimately cause us to want to
live in total agreement with Him.**

When we allow the Holy Spirit to work within us, He sets about in us to do all of these things:

- He brings life instead of death (John 6:63; Romans 8:11).
- He pours God's love into our hearts (Romans 5:5).
- He gives us everything we need pertaining to life and godliness (2 Peter 1:3).
- He blesses us with every spiritual blessing we will ever need (Ephesians 1:3).
- He seals us in God, the guarantee of His ownership and authenticity (Ephesians 1:13; 2 Corinthians 1:22).
- He sanctifies us and makes us like Him (2 Thessalonians 2:13).

- He chooses us and takes us into His family. He sets us apart for His purposes, making us holy by His Truth (John 17:17).
- He frees us from sin and fights against our sin nature (Galatians 5:17-18).
- He develops and accomplishes the fruit of the Spirit within us and makes it known through our attitudes, actions, and behaviors (Galatians 5:22-25).
- He partners with us when we determine to be dead to the slavery of sin and alive to His righteousness (Romans 8:4-11).
- He liberates us, setting us free from sin and its power (2 Corinthians 3:17).
- He gives us the character of God (2 Corinthians 3:18).
- He causes us to desire peace and holiness in our lives (Hebrews 12:14).
- He strengthens the inner man (Ephesians 3:16, 19).
- He strengthens our faith and enables us to trust God for the impossible! (Psalm 27:1).
- He renews and regenerates us (Titus 3:5; 1 Timothy 4:7-8).
- He gives us hope and confidence to receive that which we hope for (Romans 5:3-5; 15:12-13).
- He gives us comfort (John 14:16).
- He gives us assurance that we belong to His family (John 1:12; Galatians 4:1-6; Romans 8:16).
- He reveals the things of God to us (1 Corinthians 2:10-16; Ephesians 3:5; Psalm 25:14).
- He teaches us all things and causes us to remember everything Jesus told us (John 14:26).
- He teaches and imparts truth to us (1 John 4:6).
- He willingly leads and guides us (Romans 8:14).
- He bears witness of Jesus in all things (John 15:26; Acts 5:32).
- He opens heaven and brings us into God's presence (Ephesians 2:18; Psalm 16:11).
- He helps us when we don't know what to pray, and He prays for us (Jude 20; Romans 8:18-27).
- He inspires us to worship, praise, adore, love, and devote ourselves to Jesus and causes us to put our confidence in Him and not in our flesh, human reasoning, and outward appearances (John 4:23-24; Philippians 3:3-10).
- He lifts our heads and He never devalues us! (John 4:24; Philippians 3:3).
- He liberates us to love (especially the "unlovely") (Colossians 1:3-5, 8; Galatians 5:22; Romans 15:30).
- He leads us to give thanks (1 Thessalonians 2:13).
- He leads us to submit to others (Ephesians 5:21).
- He leads us to confront others when we need to (Proverbs 28:1).
- He makes us like-minded with Him and other believers (Philippians 2:2).
- He removes prejudiced attitudes and behaviors and causes us to prefer others over our own selfish motives (Philippians 2:3-5).
- He causes us to love Him, ourselves, and others (Mark 12:30-31).
- He gives us power to be His witnesses (Acts 1:8).
- He performs miracles through us (John 14:12; Hebrews 2:4).
- He always remains stable and reliable, for He is "always the same; yesterday, today and forever" (Hebrews 13:8).
- He overcomes evil by causing us to do good (Romans 12:21).
- He produces His good harvest in us (Galatians 6:7-8).

- He gives us gifts for the purpose of building one another up in the church (1 Corinthians 12:8-10).
- He appoints us to ministry (Acts 13:2; 20:28).
- He equips us for service according to His will, not man's (Ephesians 4:11, 16).
- He enables us to communicate in power to show and tell the world what Christ is like (1 Thessalonians 1:5; Acts 1:8; 1 Corinthians 2:1; Mark 16:15-20).

1 John 4:17 sums these statements up nicely. "In this [union and communion with Him] love is brought to completion and attains perfection with us, that we may have confidence for the day of judgment [with assurance and boldness to face Him], *because as He is, so are we in this world.*" Wow! Let's open our hearts to those italicized words! What a marvelous work of the Holy Spirit!

The working power of the Holy Spirit is so great! He is ready and waiting to work in us and through us. Oftentimes He is waiting for us to believe and be open to His ways. We can quench the Holy Spirit by trying to hold God to our time frame and our perception of how things should be. This causes us to close our hearts to Him and renders us incapable of receiving from Him. The Spirit of God, however, moves in ways that do not always make sense to us. He invites us and waits for us to believe. Doubt and unbelief cut us off from His blessings. They cause us to quench the Spirit and what He wants to do in us and through us (1 Thessalonians5:19).

He is the wellspring of life that lives inside of us and wants to flow out of us as His channel. He brings blessings to all who come to Him—those who hunger and thirst for more of Him! I love the verses in Isaiah 55:1-3 which says,

> Wait and listen, everyone who is thirsty! Come to the waters; and he who has no money, come, buy and eat! Yes, come, buy [priceless, spiritual] wine and milk without money and without price [*simply for the self-surrender that accepts the blessing*]. Why do you spend your money for that which is not bread and your earnings for what does not satisfy? Hearken diligently to Me, and eat what is good, and let your soul delight itself in fatness [the profuseness of spiritual joy]. Incline your ear [submit and consent to the divine will] and come to Me, hear and your soul will revive; and I will make an everlasting covenant or league with you, even the sure mercy (kindness, goodwill, and compassion) promised to David.

Indeed the Holy Spirit will do this for you and me "*simply for the self-surrender that accepts the blessing.*" (Isaiah 55:1). The key to the working of the Holy Spirit in you is your availability to Him. He is not looking for ability or "specifics." Rather, He wants hearts after His own—people whom He can use to do His great works in and through.

Questions for Study
1. Highlight or rewrite the verses that speak the most to you regarding the Holy Spirit.
2. Which verses do you need to believe, apply, and appropriate as you partner with Him?
3. Ask the Holy Spirit if there is any way in which you have quenched His working in your life because you had different expectations than His.
4. Ask Him to open your eyes and ears to any truths that He would like to share with you.

Personal Prayer

Lord, I come to You with an unveiled face, renouncing anything that I think I might know apart from Your Spirit teaching me (2 Corinthians 3:14-16). Thank You, Lord, for the work of the Holy Spirit within me, completing that which You have started (Philippians 1:6). I desire to fully cooperate with Him. I pray that You open my heart to believe and receive that which You are teaching me through Your Word. I ask You to discipline me for my good, so that I may share in Your holiness (Hebrews 12:10). Empower me to become more like Jesus and to let Your sanctifying power work within my life (2 Thessalonians 2:13). Pour out Your life into my heart, and bring a renewed level of life to me as I follow Your ways (Romans 5:5). Thank You for liberating me from the penalty of sin. I am no longer controlled by sin. Rather, I am dead to sin and live to You, full of the Holy Spirit (Romans 6:2; 8:2). I choose to believe and stand on all of the verses mentioned in this chapter. May Your Holy Spirit develop them in my life as I exchange my thoughts, ideas, and beliefs for Yours. Thank You, Jesus!

Chapter 20

Believing
He Loves Me!

When we come to grips with the unhealthy roots and fruits in our lives we find freedom. When I finally took responsibility for my own actions, reactions, thoughts, attitudes, and behaviors before God, I was both humbled and freed. I truly desired the help He had been waiting to give me all along. He didn't force Himself, but as a gentleman He waited for my invitation as He always does. In all of my self-efforts, I came to the "end of my rope." I surrendered to the fact, that I could not change myself by trying harder. I sought to surrender myself completely to Him placing every area of my life into God's hands; everything I liked about myself and everything I disliked.

Total surrender means willingly giving up all of our "back-up plans." These only contribute to the preservation and vindication of self. It is necessary to be emptied of that self-filled mindset in order to be filled with God's. Think of a glass that is full of water. It cannot be full of water and also full of coffee at the same time. Likewise, we cannot be full of ourselves and full of God all at once.

**I surrendered to the fact that I could not
change myself by trying harder.**

This process starts when we allow God to show us how much He loves us and desires to fill each of us with Himself and with that love. As for me, I knew that "God so loved the *world* that he sent His only Son," but my own personal experience lacked revelation (really knowing with my heart) of His love toward me (see John 3:16). I needed His love for me to take root in my heart and enlighten my mind. I needed to know for myself what God thought of me. I am His child and, as I faithfully continue in His Word and obey Him, He is faithful to change me by rooting and grounding me in His love.

God showed me how to personalize verses that spoke of His love for me. Let me show you what I have learned about personalizing Bible verses. When I read Scripture regarding

God's love for me out loud, I'm hearing and speaking life-giving words to myself. John 6:63 says that God's Word is Spirit and Life. God's Word flowing out of my heart, into my mouth, over to my ears, and up to my mind is like a seed taking root in fertilized, ready-for-growth soil. This kind of soil is essential if a new crop is to be harvested and change is to take place. All day long, we experience self-talk anyway, so we might as well make it productive and align our mouths with what God has to say about us. We reap what we sow (see Galatians 6:9), and if we sow the seeds of God's love into our lives we will reap His fruit of blessings. Let me be clear—personalizing Bible verses is not a formula to get what we want. Instead, it serves to mold our hearts' desires to His and what He wants.

Hebrews 4:12-13 (NIV) says,

> For the word of God is living and active. Sharper than any double-edged sword, it penetrates even to dividing soul and spirit, joints and marrow; it judges the thoughts and attitudes of the heart. Nothing in all creation is hidden from God's sight. Everything is uncovered and laid bare before the eyes of Him to whom we must give account.

As we live in God's Word, His Spirit drops verses into our hearts to meditate on, to think about, and to say out loud. This is how a double-edged sword should work. We are partners with Him. Therefore when we speak the Word that He places in our hearts, we work together with Him as a team.

Personalizing Bible verses is not a formula to get what we want. Instead, it serves to mold our hearts' desires to His and what He wants.

During this process, the Holy Spirit revealed to me a very important Kingdom Principle about God's economy. He showed me Romans 10:9-10 (NIV), which says,

> That if you *confess with your mouth,* "Jesus is Lord," *and believe in your heart* that God raised him from the dead you will *receive* salvation. For it is with your *heart* that you *believe* and are justified, and it is with your *mouth that you confess; receiving salvation.* (emphasis added)

We often associate this verse in Romans with the point of salvation; the time at which a person gives his heart to Christ. But salvation means more than the assurance of going to Heaven someday! Rather, salvation includes all of the spiritual blessings and the life that resides in Christ, which now reside in you—right now! Salvation means life as God has it! The blessings of God! These blessings include deliverance from sin, selfishness, Satan, and the system of the world. It includes our preservation; soundness; peace; wholeness; prosperity in spirit, soul, and body; our rescue; forgiveness; and general well-being in all realms: spiritually, physically, emotionally, and financially.

In order for the Holy Spirit to work in us, we must believe what God says and thinks about us in His Word. We do this by receiving His Word into our hearts and confessing it with our mouths. When we do this, we defeat the enemy of our souls: Satan. As you believe, God's Word takes root in you. You then will start to pattern your life according to this revealed belief *by putting it into practice and receive the promises.* If you do not grow weary while continuing to obey God's Word you will reap a harvest! (See Galatians 6:9.)

When we know what He thinks about us and we believe He loves us, surrendering to Him becomes a natural response. Through the transforming power of continuously *confessing, believing,* and *receiving* God's Word, we uproot all of the strongholds Satan has built in our minds that cause us to be ineffective. We become rooted and grounded in Him on the inside! (This is the picture of Hebrews 4:12-13 at work in you!). At this point, we are truly learning to live by faith (confidence in what He says about us) and not by sight (the circumstances that we physically see).

> **When we know what He thinks about us and**
> **we believe He loves us, surrendering to Him**
> **becomes a natural response.**

As we grow in our understanding of God's personal love for us, our faith begins to express itself through love. (See Ephesians 3:19.) Galatians 5:6 says that, "Faith works through love." This is a statement that can be easily misunderstood. But simply stated; when we believe God loves us, our faith will work. Therefore, receiving God's love is the first fundamental principle for establishing a life rooted in righteousness, humility, and faith. God establishes His promises through this foundation and works in our lives to give His life, light, and love to others.

Just think if you built a house, you would start with the foundation in the basement so that the entire house would be able to withstand the elements. So it is with our lives. We must build on the foundation of God's personal love for each of us, the love He revealed on the cross and in His Word, in order to withstand the pressures of this life that are constantly coming against us.

> **When we believe God loves us,**
> **our faith will work.**

In Matthew 7:24-27, Jesus shares this teaching:

> So everyone who hears these words of Mine and acts upon them [obeying them] will be like a sensible (prudent, practical, wise) man who built his house upon the Rock. And the rain fell and the floods came and the winds blew and beat against that house *(you)**; yet it *(you)** did not fall because it *(you)** had been founded on the Rock! And everyone who hears these words of Mine and does not do them will be like a stupid (foolish) man who built his house upon the sand (your own way of doing things, your own resources and worldly standards all of which can vanish in an instant).* And the rain fell and the floods came and the winds blew *(and the storms of life)** beat against that house, *(you)** and it *(you)** fell—and great and complete was that fall of it *(you)*.*

Questions for Study

1. What personal responsibility did I choose to accept in my own life that God asks each of us to do?
2. What does total surrender mean?
3. What does it mean to personalize Scripture?
4. What important Kingdom Principle is mentioned in this chapter?
5. Explain the concept of the double-edged sword as it relates to our partnership with Christ, which is the picture of Hebrews 4:12-13 working in you.
6. According to Galatians 5:6, how does faith work?
7. Receiving God's love is the beginning and fundamental principle for establishing what?
8. What type of house do you live in . . . sand or Rock?

Personal Prayer

Lord, I believe that You love me! (John 3:16). According to the riches of Your glory, please strengthen me with power through the Holy Spirit in my innermost being. May You live in my heart through faith. May I become rooted and grounded in your love for me so that my faith will work. Help me to understand the breadth and length and height and depth of this love and to know Your love that surpasses anything that I could or have already learned on my own. Fill me up to all the fullness of God in every area of my life (Ephesians 3:16-19). Thank You, Lord, for this power that works within me (Acts 1:8)! I willingly surrender all of my faculties to You (Romans 12:1-2).

Chapter 21

The Word of God

———•———

*H*aving turned to Christ in repentance and faith, followers of Jesus Christ need to understand and value the importance of God's spoken Word—the Bible. God Himself places such high value on His Word that He speaks of it throughout the Bible. Proverbs 30:5 tells us that, "Every Word of God is tried and purified." Isaiah 55:11 says, "So shall My Word be that goes forth out of My mouth: it shall not return to Me void [without producing any effect, useless] but it shall accomplish that which I please and purpose, and it shall prosper in the thing for which I sent it."

God's Word describes His character and His will for us. The Holy Spirit uses it to transform each of us.

**God's Word describes His character and His will for us.
The Holy Spirit uses it to transform each of us.**

God's Word renews and liberates us. For example, if we look in a mirror we can see to get the dirt off of our faces. Similarly, if we look into God's Word, we can see the entanglements of our hearts. Second Corinthians 3:17, 18 says,

> Now the Lord is Spirit, and where the Spirit of the Lord is, there is Liberty (emancipation from bondage, freedom). And all of us as with unveiled face, [because we] *continued to behold [in the Word of God]* as in a mirror the glory of the Lord, are constantly being transfigured into His very own image in ever increasing splendor and from one degree of glory to another; [for this comes] form the Lord [Who is] Spirit.

Look at the promise revealed in this verse. If we will *live, continue,* and *remain* in God's Word, then He will change us to increasingly look like Him. Cooperating and working with God while He untangles us requires us to be patient with both Him and with ourselves while

He does it. John 8:31-32 reveals the same truths. As we remain in God's Word and hold on to the truth, He will use the Word to set us free.

James 1:21 specifically reveals how God intends to heal our souls (mind, will, attitude and emotions). It tells us the following:

1. "Get rid of all uncleanness and the rampant outgrowth of wickedness." We must *choose* to stop doing things our way and choose to identify with God's ways in thought, word, and deed.
2. "In a humble (gentle, modest) spirit, receive and welcome the Word." We must choose to admit our need for help, believe that He is willing and able to help, and then receive His help by grace.
3. "This Word implanted and rooted (in our hearts) contains the power to save our souls." It's so important for us to believe God's Word and hold onto it, especially when our circumstances seem to dictate something completely different. We must choose to speak God's Word during difficult situations. The Holy Spirit plants the Word in us and we are to repeat it aloud. As we repeat the Word, we are nourishing and watering it, believing its truth.

Spending time at the feet of Jesus should be every believer's highest priority. This means reading His Word, meditating on it, studying it, and speaking it out loud. Joshua 1:8 verifies this fact when it says, "This Book of the Law *shall not depart out of your mouth,* but you shall *meditate on it day and night,* that you may *observe and do* according to all that is written in it. For *then you shall make your way prosperous,* and then you shall deal wisely and have good success (emphasis added). It is interesting to note that the word meditate means not only to think about, but to also mutter aloud.

**Spending time at the feet of Jesus, reading His Word,
meditating on it, studying it, and speaking it out loud,
should be the highest priority of every believer.**

God's recipe for success includes three conditions for us followed by three promises from Him:

Condition #1: The Book of the Law shall not depart out of your mouth.

Condition #2: Meditate on it day and night! (Think about the verse and speak that Word out loud).

Condition #3: You must observe and do according to what is written in it. (Your obedience to the Word shows God that you love Him).

Promise #1: Your way will be prosperous.

Promise #2: You will deal wisely.

Promise #3: You will have good success.

Remember, if you sow God's Word into your life by believing it, speaking it, and doing it, then you will reap the harvest that gives life. If you are not sowing the Word of God into your life in every area, situation, and relationship, then you cannot expect the promises. Mark 4:24 says, "And He said to them, Be careful what you are hearing. The measure [of thought and study] you give [to the truth you hear] will be the measure [of virtue and knowledge] that comes back to you—and more [besides] will be given to you who hear!"

Like medicine, The Word of God acts as a healing ointment that springs up into our wounded souls as we pour it into our hearts. The Holy Spirit then takes this medicine and activates and disperses the healing power within.

Like medicine, the Word of God
acts as a healing ointment that springs up
into our wounded souls as we pour it into our hearts.

It is necessary to understand that *the Word and the Spirit work together inside* the believer to bring about the healing. Without the Spirit of God, the Word of God leads believers to legalism and bondage. On the other hand, those who claim to follow only the Spirit of God without the use of His Word end up creating fantasy or emotionalism. Neither is able to rightly divide the truth of God's Word. For in cases such as these, the mind has enlightened the spirit. This cannot be! For, *it is the Spirit of God that enlightens the spirit in man which opens the mind and exposes the Truth.* Proverbs 20:27 says, "The spirit of man [that factor in human personality which proceeds immediately from God] is the lamp of the Lord, searching all his innermost parts." Romans 8:6 says, "Now the mind of the flesh *[which is sense and reason without the Holy Spirit]* is death [death that comprises all the miseries arising from sin, both here and hereafter]. But the mind of the [Holy] Spirit is life and [soul] peace [both now and forever]."

The Holy Spirit is our teacher. He alone reveals and leads us into the truths of God's Word (see John 14:26). When we fail to yield to and unite with the Holy Spirit, then our Biblical interpretations take root only in our minds. When we sit before God with His Word in hand, it is imperative that we ask the Holy Spirit, and the Holy Spirit alone, to lead, teach, and guide us. We must be willing to renounce any other former beliefs, teachings, or methods. Because our finite minds cannot understand an infinite God, we must open our hearts up to the Holy Spirit, that He may enlighten our minds to God's truths.

When we sit before God with His Word in hand,
it is imperative that we ask the Holy Spirit
to lead, teach, and guide us.

Remember, one of the tricks of the enemy is to take God's Word and twist it ever-so-slightly, deviating from the intended truth(s) in order to incorporate sin and bondage. The interpretation of Scripture must always agree with the nature and character of Jesus Christ as revealed in His Word through the power of His Holy Spirit. This is why it is so important to spend time getting to know Jesus personally. Doing so helps us to interpret the Scripture according to the character of Christ. John 4:24 says, "God is a Spirit (a spiritual being) and those who worship Him must worship Him in spirit and in truth (reality)." As we get to know Him and study His Word, we worship Him from our hearts—our spirit—in accordance with the integrity, virtue, and character of Christ.

The interpretation of Scripture must always agree with the nature and character of Jesus Christ.

Look at the power of God's Word that we have at our disposal! God brought *everything* into existence by His spoken Word! Likewise, our words have the power to bring about things. Proverbs 18:21 says, "*Death* and *life* are in the power of the tongue, and they who indulge in it shall eat the fruit of it [for death or life]." In John 6:63 Jesus said, "The words (truths) that I have been speaking to you are spirit and life."

Remember Hebrews 4:12, which tells us that God's Word is sharper than any double-edged sword? God places His Word in our hearts, and we are to ponder, believe, and repeat it out of our mouths. His Word knits together His Sprit with ours to establish His will and purposes within us, in order that we may have life—life as God has it. The opposite of this is true as well. If our speech is in agreement with Satan, our words will then sow seeds of destruction, bringing about death.

The Word of God causes us to change as it is implanted in our hearts. When we begin to obey the Word, it takes root in our souls and bodies, aligning them to the Holy Spirit. Thus, we are being "linked" together, spirit, soul, and body, to the direction of the Holy Spirit.

Please note that God does not require us to read several chapters each day to fulfill any quotas. That, in and of itself, is the misuse of God's Word. Rather, He knows the thoughts and intentions of our hearts. He determines whether or not we are reading His Word to impress Him, or because we want to know Him more personally.

Questions for Study

1. Do you value the Word of God so much that you set aside special time each day to read, study, and meditate on it? We cannot become like Christ if we do not water ourselves with the Word of God.
2. What is the device that the Holy Spirit uses to bring about transformation within each of us?
3. According to 2 Corinthians 3:17, 18 how are we are being transfigured into the image of Christ?
4. What should be the number one priority of every believer?
5. What is God's recipe for success?
6. What two things must work together within the believer to bring about the soul's healing?
7. The interpretation of Scripture must always be in accordance with what?
8. How are we "linked," spirit, soul, and body, to the direction of the Holy Spirit?

Personal Prayer

Thank You, Lord, for Your Word and the power it contains to save my soul! (James 1:21). Rid me of all uncleanness and wickedness. Help me to hide Your Word in my heart so that I might not sin against You (Psalm 119:11). I come to You on Your terms—with unveiled face. Empty me of what I think I know about You so that I can be filled with the knowledge of Your truth. As I live in Your Word, Lord, change me into Your image, from one level of glory to another (2 Corinthians 3:18). Give me the desire to sit at Your feet, reading Your Word, meditating on it, and speaking it out loud (Luke 10:19; Proverbs 18:21). Help me to observe and do according to all that is written in it, for then my way shall be prosperous. Then I will deal wisely, and have good success (Joshua 1:8).

Chapter 22

Personalizing God's Word Establishes Us in His Love

I am learning that the more time I spend hearing and studying God's Word, the more deeply I trust Him. I become more rooted and grounded in God's love as I spend time meditating on Scripture and praying. When I meditate on Scripture, I repeat it over and over in my mind and I mutter it aloud. When I pray, I converse with God about everything in my life. To me, this is the picture of Mark 4:24-25 which says,

> And He said to them, be careful what you are hearing. The measure [of thought and study] you give [to the truth you hear] will be the measure [of virtue, power* and knowledge] that comes back to you—and more [besides] will be given; and from him who has nothing, even what he has will be taken away [by force].

What an amazing promise! God is concerned with every detail of your life. He cares about everything that concerns you. He wants you to share your life with Him. I am discovering that the more I believe in God's love for me and seek after His heart, (His priorities), the more He shows me about Himself. Remember, He is no respecter of persons. He is waiting for you to believe that He loves you and to seek Him for the sake of relationship and fellowship. Many times we talk to God when we need something or have a request. However, He wants to reveal Himself to us so that we will find all that we need is in Him. As we spend time getting to know Him more intimately, He will do just that. We have to become more like Mary, who sat at Jesus's feet visiting with Him, and less like Martha, who ran around in busyness rather than getting to know Him. (See Luke 10:38-42.)

I love the promises of the following two verses:

- Psalm 25:14 says, "The secret [of the sweet, satisfying companionship] of the Lord have they who fear (revere and worship) Him, and He will show them His covenant and reveal to them its [deep, inner meaning]."

- Psalm 32:8 says, "I [the Lord] will instruct you and teach you in the way you should go; I will counsel you with My eye upon you!"

Let's look at the love God has for each of us as He has revealed it to us in His Word. God's love is called *agape* love, which denotes a pure, innocent love that is spiritual in nature. It also means that God has our very best interest at heart at all times.

- God is love: or God = love (1 John 4:8).
- And this is love, "Not that we loved God, but that He loved us and sent His Son to be the propitiation (the atoning sacrifice for our sins. (See 1 John 4:10.)
- God's love is about *sacrifice*. He *chooses* to love people no matter what. Even while we were yet sinners, God *sacrificed His Son and chose* to love us. (See Romans 5:8 and John 3:16.)

Let's look closely at *agape* love.

1. Agape love is unconditional, sacrificial love. It means choosing to love those who are unlovable, including yourself, through the power of the Holy Spirit. Whether you realize it or not, self is the person that is hardest to love. Christians everywhere desperately need to learn how to love themselves in a healthy, balanced, and God-honoring way. His Word rooted in us teaches us how. As we learn to love ourselves the way God does, we will truly be able to love others in this way. Remember, God's Word, which is love, when implanted in us has the power to save and heal our inner selves.
2. Agape love is undefeatable! It never fails. Based on choice, rather than feelings or emotions, it gives freely without asking or expecting anything in return. It always seeks the highest good of the other person, no matter what he or she does. (See 1 Corinthians 13.)
3. Agape love has no conditions. One of the things I love most about God is how He sees what we can become if we will trust Him with our lives rather than looking at where we are right now. He knows that if we will simply receive His unconditional love, we will see for ourselves that He has truly made us "more than conquerors." He knows that we will do "greater things than these," and that we will "continue to bear fruit even into old age." Truly, He longs for us to believe these things so that it will become a reality to us.

When God's love takes root inside of you, it changes who you are and how you view yourself. It allows you to see yourself, your past and your future, from God's perspective, which is always hope-filled and positive.

**When the love of God takes root inside of you,
it changes who you are and how you view yourself.**

Look at this incredible promise in Romans 8:28 that is ours to claim if we choose to partner with God. It says, "We are *assured* and *know* that [God being partner in our labor] all things work together and are] fitting into a plan] for good *to and for those who love God* and are called according to [His] design and purpose." How do we become recipients of such grace? God gives grace to the humble in spirit. This means we continuously admit our need for His help. It means believing in our hearts that God is willing and able to help. It means confessing with our mouths that He completely (in spirit, soul and body), rescues us from the dominion of darkness.

I want to share with you some of the verses (in paraphrased form) that the Holy Spirit led me to personalize and to pray over my life. I also pray them over the lives of others. I encourage you to ask the Holy Spirit to show you the verses He wants you to personalize to help root and ground you in His love. It is important to insert your name in the Scriptures, allowing verses to become your personal letter from God Himself to you.

- John 1:12—Because I have received Him and I believe in His Name, He has given me the right to become His child; I am God's child, I belong to Him and Him only.
- Jeremiah 1:5—Before I formed you in the womb, Lisa, I knew you! Yes, before you were born, I set you apart for Myself, that you might become a spokeswoman for Me.
- Psalm 139:14, 16—Lisa, you are fearfully and wonderfully made! Lord, your works are wonderful! Your eyes saw my unformed body and all the days ordained for me were written in Your book before one of them came about.
- Ephesians 1:16, 17-19—I keep asking that the God of my Lord Jesus Christ, the glorious Father, may give me the Spirit of wisdom and revelation, so that I may know You better. I pray also that the eyes of my heart may be enlightened in order that I may know the hope to which You have called me, the riches of Your glorious inheritance in the saints, and Your incomparably great power because I believe.
- Ephesians 3:14-21—Lord, I kneel before You, and I pray out of Your glorious riches, that You would strengthen me with power through Your Spirit in my inner being, so that You may live in my heart through faith as I place my confidence in Your ability. I pray that I would be rooted and established in You and have power with all the saints, to grasp how wide and long and high and deep is Your love for me! I want to know Your love personally; Your love that surpasses head knowledge—that I may be filled to the measure of all the fullness of You. Now to You, Lord, You who are able to do immeasurably more than all I could dare ask, think, or imagine, according to Your power that is at work in me! To You be the glory!
- Ephesians 5:1-2—I am an imitator of You. I am a dearly loved child, and I live a life of love. Just as You have loved me and gave Yourself up for me, I now give all of myself up to You as a fragrant offering and living sacrifice.
- Philippians 1:9-11—And this is my prayer; that my love may abound more and more in knowledge and depth of insight, so that I may be able to discern what is best and may be pure and blameless until You come to get me. I want to be filled with the fruit of righteousness that comes through You as I lay aside myself and live in You.
- Colossians 1:9-14—I am asking You, Lord, to fill me with the knowledge of Your will (Your way of thinking, speaking, and doing) through all spiritual wisdom and understanding. I pray that I may live my life worthy of You and may please You in every way, bearing fruit in every good work, growing in the knowledge of Your love for me, being strengthened with all power according to Your glorious might so that I may have great endurance and patience, and joyfully give thanks to You, who has qualified me to share in Your inheritance! For You have rescued me from the dominion of darkness and brought me into the kingdom of the Son You love, in whom I have redemption, the forgiveness of sins!

- Ephesians 5:18 and Acts 1:8—I am not filled or drunk with the ways of this world, for that is debauchery and lawlessness; but I am ever filled and stimulated with Your Holy Spirit. I receive and welcome Your grace; the empowerment, ability, efficiency, and might of Your Holy Spirit, who enables me, to be Your witness wherever I go.

Questions for Study

1. Are you willing to spend time in God's Word in order to become rooted and grounded in Him? If so, how will you approach this? List any helpful habits that will encourage you in your commitment.
2. Are you seeking after God for Himself and His priorities or are you only concerned that He tend to your concerns?
3. What promises does God make to us in Psalm 25:14 and 32:8?
4. Define agape love.
5. What helps us to receive God's grace?
6. Why is it important to insert your name into Scriptures?
7. List the verses that the Holy Spirit is asking you to speak over your life. (Example: If you struggle with being kind, look up Scriptures relating to kindness. If you are anxious or tend to worry a lot, look up Scriptures about God's peace).

Personal Prayer

Lord, thank You that while I was yet a sinner You chose to love me (Romans 5:8). I receive Your love in simple, childlike faith. I believe in Your Name. Thank You for giving me the right to become Your child. I am Yours, and I belong to You and You only (John 1:12). Thank You, that before I was formed in the womb, You knew and approved of me despite all of my mistakes (Jeremiah 1:5). Help me to love myself in a healthy way as You would want me to do. Forgive me for trying to be the guide of my own life. I know that I can never do life apart from You (John 15:3-5). Thank You that You will instruct me and teach me in the way that I should go. Counsel me, Lord, with Your eye upon me (Psalm 32:8). Help me now to become an imitator of Your love because I know that I am Your dearly loved child. I give myself up to You as an offering and living sacrifice (Ephesians 5:1-2; Romans 12:1).

Chapter 23

God, His Love, and Me

God *is* love. Therefore, God equals love. Love defines who God is. It's not something He does for us because we behave well or never make mistakes. No, God is love, and he loves us—imperfections and all. Because of who He is, He can deal with us only through love. God loves everybody. Furthermore, the only sin we could ever commit that He would not forgive is choosing to disregard His plan of salvation, which stems from His immeasurable love for each of us. (This is called blasphemy against the Holy Spirit).

As believers in Christ, God has called us to demonstrate the love of Jesus to a dying world. In order to do this, though, we must first receive His love into the innermost parts of our beings, which is our spirit. As the saying goes, "You can't give away something you don't have." Everything regarding God, Jesus, and the Holy Spirit hinges on love. Therefore, it must become the main concern, theme, and foundation of our lives as well.

Remember, we receive by simply believing, and as we believe we then receive. In God's economy, we have to believe first. Then we will see the results of that belief. After all, it doesn't take faith for us to believe in something we can see. Rather, it is required for the things which we cannot see.

**We receive by simply believing,
and as we believe we then receive.
In God's economy, we have to believe first.
Then we will see the results of that belief.**

Psalm 127:1 says, "Except the Lord builds the house, they labor in vain who build it." Read the sentence again and replace the word "Lord" with the word "Love" because God equals love. "Except Love builds the house, they labor in vain who build it." In order to grow closer to God in our daily lives, we must grasp this truth—individually, within our homes, within our neighborhoods, at work, and at church. If we are not becoming people who are rooted and grounded in God's love, then nothing we do will amount to anything. God calls work done without love

111

vanity. In other words, if we continue doing good deeds out of obligation rather than out of a heart that is filled with the love of the Godhead, we are working to no avail.

Learning to walk in love the way God desires begins with us knowing that we are loved by Him. It helps to observe, study, pray, and think about the life of Jesus found in the Gospels. We can learn to love by knowing how He acted, reacted and lived while on earth. Ephesians 5:1-2 says,

> Therefore, be imitators of God [copy Him and follow His example] as *well-beloved children* [imitate their father]. And walk in love [esteeming and delighting in one another] as Christ loved us and gave Himself up for us, a slain offering and sacrifice to God [for you, so that it became] a sweet fragrance.

These two verses teach us what it means to walk in love. They tell us to do the following:

1. Imitate God because you believe that you are loved by Him.
2. Nurture His love within you by reading His Word and submitting to His Spirit (obedience).
3. Do this so you can:
    *   Esteem and delight in other people and walk in the Light as He is in the Light (see 1 John 1:7).
    *   Give up your ways for His and your rights for the sake of another.

Matthew 22:37-40 says,

> You shall love the Lord your God with all your heart and with all your soul and with all your mind (intellect). This is the great (most important, principal) and first commandment. And a second is like it: you shall love your neighbor as [you do] yourself. These two commandments sum up and upon them depend all the Law and the Prophets.

Remember, if God commands us to do something, He also gives us the grace to do it. First John 4:10 explains this grace: "In this is love: not that we loved God, but that He loved us and sent His Son to be the propitiation (the atoning sacrifice) for our sins." In other words, we are to recognize, appreciate, and receive God's love for us first. We must decide to be completely His. Then, we can love Him with all our heart – the core of our being, – as well as with our souls – our mind, will, attitudes, and emotions, – realizing that everything we own belongs to Him. This includes our time, money, hopes, dreams, and aspirations. Every part of us belongs to Him and others will see the love of Christ displayed through our bodies by our consistent godly actions. Loving and trusting God will give Him the proper Lordship over all of our being! God's great love for us is what caused Him to give up His Son for our ransom. We imitate this love while at the same time receiving His love for us. As we progress in this we will love others as we love ourselves because our hearts are in tune with His.

This is the key: If we do not receive His love for us we will not have a healthy, balanced, or proper love for ourselves. Then we will never be able to love God, or anyone else, the way we were designed to. (Refer back to Chapter 20 entitled, "Believing He Loves Me.") By meditating on and declaring God's love for yourself, you will get rooted in it! "God loves me!" and "I love me!" are two phrases that need to come out of our mouths regularly.

**By meditating on and declaring God's love for yourself
you will get rooted in it! "God loves me," and "I love me!"
are two phrases that need to come out of our mouths regularly!**

Notice the shape of the cross. It pictures Jesus' love coming down on us. We take this love in, receive it, then give and lavish it back upon Him. This is our starting point! Now we are able to reach out to the world because of the confidence and security we have within this reciprocated love cycle. Let's look at this love cycle more in depth.

1. The first step is God's love coming down to us.
2. Christ demonstrated His love to us by choosing to lay His life down for us.
3. We demonstrate our love back to Him by receiving His free gift of love into our heart and spending time developing that love relationship as we obey His voice.

Becoming rooted and grounded in God's love takes time, effort and life-long dedication to Him. Simply punching in and out of church each week "doing our duty" is not going to make God-things happen in our lives. Quite often this is where so many people fail. They fail because they do not take the time to study God's love and receive it into their spirits on a day-to-day basis. When we believe God has a good plan for us, regardless of bad things that may happen, we realize our need for this daily time with Him and we start to receive His love into our being by believing His Word. Ephesians 3:17 attests to this fact. It says, "May Christ through your faith (belief and confidence in God), [actually] dwell (settle down, abide, make His permanent home) in your hearts! *May you be rooted deep in love and founded securely on love.*"

If you choose not to become rooted and grounded in God's love, you forfeit a life of stability and security. Your root system will be weak and easily plucked up when the storms of life come around. Inevitably, you will resort back to your own way of living.

Ephesians 3:18-19 explains why we are to become rooted and grounded in God's love. When we do so, six things happen. First, we have power over the enemy, because we know our sins are forgiven and we have right-standing with God. Second, we are strong during tests, temptations, and trials because we know God loves us and has our best interest at heart. Third, we experience the full package of God's love—the breadth, length, height, and depth—made available through salvation. Fourth, we personally know the love of Christ and each facet of His salvation (forgiveness of sins, rescue, deliverance, healing, wholeness, soundness, blessings, provision, peace, and well-being). It becomes more than mere head knowledge. Rather, personal experience teaches us all that salvation encompasses. Fifth, we become filled throughout our entire being (spirit, soul, and body) to the fullness of God and all that He is! Finally, we allow God to grow our entire being, wholly filled and flooded with God Himself.

Ephesians 3:20-21 explains what happens when we take His love into our inner being:

1. He is able to carry out His purpose within us (the good plan He has for our lives).
2. His plan is always far over and above all that we could dare ask, think or imagine, even beyond our highest prayers, desires, thoughts, hopes, and dreams.
3. He will receive the glory, and the world will be drawn to Him.

The complete cycle looks something like this:

1. He loves me first.
2. I receive His free gift of love into my heart.
3. I give love back to Him by acknowledging and confessing my sins and praising Him for giving me righteousness, forgiveness, healing, and blessings instead. I enjoy praying, spending time with Him, and obeying Him daily because of His love, grace, mercy, and loving-kindness for me.
4. As I do this, His love inside of me grows, and I get rooted in it.
5. He untangles and delivers me from sin, selfishness, Satan, sickness, and the system of the world.
6. He fulfills His good plan for my life.
7. He receives the glory.
8. Others are drawn to Him because of my faith, patience, perseverance, and obedience to Him.

I cannot stress enough how important it is to receive God's love in order to become true imitators and disciples of His. When we believe that God loves us, nothing can harm us or separate us from the security and power found within that love. As we open our hearts up to Him, He delivers us from the enemy's entanglements. Even though we are not free of troubles, necessarily, we are free from the power that Satan wants to exert over us *during* our troubles. As such, we are true witnesses of the character and love of Christ. John 13:35 says, "They will know we are Christians by our love . . ." because we know that we are beloved by God.

God's power and purpose for our lives can only be acquired through complete devotion to Him and the believing and receiving of His love which always works through faith, (see Galatians 5:6). That is, our faith works when we believe that we are loved by Him. Truly, we need to open our mouths and declare God's Word back to Him in prayer.

On a side note, if you find yourself struggling with believing that God loves you, it is guaranteed that your love walk and prayer life are struggling too. This will affect your relationships, your health, your finances, and every area of your life. Love requires us to place our total trust in God. It demands that we sacrifice what we think, want, feel, hear or see in the physical realm and cling to the Word and Spirit of God. It means that we trust God to fulfill His promises in our lives, and thus enable us to reach a lost world.

This book is designed to teach us how to walk in love and become rooted, grounded, and secured in God Himself. God uses our submission to Him to reach out and love others through us. Once we become rooted in His love, we can respond and react to people as He would, rather than reacting from our personal offenses and unforgiveness. This whole process is about "taking off the old" way of doing things and "putting on the new." It can happen only as we believe and receive God's gift of love into our innermost being.

Consider these statements:

- We all know people we want to see saved or changed.
- We all want to have victory in our lives and power over the enemy.
- We all want to see our children and loved ones walk with the Lord.
- We all desire to reach out to our neighbors and community for Christ.
- We all desire for our churches to grow spiritually.

Dear brothers and sisters in Christ, we must give up trying to do God's work in other's lives by trying to change them. We must abandon our selfish efforts toward manipulation. These are works of the flesh. Instead, let's start to live by the new commandment he gave us by loving God, others, and ourselves the way that He loves us. Everything depends on our obedience to this! God has done His part by loving us and allowing us to partner with Him. He is waiting for His people's cooperation. He wants people without the spots of sin, the wrinkles of division, or the blemishes of pride. God is looking for people who will dare to believe that He loves them and accepts them, and whose sins He remembers no more. This is a body of people that lives with a clear conscience, understanding the righteousness they have in Christ.

Questions for Study

1. Finish the equation: God = ?
2. Do you really know in your heart that God loves you, imperfections and all? Do you really believe it? Write out Jeremiah 1:5 and John 3:16.
3. How are we to show the love of Christ to a dying world?
4. What is the main theme, concern, and foundation of the Godhead? Is it your main theme, concern, and foundation?
5. Write out and meditate on 1 John 1:7. Do you agree that this verse lived out will help evangelize the world?
6. What is the key to loving our neighbor as we love ourselves?
7. Write out the complete love cycle.
8. What is the greatest commandment given to us by Christ? How are we able to keep this commandment?

Personal Prayer

Lord, I realize that You are love, and therefore You deal with me only through love (1 John 4:8). Thank You for loving me first and reaching down to me through Christ (1 John 4:10, 19). Forgive me for the many times I have chosen to walk in selfishness rather than in love. Your Word says that perfect love (sacrifice) casts out all selfishness (1 John 4:18). Lord, I realize that I cannot love as You do unless You fill me with Your love. I receive Your love into my inner-most being. Please establish me in love and root me and ground me in love, so that I may be an imitator of You (Ephesians 3:18-19, 5:1-2). Help me to do my part by declaring Your love for me. I realize that unless You build me up in love, I am laboring in vain by simply trying harder (Psalm 127:1). Help me learn to love You from the inside out, with all of my heart, soul, and body, realizing that every part of me belongs wholly to You (Matthew 23:37-40; Romans 12:1-2). Please be the Lord of my life and help me to submit my belongings to You as well, including my money, time, hopes, dreams, and aspirations. Help me to love myself in a balanced way so that I can love my neighbor (Mathew 22:37-40; Romans 12:1-2). Help me to respond to others as You would, and not from my own fleshly reactions of offense and unforgiveness. Help me to love others without being infected by them, but affecting them with Your love emanating out from within me. Then I will be a true witness of Your character, and the world will know that I am Yours by my love toward others. Holy Spirit, please help me to walk in the light of Your love so that I will have fellowship with others.

Chapter 24

What Does God's Love Working in Us Look Like?

———————❧———————

*I*n the last chapter we discussed the importance of receiving God's love into our inner-most being. When we realize it is God who reaches down to us through the Cross of Christ rather than us initiating the relationship, we receive the love of Christ into our hearts. (See 1 John 4:19.) We, in turn, love Him back and are then able to reach out to others with His unconditional love. Through the childlike and simple belief that He loves us unconditionally, Jesus Christ's love working in us causes us to trust Him. This childlike faith leads us to growth and releases His good character and plan into our lives.

The world bases its love on conditions. It says, "I'll love you if . . ." and usually, when a person fails to live up to the "ifs," the relationship is over. Sadly, many Christians live (and love) like this, as well. It happens when we choose to love others according to the mind of our flesh rather than that of the Holy Spirit. Why does this happen? Oftentimes, as Christians, we don't realize our own need to be untangled and set free from wrong mindsets—a stubborn, selfish will and emotions completely out of sync with Christ's.

The mind of the flesh consists of selfish thoughts and motives regarding relationships. It thinks, "What's in this for me?" and "What can you do to make me happy?" Usually, once the minute disappointment sets in or desire is left unfulfilled, the "love" goes out the window and the search for another fix is on the mind. The Holy Spirit is working to remove this from our lives. He wants to take off our old way of doing things and replace it with love for Him, our-selves, and others. Colossians 3:12 says,

> Clothe yourselves therefore, as God's own chosen ones (His own picked representatives) [who are] purified and holy and well-beloved [by God Himself, by putting on behavior marked by] tenderhearted pity and mercy, kind feeling, a lowly opinion of yourselves, gentle ways, [and] patience [which is tireless and long-suffering, and has the power to endure whatever comes, with good temper].

There are two main reasons we *choose* not to love another person:

1. We are selfish and apathetic, or
2. We are focused on an offense that this person previously committed against us.

Do we realize that the choice to not love another person as Christ loves us severs us from all of His good plans and blessings? When the whole body of Christ finally grasps that concept, the bars of sin, pride, and discrimination will break from each one of us. Encouragement will abound. We will no longer view each other according to the outer appearance of race, gender, social status, economic status, age, or denomination. Instead, we will be truly one in Christ—equally sharing His blessings and benefits with one another. We will encourage each other to use our gifts and become like Him in all ways of life. We will be a church without spot, wrinkle or blemish—the blameless bride of Christ! This is the body of Christ as He intended, and following Christ means becoming like Him and doing what He did—preaching, teaching, healing people, and setting people free from the wiles of the enemy. It's about encouraging people to trust in Him and take on His identity. Following Jesus Christ involves teaching people how to obey Him and helping people become His disciples. As we do this, we need to pay attention to His Word, allowing His Spirit to lead us.

Every day of His life, Jesus went about doing good. Full of the Holy Spirit, He ministered to people and He allowed others to minister to Him. (See Acts 10:38.) Jesus loved them all. The door into His heritage is open to every man, woman, child, slave, free, Jew, and Gentile. Truly, every follower of Christ is to become a minister of His grace. We too, should allow others to minister to us. Jesus welcomed everyone who desired to do so for Him. Sometimes, one of the hardest things for us as Christians is to let another person serve us. This is the compassion that motivated Christ and causes the love cycle to continue. Loving and seeing others as Jesus does equips us to minister and meet needs. The Holy Spirit Himself places His people in the church where He wants them because He knows the gifts He has placed within each person. We truly need His help in this area.

Colossians 3:14 says, "And *above all these* [put on] love and enfold yourselves with the bond of perfectness [*which binds everything together completely in ideal harmony*.]" It's hard to find this God-like harmony within ourselves, within our homes, or within our churches when we have not yet "put on" the love of Christ. But Paul gives us a strategy in Colossians 3:12-17 to help us live for God day by day:

1. Put on a heart of compassion, kindness, humility, gentleness, and patience.
2. Forgive and bear with one another.
3. First and foremost, let love guide your life.
4. Let the peace of Christ rule in your hearts, and always be grateful.
5. Keep God's Word in your heart at all times and in all circumstances. Keep a godly disposition towards one another.
6. Be thankful.
7. Live as true representatives of Christ Jesus through the power of the Holy Spirit.

The love of Christ at work in our lives will cause us to live differently. We will find the following to be true:

1. Fear is gone as we rest and trust in Him.
2. We mature in Him as He brings us to perfection and grows Christ-like character in us.
3. We become confident in who God has made us to be, believing He has provided us with every spiritual blessing that Jesus has and trusting that we are joint heirs with Him.
4. We start to desire His pleasure more than we want to please man.
5. We live our lives according to the Holy Spirit's will rather than that of our flesh.
6. We start to love other people the way He does.
7. We learn to despise sin in our lives, and we become untangled from it.
8. We want to help others know Him intimately and His unconditional love.
9. We become filled with grace, giving ourselves and other people a "break."
10. We stop smothering people and start encouraging them instead.

God loves us with unconditional love called *agape love*. This is how we should choose to love others. This kind of love sacrifices self-will for that of another. It chooses selflessness without condition. Agape love will confront and encourage others to live in right standing with God. Love, God's way, seeks the welfare of others and works no ill towards anyone. It looks for opportunities to do good to all. Agape love changes everything and everyone it touches. It *never* fails. God's love, working in us, brings others to repentance. In fact, our lives become victorious and powerful when we focus on loving people as Jesus did. *We do this by partnering with Him, submitting to Him, and allowing Him to cleanse us first from all of our impurities.* He makes us as funnels through which His love comes in and flows out without the interruption of a contaminated soul (mind, will, attitudes, and emotions). When the life of God Himself becomes the fragrance of our hearts, we live as He intended.

> **We are to be funnels through which His love comes in**
> **and flows out without the interruption of a contaminated soul.**
> **When the life of God Himself becomes the fragrance of our hearts,**
> **we live as He intended.**

First Corinthians 13 is often called the love chapter. It reveals the truth of God's sacrificial agape love so that we can love likewise. It would do us well to read this chapter as our prayer every morning before we attempt to go through our day.

The first three verses of this chapter read like an impressive spiritual resume. However, every last bit of it is considered as nothing if not done in accordance with God's love. Just think about that! We can impress people with our so-called spiritual resume, but if our hearts do not reflect God's love, He is not impressed.

Verses four through six tell us that:

- Love endures long.
- Love is patient.
- Love is kind.
- Love is never envious.
- Love is never jealous.

- Love is never boastful.
- Love is never big-headed.
- Love never acts disrespectfully or hot-headed.
- Love is not conceited.
- Love is not arrogant.
- Love is not rude.
- Love is not unmannerly.
- Love does not insist on its own rights.
- Love does not insist on its own way.
- Love is not touchy or irritable.
- Love is not self-seeking.
- Love is not fretful or afraid.
- Love is not resentful.
- Love takes no account of the evil done to it.
- Love doesn't keep track of a wrong done to it.
- Love does not rejoice at injustice, prejudice, or discrimination of any kind.
- Love does not rejoice at unrighteousness.
- Love rejoices when right and truth prevail.
- Love bears up under anything and everything that comes.
- Love is quick to believe the best of every person.
- Love persists under all circumstances.
- Love endures everything without weakening.
- Love never fails.
- Love never fades out.
- Love never becomes obsolete.

Love is the greatest of all!

Read back through this list and put God's name in the place of the word love. Now understand that this is who He is. Love is the very character of God, and it's how He chooses to respond to every one of us.

Now, read back through the list again and place the word "I" in the place of love. After all, God is our standard. He is at work in us and He is who we desire to imitate. Therefore, we must also see ourselves and speak of ourselves as patient, kind, enduring, forbearing, longsuffering, and so forth. As followers of Christ, our purpose is to become like Him. We are called to receive His love and respond out of that love. We are called to partner with His Holy Spirit, believing that in Him all things are possible. As we do, He will change us from one level of His glory to another! The soul will no longer be a stumbling block because we will choose daily to submit our will to the Holy Spirit and obey Him. God's love cleanses and purifies us. As such, we become His vessels, His children, who draw a dying world to Himself.

First Corinthians 14:1 says, "Eagerly pursue and seek to acquire [this] love [make it your aim, your great quest]." Just think how rewarding it would be if everyone in the body of Christ took personal responsibility for his or her own love walk with Christ—no blaming the pastors or fellow church-goers. No pointing the finger at spouses or parents. No bad-mouthing our employer or employees. Instead, imagine each of us committing to the studying, reading, praying, and desiring of God's love in our lives and making it be the governing rule of our hearts and minds at all times. If we seek God's love first, the blessings will always follow (see Deuteronomy chapter 28). Get alone with God each day and allow Him to transform your total being to look like His. Devote yourself to living as He desires, depending on His teachings for guidance and trusting His Holy Spirit for power. Let His life become your life.

Questions for Study
1. What is the love of the world based upon?
2. What are we really choosing when we choose not to walk in love towards another person?
3. What is the point of Christianity?
4. Is there anyone in your life discouraging you from becoming like Christ and doing what He did? Is that someone you?
5. Who alone places and equips people within the body of Christ and why should it be this way?
6. What is the strategy for daily living that Paul recommends to us in Colossians 3:12-17? Are you asking for God's grace to help you do this?
7. What must we do in order to live a powerful and victorious life in Christ?
8. Are you eagerly pursuing the love walk?
9. Is love your highest aim?

Personal Prayer
Lord, forgive me for trying to love people unconditionally when I have yet to receive Your love for me. Your Word says that Your mercy is new every morning (Lamentations 3:22-23), and I need Your mercy to help me walk in love each day and in every situation. I desire to show the agape, unconditional love to others that You have shown to me. Help me to be a funnel through which Your love comes in and flows out, uninterrupted by a contaminated, selfish soul. May Your life and Your love become the fragrance of my heart. Your love, working in me, is patient, kind, enduring, not envious, jealous, boastful or vainglorious. It is not conceited, arrogant, rude, or haughty. Your love, working in me, is not unmannerly, it does not insist on its own rights or ways. Your love is not touchy, prideful or self-seeking. Please help me to love like this. It is not fretful, afraid, or resentful, and it takes no account of a wrong suffered. It is not easily offended. It does not rejoice at injustice, prejudice or discrimination of any kind, nor does it rejoice in unrighteousness. Love rejoices when right and truth prevail. Love bears up under anything and everything that may come, and love is always ready to believe the best of every person. Love's hopes are fadeless under *all* circumstances; love will endure everything You ask me to face, without weakening. Love never fails, fades out or becomes obsolete. Your love, working in me, is the greatest thing of all, and it is what You desire most (1 Corinthians 13)! Help me to eagerly pursue and acquire this love. May I make it my aim (1 Corinthians 14:1).

PART FOUR:

*Understanding
the Function of Our Mind
Will, and Emotions*

Chapter 25

The Mind

───────◆───────

When God gave each of us our mind, He gave us a wonderful and complex tool. With our minds, we have the ability to reason, think, remember, feel, imagine, intend, purpose, agree, disagree, change, and form opinions. Having been created in God's image, we are different from every other creature He made. (See Genesis 1:27). The Lord knows well all the deep recesses and complexities of our minds. Whether we are conscious of them or not, our private inner conversations are no secret to Him. He made us, and He knows all things. The following verses attest to this:

- Psalm 139:1-3: "O Lord, you have searched me [thoroughly] and have known me. You know my down-sitting and my uprising; you understand my thoughts afar off. You sift and search out my path and my lying down, and you are acquainted with all my ways."
- John 2:24-25: "But Jesus [for His part] did not trust Himself to them, because he knew all [men]; and He did not need anyone to bear witness concerning man [needed no evidence from anyone about men], for He Himself knew what was in human nature. [He could read men's hearts]."

The mind is also the mechanism where we process and filter everything in life. All that happens to us sifts through the mind. Consequently, we view God, self, and others through that filtering system. In other words, we do not merely live, based on the facts of our past, but we function by our interpretations or memories of these facts.

For example, two children growing up in the same family will have two completely different interpretations of the facts that have occurred within their family. While we cannot change the facts of our pasts, we can allow the Holy Spirit to alter our interpretations; that's how healing comes. The Holy Spirit led Joseph to forgive his brothers' hate crimes. That's how he was able to say in Genesis 50:20; "As for you, you thought evil against me, but God meant it for good, to bring about that many people should be kept alive, as they are this day." He can lead you to do the same, if you let Him.

Despite whatever insecurities, injustices, discouragements, or abuses that you may have suffered to your mind or body in the past, God can turn those negative experiences into positive outcomes for you as well as for others. It's up to you to decide whether you will partner with His Spirit and believe what God says about you in His Word. This will lead you into all truth. It will also lead you out of those hidden and buried places within your mind and heart that keep you locked in because of your past experiences.

**Despite whatever insecurities, injustices,
discouragements, or abuses that you may have
suffered to your mind or body in the past,
God can turn those negative experiences into positive outcomes.**

In the New Testament, the mind is described as either good or evil. We can have the mind of Christ or the mind of the flesh. The "good" mind is renewed through the Holy Spirit with God's Word. Romans 12:2 says,

> Do not be conformed to this world (this age), [fashioned after and adapted to its external, superficial customs], but be transformed (changed) by the [entire] renewal of you mind [by its new ideals and its new attitude], so that you may prove [for yourselves] what is the good and acceptable and perfect will of God, even the thing which is good and acceptable and perfect [in His sight for you].

The Message Bible says it like this:

> So here's what I want you to do, God helping you: Take your everyday, ordinary life—your sleeping, eating, going to work, and walking around life—and place it before God as an offering. Embracing what God does for you is the best thing you can do for Him. Don't become so well-adjusted to your culture that you fit into it without even thinking. Instead, fix your attention on God. You'll be changed from the inside out. Readily recognize what He wants from you, and quickly respond to it. Unlike the culture around you, always dragging you down to its level of immaturity, God brings the best out of you, develops well-informed maturity in you.

As believers, we have received the mind of Christ! Ponder that thought for a minute!

1 Corinthians 2:16 verifies this: "But we have the mind of Christ and do hold the thoughts (feelings and purposes of His Heart)." The Holy Spirit puts these thoughts and purposes into action in our lives. (See 1 Corinthians 2:11-13.)

Romans 8:6 says, "Now the mind of the flesh [which is sense and reason without the Holy Spirit] is death [death that comprises all the miseries arising from sin, both here and hereafter]. But the mind of the [Holy] Spirit is life and [soul] peace (both now and forever)." Our purpose as Christians is to display the new nature and the fruit of the Spirit that God has given to us. Our renewed mind and new nature gradually becomes our habitual behavior as we choose to worship God regardless of our circumstances. As we do this, we become teachers, leaders, and encouragers to those around us.

The mind of Christ—the positive, life-giving, good mind—directed by God's Spirit, must be renewed each day with the Word of God. The negative, evil mind of the flesh, which is directed by our physical senses, (what we can see, touch, taste, hear, and smell) is then slowly put to death. By depriving it of the authority to direct our thoughts, words, attitudes, and actions we starve it to death. Sin has corrupted the evil mind, just as it has the rest of man's nature. If we do not renew our minds with God's Word it is only natural that we will follow the dictates and desires of the flesh, along with our physical senses. That mind pursues what it wants, thinks, and feels with no consideration of the mind of Christ, His Holy Spirit and His Word. The following verses help to clarify this:

- Romans 1:21: "Because when they knew and recognized Him as God they did not honor and glorify Him as God or give Him thanks. But instead they became futile and godless in their thinking (with vain imaginings, foolish reasoning and stupid speculations) their senseless minds were darkened."
- Romans 8:7: "[That is] because the mind of the flesh [with its carnal thoughts and purposes] is hostile to God, for it does not submit itself to God's Law: indeed it cannot."
- 1 Corinthians 2:14: "But the natural, non-spiritual man does not accept or welcome or admit into his heart (mind) the gifts and teachings and revelations of the Spirit of God, for they are folly (meaningless nonsense) to him; and he is incapable of knowing them [of progressively recognizing, understanding and becoming better acquainted with them] because they are spiritually discerned and estimated and appreciated."

The enemy will absolutely seek to devour the unattended, out-of-balance mind as his main meal. This is especially true for Christians. Please understand that our battle does not stop at salvation. In truth, salvation is just the beginning. Our minds are renewed as we dethrone the natural mind, which is led by our physical senses, and replace it with a faith-filled mind, which is led by God's Spirit and His Word. If Satan can control our thoughts, he will control our lives. The mind is his battleground, the place where he wages war against you. To simply acknowledge that fact will not rescue you from him. A fight rages inside each of us right now. Which powerful source will you side with? Christ and His life-giving power? Or Satan and his death-giving power?

Proverbs 4:23 tells us that the wellspring of life flows from our hearts/spirits. If our hearts do not agree with the Word and the Holy Spirit, then neither will our minds. If we choose to remain in this condition, we are rendered powerless. However, embracing, and obeying, the Word of God and the Holy Spirit enlightens and transforms our entire person—spirit, soul, and body (in that order), into the image of Christ. We must learn to align our minds of the flesh by submitting them to the direction of the Holy Spirit which is in agreement with God's Word.

Questions for Study
1. What are some of the things your mind has the ability to do?
2. What does it mean to be created in God's image?
3. Are your private thoughts kept secret from God?
4. We do not live solely according to the facts of our past, but with_____.
5. We cannot change the facts of our pasts, but what happens if we team up with the Holy Spirit?
6. According to the New Testament, what is the "good" mind?

7. Even though you are a Christian, if Satan can control your thoughts, he will control your_____.

Personal Prayer

Lord, Your Word says that the mind of the flesh with its carnal thoughts and purposes is hostile to God. It does not submit itself to Your laws, and indeed it cannot (Romans 8:7). Forgive me for placing my own sense and reasoning above the truth of Your Word (Romans 8:6). Please deliver me from my carnal mind and my way of thinking apart from You. Thank You for giving me the mind of Christ (1 Corinthians 2:16). Please empower me through the Holy Spirit to put Your thoughts and purposes into action in my life. Lord, I come against Satan's attempt to control my life through my thoughts. Help me to keep my heart and mind fixed on You, for as a person thinks in his heart so is he. (Proverbs 4:23).

Chapter 26

The Faith-Filled Mind

⸺⸺⸺⸺⸺⸺⸺⸺⸺⸺⸺⸺

The faith-filled mind is full of good judgment, discernment, and disciplined thought patterns. Second Timothy 1:7 describes this mind. It says, "For God did not give us a spirit of timidity (of cowardice or craven and cringing and fawning fear), but [He has given us a spirit] of power and of love and of calm and well-balanced mind and discipline and self-control." Because God's Spirit has enlightened the faith-filled mind, it understands and makes the right (God-inspired) decisions in everyday life. The faith-filled mind is peaceful, stable, steadfast, and unwilling to compromise any God-given truth.

Developing this faith-filled mind requires every kind of effort and determination on our part because the enemy is always at war with our new nature. Make no mistake, he will do everything within his power to derail anyone whose mind is full of faith. James 1:21 says, "So get rid of all uncleanness and the rampant outgrowth of wickedness, and in a humble (gentle, modest) spirit receive and welcome the Word which implanted and rooted [in your hearts] contains the power to save your souls." It is absolutely essential to welcome and instill God's Word into your mind so that the Holy Spirit can release you from the old nature of wickedness. He uses our faithful and obedient response to God's Word to release us from old mindsets, habits, ways of thinking, and speaking. Without a doubt, this is a process which requires much patience as the Holy Spirit works within us to remove the plaque from our hearts and out of our minds.

Being patient is a necessity
as the Holy Spirit works within us
to remove the plaque from our hearts
and out of our minds.

As Christians, we are apt to miss this. So often we conform to new rules, trying to do this transforming, plaque removing part on our own. Instead, we must surrender ourselves to God and put to death all wrong and negative thinking patterns. We need our thoughts, words, attitudes, and deeds to be retrained according to Christ. This can only be accomplished as we cooperate with the Holy Spirit, allowing Him to change us from the inside out. Let's revisit

Romans 12:1-3. The Message Bible gives us a simple picture of what this transformation looks like. It says,

> So here's what I want you to do, *God helping you:* Take your everyday, ordinary life—your sleeping, eating, going-to-work, and walking-around-life—and place it before God as an offering. Embracing what God does for you is the best thing you can do for Him. Don't become so well-adjusted to your culture that you fit into it *without even thinking.* Instead, *fix your attention on God.* You'll be changed from the inside out. Readily recognize what He wants from you, and quickly respond to it. Unlike the culture around you, always dragging you down to its level of immaturity, God brings the best out of you, develops well-formed maturity in you.

Let's look at these vital transformation steps that these verses give us.

- Place your life before God—__all__ of you. Take your sleeping, eating, going to work, walking around, everywhere you go, and place it before God as an offering. Invite Him into your everyday life to be with you, to teach you and to show Himself to you, no matter what you are doing or where you are going.
- What does God want from you? Embrace Him by spending time with Him—reading, studying, and meditating on His Word. Embrace His Spirit's teaching by doing it! Hear it, receive it, learn it, and obey it—then do it. That's what real faith does; it acts like the Word is true! Do not consider doing things any other way except His way.
- Take off your of-this-world nature and put on the ways of Christ. Don't keep doing things the way the world does, self-centered and uninterested in God.
- Instead, fix your attention on God. Place and set your mind on Him and keep it there. As you continue to do this, He will change you from the inside out.
- Readily recognize His ways. That is, recognize His character and start acting like His Word is true in your own situations and relationships. The best place to begin this practice is in your own home.
- Quickly obey His ways by willingly exchanging your ways for His.
- Resist the culture around you and what everyone else is doing. They intend only to bring you down to their immaturity and impurity.
- Grab hold of God and hang on to His ways, which are expressed through His Word. His Spirit will bring out the best in you and develop Christ-like maturity in you.

The faith-filled mind literally undresses self from the old ways and pushes them far away. It chooses to put on Christ's character through His empowering grace. The key to this fundamental growth is learning to practice the principle described in 2 Corinthians 10:5 in every situation. It says, " . . . and we lead every *thought and purpose* away captive into the obedience of Christ."

A faith-filled mind is a spiritually-resting mind —not a worried mind.

A faith-filled mind is a spiritually-resting mind—not a worried mind. Look at the promise of Isaiah 26:3, "You will guard him and keep him in perfect and constant peace whose mind (both its inclination and its character) is stayed on you, because he commits himself to you, leans on you, and hopes confidently in you." Surely, as long as our attention and intentions are fixed on those of Christ's, He will bless us with His peace. This means that when the world seems to cave in on us, we can remain stable because our attention is not on the problem. Rather, our attention is on the solution—Jesus Christ!

Philippians 4:6-8 tells us this:

> Do not fret or have *any* anxiety about anything, but in every circumstance and in everything, by prayer and petition (definite requests), with thanksgiving, continue to make your wants known to God. And God's peace [shall be yours, that tranquil state of soul assured of its salvation (deliverance)* through Christ, and so fearing nothing from God and being content with its earthly lot of whatever sort that is, that peace] which transcends all understanding shall garrison and mount guard over your hearts and minds in Christ Jesus. For the rest, brethren, whatever is true, whatever is worthy of reverence and is honorable and seemly, whatever is just, whatever is pure, whatever is lovely and lovable, whatever is kind and winsome and gracious, if there is any virtue and excellence, if there is anything worthy of praise, think on and weigh and take account of these things [fix your minds on them].

These verses give explicit instructional training for renewing our minds and filling them with faith.

- "Do not fret or have any anxiety about anything." We need to stop worrying, and quit talking about our problems. As we talk about them continuously, we make them bigger.
- Instead of worrying and talking about our problems, we are told to take our requests to God, all the while giving Him thanks and praise as we do so.
- As we praise Him, He will release His peace into our minds and will give us rest as He assures us that He will work things out for our good.
- This peace received will guard our hearts and keep us confident in Christ, even in situations of turmoil. This is the peace that operates in the midst of a crisis. Remember, whatever your focus is on is what you are placing your trust in.
- The final section of this Scripture tells us what we are to think about instead. It says to focus on whatever is true, worthy of reverence, honorable, seemly, just, pure, and lovely. We are to keep our minds set on these very things. When I began saying to God, "Lord, You are the only One that is true, worthy of reverence, noble, honorable and lovely," He instantly impressed in my heart the importance of keeping my mind on Him despite my circumstances. I realized that although my circumstances were subject to change, God might choose to allow me to walk through them instead, empowering me by His grace.
- We must be mindful of the things that we think about. If our thoughts are opposed to the character and Word of Christ, we will be led into many problems.

Put these three things into practice today:

1. Think before you act. Don't impulsively react to a situation. Rather, quiet yourself inside and out, and tune in to the solution—Jesus Christ. He is the One that is able to empower you to respond as He would.
2. Choose to react as Christ would—with discipline and self-control.
3. Think first on the things that are honorable, true, worthy of reverence, pure, lovely, and just.

By doing these things you are retraining your mind! Your behavior will start to manifest the character and the mind of Christ as you reject old ways and replace them with Christ's ways, modeled through the fruit of His Spirit. Remember to receive God's empowering grace for yourself as He walks you through this day-to-day process of renewing your mind.

Questions for Study
1. What is a faith-filled mind?
2. According to James 1:21, what is the first step toward developing a healthy, balanced, and faith-filled mind?
3. Why must the Word of God be implanted in your mind?
4. Looking at the steps toward transformation given in Romans 12:1-3 (MSG), which steps are you already practicing? To which steps do you need to be more committed?
5. Write out 2 Corinthians 10:5. It is a key verse in the process of renewing your mind. Do you practice what it says?
6. When the world is caving in on you, how are you able to remain stable?
7. According to Philippians 4:6-8, what things should you think about consistently?
8. According to these explicit training instructions, why do you think the first step is so important for growth to occur in a faith-filled mind?

Personal Prayer
Lord, help me to have a faith-filled mind that is full of good judgment, discernment, and disciplined thought patterns. You have said in Your Word that You did not give me a spirit of fear, but of power, love, and a calm and well-balanced mind, along with discipline and self-control (2 Timothy 1:7). Help me to do my part and to pay attention to what I am feeding my mind. Help me to undress myself from my old ways of thinking and push them far from me, as I choose to focus on, and put on, the character of Christ. Teach me how to lead every thought captive and line it up with the truth of Your Word. May everything that I think, say, and do be in accordance to Your will (2 Corinthians 10:5). I am not anxious about anything, but in every circumstance and in everything, I choose to pray first! I am thankful that You hear my cries, and I will continue to make my wants known to You. I receive the peace that is mine, that tranquil state of assurance that You will deliver me. Help me now to rest and think only of those things which are true, worthy of reverence, honorable, and seemly, whatever is just, pure, lovely, kind, winsome, and gracious. Help me to think of these things which are virtuous, excellent, and worthy of praise and to fix my mind on them (Philippians 4:6-8)!

Chapter 27

The Obedient
Mind and Will

---

*F*aith and obedience go hand in hand. Good intentions do not make us obedient. Sometimes a problem arises and we know that the first thing we should do is pray about it. In reality, however, it is often the last thing we do. Knowing and doing are two very different things. This chapter will walk us through what to do, when faced with a crisis. If we begin practicing these steps when there is no crisis, we will be more likely to follow them when one arises.

One amazing thing about our mind is how it acts as a computer. It has the ability to pour forth the information it has been given. Part of retraining our minds is the willingness to disengage from old patterns and replace them with new ones. Thus, we need to reprogram the computer of our mind by focusing on Who we want to become like and ultimately that is Jesus. The story of King Jehoshaphat serves as a great model for practicing this strategy in our own lives. By studying it, we can learn how to handle every situation in which we find ourselves. Second Chronicles 20 describes Jehoshaphat dealing with an entire army of people. In our lives, the "armies" we battle are often armies of negative mindsets, bad attitudes, self-pity, bitterness, unforgiveness, and insecurities. However, when we allow God to heal our wounds and conform our wills and ways to His, we change the course of the battle. Then He can work on our behalf to defeat the "negatives" in our lives.

> **The army working against us
> is often our negative mindsets,
> bad attitudes, self-pity, bitterness,
> unforgiveness, and insecurities.**

King Jehoshaphat found himself surrounded by enemies. The Moabites, the Ammonites, and the Meunites all came against him, and Jehoshaphat was afraid. Quite often, fear is also our first reaction when we are in a difficult situation. It's easy to get distracted and forget that people are not the enemy. Although the enemy may work through people, to come against you,

Satan is the real enemy, not people. (See 2 Corinthians 10:3.) Jehoshaphat may have felt fear, but he did not allow it to paralyze him. Rather, verse three tells us:

- *He set himself* determinedly to seek the Lord.
- *He proclaimed a fast* in all of Judah.

Jehoshaphat *was seriously determined to hear from God.* In his time of need he turned toward God. As believers, we too, are called to turn toward God. The "fasted" lifestyle is equally important. This means that we live pure and holy lives on a daily basis. Fasting is not simply abstaining from food. Perhaps God would have you "fast" from a television show in order to spend time with Him. Or maybe He wants you to "fast" from a critical attitude, or a gossiping tongue.

Verse four tells us that Judah gathered the people together to ask the Lord for help. Likewise, we are to:

- *Ask the Lord for help.* One of the shortest yet most powerful prayers we can pray is, "Holy Spirit, help me!"

Verse five indicates that Jehoshaphat stood in the house of the Lord. That is exactly what we are to do.

- *Stand in the presence of God.* Remember, because His presence is within us, we can do this anywhere, anytime.

Verses six through eight tell us that Jehoshaphat repeated out loud the wonderful things that God had already done, proclaiming His power and might. Despite our situations, we must do this, too.

- *Repeat all the wonderful things God has done for us. Proclaim His power and might.* As we proclaim God's deeds, power and might, we remind ourselves of His ability. Thus building our confidence in Him makes it easy to place our trust in Him.

We learn from verse nine that we are to:

- *Cry out to God in our affliction and He will hear and save us.* Please note that there is no time frame given here. God will deliver you, but you must be willing to allow Him to determine when that perfect time is. Our job is to remain faithful to Him. In other words, we have to take our eyes off of the problem and focus on the solution: Jesus. Quite often, He is perfecting our faith and working on our character as we wait.

In verse 12, we see that Jehoshaphat humbled himself. He verbalized his inability to stand against this great company without God's help.

- *Humble yourself before God, admitting your need for His intervention, and keep your eyes on Him.* We must understand that we are no match for the devil without Jesus, but we are more than conquerors with Him!

Verse 14 says the Spirit of the Lord came upon Jahaziel and, through him, told Jehoshaphat not to be afraid or dismayed, for the battle was not his, but the Lord's.

- *The battle is not yours. It belongs to the Lord.* There may be times in your life when God will use other people to speak words of encouragement into your life. However, do not seek other people and their opinions before seeking the Lord. Whatever anyone tells you, you must take that word back to the Lord and test it according to the Word of God and the character of Jesus Christ.

**Do not seek other people and their opinions
before seeking the Lord.**

Jehoshaphat was then told in verse 17 to "take your position, and stand still, and see the deliverance of the Lord. . . . Fear not . . ." Keep standing.

- *Take your position, stand still, and see the deliverance of the Lord. No matter how afraid you might feel, keep standing and keep believing.* It's easy to think that standing still is doing nothing. Actually, though, standing still spiritually means waiting on God to deal with the situation as we go about our lives.
- Being still or quiet inside enables and empowers us to hear the Holy Spirit's direction. It allows us to keep going about our business. To keep standing in this truth means to keep on believing, expecting, and waiting on God to deliver us *without taking matters into our own hands*.

The picture of Jehoshaphat in verse 18 shows him bowing his head with his face to the ground, worshipping.

- *Continue to bow your head with your face to the ground and worship the Lord while you wait and depend on His deliverance.*
- All too often we quit and give up in the middle of a battle or situation. This should not be! This is when it is important to dig our heels in and set our faces like flint determined to praise Him even more!

Verse 20 tells us to do this very thing: "Believe in the Lord your God and you shall be established; believe and remain steadfast to His prophets (His Word)* and you shall prosper!"

- Praising the Lord increases our belief and confidence in Him.
- *Believe in the Lord your God and you shall be established! Remain steadfast to His Word.*

Verse 21 encourages us to keep singing praises to the Lord.

- *Keep singing praises to the Lord. Thank Him for His mercy and loving kindness that endures forever.*

133

Verse 22 tells us that "when they began to sing and to praise, the Lord set ambushes against the men that were attacking them and they were self-slaughtered!"

- As we sing and praise God, the Lord sets up ambushes in our defense. *Praise to God causes Satan confusion, and he ends up slaughtering himself.*
- Verse 25 tells us that when Jehoshaphat and his people came to take the spoil, it was more than they could carry away! If we wait on the Lord and continue to praise Him in the process, He will defeat the enemy and work the situation out for our good.

In verse 26 Jehoshaphat and all the people blessed the Lord.

- *Continue to bless the Lord with praise and singing filled with joy!*

Verse 29 tells us that, " . . . the fear of God came upon all the kingdoms of those countries when they heard that the Lord had fought against the enemies of Israel."

- *If you are faithful to God and react to life in this way, other people will see the Lord working on your behalf and will fear Him as well.*

Verse 30 says, "So the realm of Jehoshaphat was quiet, for his God gave him rest round about." I believe God gave Jehoshaphat rest in every realm of his life—spiritually, physically, mentally, financially, and socially. Truly, the Kingdom of God alive and active inside of us is righteousness, peace and joy in partnership with the Holy Spirit. (See Romans 14:17.)

- *Peace and rest in all realms; spiritually, physically, mentally, financially, and socially for you.*

Questions for Study
1. On a blank sheet of paper, write out the steps that we learned from Jehoshaphat and put them in a place where you will be reminded of how to react to the situations you face in your everyday life.

Personal Prayer
Lord, I realize that faith and obedience go hand in hand. Forgive me for the times that I have allowed my "good intentions" to count as obedience. I realize now that they do not, and I renounce them as sin. Forgive me for the times that I have stubbornly remained in my negative mindsets, bad attitudes, self-pity, bitterness, unforgiveness, and insecurities. I realize this is not the obedient mind and will from which You desire for me to operate. I admit that all the excuses which allow me to wallow in this behavior are sin. I realize that when people come against me, Satan is the real enemy behind the scenes, not people (2 Corinthians 10:3). Help me to be like Jehoshaphat, who did not allow fear to paralyze him and disobey You. Instead, he set his mind to seek You, and he was determined to find You (2 Chronicles 20). I, too, desire to be like that. Help me to have conversations with You before I seek other people and their opinions. That is what You desire from me.

Chapter 28

The Mouth

———————————•———————————

The mind, the mouth and the outcome of our lives are tightly woven together. The Word of God has much to say about our mouths and how we are to use them. I believe the two biggest struggles for Christians are the areas of the mind (our thoughts) and the mouth (our words). The next two areas of great battle are our attitudes and emotions. In fact, if our minds and mouths are out of balance with the Word of God, our attitudes and emotions will follow suit. The reverse of that is true, as well.

It is much easier to think negative thoughts and speak negative words than it is to think and speak positively. That is because the natural inclinations of the mind and mouth, without the Holy Spirit, are prone to negativity. The sad reality is that a negative Christian often believes that he is just wired that way. This can be true to an extent. Some of us have to work harder at being more positive than others. However, negativity as a whole is the result of a wrong and unregenerate mindset. We only need to compare ourselves with Christ. Jesus didn't have a negative mindset. Neither should we. There are no excuses.

God refers to us as a "garden, field, and vineyard under cultivation." (See 1 Corinthians 3:9.) The mind and the mouth require constant weeding, pruning, and tending in order to mature. As ambassadors of Christ, we must learn only to speak what is of faith, permissible, and in accordance with His Word and character. Consider the following example. If you were an ambassador for the American government in a foreign country, you wouldn't think of speaking your own will and agenda. You would only speak what you had been commanded. Why? Because you would understand your assignment and would have a healthy respect for the wishes of your employer as well as a healthy fear of losing your job should you fail to fulfill your responsibilities.

Look at what Paul said to the Corinthians in 1 Corinthians 3:1, "However, Brethren, I could not talk to you as to spiritual [men], but as to non-spiritual [men of the flesh, in whom the carnal nature predominates], as to mere infants [in the new life] in Christ [unable to talk yet!]." Obviously these people could talk, but I believe that Paul was making the point that the Corinthians' conversations resembled the way people in the world spoke. He called out the way they responded to situations—in accordance with their flesh. They were allowing their carnal nature to dominate their speech. Keep in mind, these people were saved. However, their conversation showed no signs of regeneration. Unfortunately, this is the case with many of us today. Sure, we can go to church and be with the circle of our Christian friends and even say the right Christian words. Come Monday, however, it's easy to speak in agreement with the people at work. Perhaps we take advantage of opportunities to indulge our flesh in negative talk, complaining about the work environment or sharing dirty jokes. This should not be.

Look at verse four. It says, "For when one says, I belong to Paul, and another, I belong to Apollos, are you not [proving yourselves] ordinary (unchanged) men?" Paul says this type of talk creates division when, in fact, a Christian's speech should create unity, filled with grace and seasoned with salt. The words of a believer should make others thirsty for the wellspring we have within us. The words we speak are seeds that will produce a harvest of either good or evil. Proverbs 18:21 says, "Death and life are in the power of the tongue, and they who indulge in it shall eat the fruit of it [for death or life]." Matthew 12:37 tells us, "For by your words you will be justified and acquitted, and by your words you will be condemned and sentenced." Take a moment and let those words settle in your mind.

Just as our minds need the Word of God to renew them, our mouths need the same help. Our words produce our thoughts, and our thoughts produce our words. Furthermore, our bodies act accordingly to the inner meditations and words that we speak, for good or bad, for life or death. Proverbs 18:20 attests to this. It says, "A man's [moral] self shall be filled with the fruit of his mouth; and with the consequence of his words he must be satisfied [whether good or evil]."

Our words produce our thoughts,
and our thoughts produce our words.

James 3:5-6, 8-11 speak explicitly about the tongue.

> Even so the tongue is a little member, and it can boast of great things. See how much wood or how great a forest a tiny spark can set ablaze! And the tongue is a fire. [The tongue is a] world of wickedness set among our members, contaminating and depraving the whole body and setting on fire the wheel of birth (the cycle of man's nature), being itself ignited by hell. But *the human tongue can be tamed by no man.* It is a restless (undisciplined, irreconcilable) evil, full of deadly poison. With it we bless the Lord and Father, and with it we curse men who were made in God's likeness! Out of the same mouth come forth blessing and cursing. These things, my brethren, ought not to be so. Does a fountain send fourth [simultaneously] from the same opening fresh water and bitter?

Taming the tongue is a learned process, one which we cannot do alone. Verse nine speaks of "blessing the Lord." It means to speak well of Him and like Him. To "curse men made in God's image" means to speak evil of others. James tells us that blessings toward God and curses toward man should not come from the same mouth. The fountain within is corrupt and needs cleansing.

Chances are your experiences can attest to that truth. Each one of us has witnessed, felt, and even inflicted pain caused by the tongue. When someone wrongs us, we totally justify our negative, destructive speech because we are offended. No doubt, it is difficult to speak well of someone when they've wronged us. It is difficult to refrain from spreading the injustice with our tongues. Yet think of all the trouble that could be avoided if we would choose to control our mouths. Imagine the pain that could be eluded if we refused to speak the negative, insisting instead on speaking words that give life. As with the mind, it takes work, effort and determination to retrain our speech patterns and disengage from old ones. Our lives however, and the lives of others depend on it!

Proverbs 15:4 says, "A gentle tongue [with its healing power] is a tree of life, but willful contrariness in it breaks down the spirit." In other words, if we speak with the law of kindness on our tongue, we will not only heal our situations, but we ourselves will find healing. If we willingly speak contrariness, however, our words will break down and neutralize the faith that God has put in us. It will do this to the faith of those who listen to us, as well.

Oftentimes we quench the work of the Holy Spirit with our minds and our mouths. When we enter into negative conversation about others, we may feel good for the moment, but our internal well is muddied. The flow of the Spirit into and out of our lives gets blocked and our faith becomes ineffective.

When we enter into negative conversation,
we quench the work of the Holy Spirit
with our minds and our mouths.

Ephesians 4:29-32 speaks directly to this. It says,

> Let no foul or polluting language, nor evil word nor unwholesome or worthless talk [ever] come out of your mouth, but only such [speech] as is good and beneficial to the spiritual progress of others, as is fitting to the need and the occasion, that it may be a blessing and give grace (God's favor) to those who hear it. And do not grieve the Holy Spirit of God [do not offend or vex or sadden Him], by Whom you were sealed (marked, branded as God's own, secured) for the day of redemption. Let all bitterness and indignation and wrath (passion, rage, bad temper and resentment (anger and animosity) and quarreling (brawling, clamor, contention) and *slander (evil-speaking, abusive or blasphemous language) be banished from you,* with all malice (spite, ill will, or baseness of any kind). And become useful and helpful and kind to one another, tenderhearted (compassionate, understanding, loving-hearted), forgiving one another [readily and freely] as God in Christ forgave you.

We must realize that every time we choose to argue with someone or speak ill of someone, the work of the Holy Spirit stops. Any time the enemy dangles the carrot of strife and arguing in front of you, don't take the bait! Refuse it and submit your mouth to the Holy Spirit to speak life (faith) into the situation instead. Of course, problems must be discussed. Conflicts will come. I am not suggesting that they won't. However, I believe that all too often, we find ourselves out of balance in this area. We are quick to run to everyone else to talk about the situation before we speak to God about it. We must learn to speak to God first. We need to vent with Him, and ask for His help. When we do, He will lead us in the way of peace and remind us that He is our vindicator. When we pray instead of criticize, we invite God into the circumstances instead of Satan. I once heard the Lord say to me, "I'm not showing you this situation to judge it, but to pray about it, so that I can intervene." He desires to do the same thing with you when you encounter a situation.

Make this an area of priority in your life (right next to spending time with God). Submit your mouth to the control of the Holy Spirit. Ask Him to nudge you every time you overstep His boundaries in your thoughts and speech. Truly, our speech reveals the attitudes within our minds and hearts.

Questions for Study
1. Did Jesus have a negative mindset? Do you?
2. In what ways do your mind and mouth need to be weeded and pruned?
3. Pay attention to your thoughts and speech this week. Do they bring life or death to your circumstances? Are they filled with faith or your own judgment?
4. Write out Matthew 12:37. What does this verse mean to you?
5. Would you consider your life good or bad? Consider your thoughts and your speech. Are you eating the fruit of your words?
6. What grieves the Holy Spirit?
7. Next time you have a conflict and you want to spout off, or not deal with the situation at all, ask the Holy Spirit to remind you to come to Him first. Record what happens!

Personal Prayer
Lord, help me with my mouth and how I choose to use it. I know that the tongue can be tamed by no man (James 3:8), but I do believe that it can be tamed by You. Therefore, I surrender my mouth to be used for Your glory. Since I am Your ambassador, Lord, help me to be in constant contact with You, so that I will use my mouth in accordance with Your will (2 Corinthians 5:20). Lord, Your Word says that death and life are in the power of the tongue. It says I will eat the fruit of my words, whether they are for death or for life (Proverbs 18:21). So help me, Lord, to choose life with my lips! Forgive me for the times I have quenched and negated the work of the Holy Spirit with negative speech. Let no foul or polluting language, no unwholesome or worthless speech come out of my mouth (Ephesians 4:29-32). Cleanse me now, Lord, with Your refining fire, and let the words of my mouth and the thoughts within my heart be pleasing in Your sight (Joshua 1:8; Psalm 19:14). Help me to focus on Your Word and not a wicked report.

Chapter 29

The Faith-Filled Mouth

―――――――――•―――――――――

aith walking requires faith talking. If we are going to walk in faith, therefore, we need to forsake the voices of our flesh—our unrenewed minds, our physical senses, and our lower nature. We discussed in the last chapter, how our spoken words are seeds which grow into either life or death. Unless we learn to renew our minds and our mouths daily with God's Word, we will struggle with believing and speaking in faith. When we pray, whether for ourselves, for other people, or for situations, we must then trust God with those things and speak about them in faith. The point is we need to say what we pray. For example, if we pray for a wayward child to change, then in conversation say, "I don't think that child of mine will ever change!," we are acting and talking like hypocrites.

It's easy to believe we're just speaking the truth, but the real Truth is what God's Word says. Our situations are subject to change when God's Word is applied, believed, obeyed and spoken. That's what it means to walk by faith, rather than by sight. We must act like what we believe in God's Word is true *before* we see the actual manifestation of it. This walking by faith means we are also to speak about ourselves by that same faith. It means we are to speak of other people, and our situations, according to our faith. We must not make the mistake of mixing our human reasoning and unbelief with our God-given faith. When we do this, we cancel out what faith is trying to accomplish. God's Word is faith.

**When we pray, whether for ourselves, for other people,
or for situations, we must then trust God with those things and
speak about them in faith. The point is we need to say what we pray.**

Romans 4:17-24 highlights the life of Abraham as a great example to model in our lives. As it is written, I have made you the father of many nations. [He is appointed our father] in the sight of God in Whom he believed, Who gives life to the dead and speaks of the nonexistent things that [He has foretold and promised] as if they [already] existed." [For Abraham, human reason for] hope being gone, hoped in faith that he should become the father of many nations, as he had been promised. So [numberless] shall your descendants be. He did not weaken in faith when he considered the [utter] impotence of his own body, which was as good as dead because he was about a hundred years old, or [when he considered] the barrenness of Sarah's [deadened] womb. *No unbelief or distrust* made him waver (doubtingly question) concerning the promise of God, *but he grew strong and was empowered by faith as he gave praise and glory to God, fully satisfied and assured that God was able and mighty to keep His word and do what He had promised.* That is why his faith was credited to him as righteousness (right standing with God). But [the words], it was credited to him, were not written for his sake alone, but [they were written] for our sakes too. *[Righteousness, standing acceptable to God] will be granted and credited to us also who believe in (trust in, adhere to and rely on) God* Who raised Jesus our Lord from the dead.)

Let's look at these verses more in depth.

God gives life to the dead and speaks of the nonexistent things as if they already existed.

- A faith-filled mouth speaks words of life into seemingly "dead" situations. It does this by speaking things that are not as though they are. We are to view ourselves and other people as God does. It is equally important to speak about ourselves and others as God would—in accordance with His Word. Do not focus on where you are at the moment, but where God's grace is taking you. For example, my own natural tendency (without God) is to speak harshly when I'm upset. God wanted to change this in my life because such strife does not match His character. So instead of focusing on what I was doing wrong (speaking harshly when I was upset), and trying not to, I started looking to God's grace and where He was taking me. He's changing me to be more like Jesus and as I stare at Him, progressively my tone of voice changes. On a side note, if we're really honest, we will have to admit that most of the time we get upset because we're not getting our own way.
- I started praying Proverbs 31:26 for myself. "I open my mouth in skillful and godly Wisdom, and on my tongue is the law of kindness as I give counsel and instruction." It soon became evident in my life, but first I had to speak it in faith and allow no unbelief to enter my thoughts. I went to the "medicine cabinet" of God's Word. I chose to agree with it and saw it as God's will for me. As a result, I spoke it. I believed it. Eventually, I was changed. Through the empowerment of the Holy Spirit, I went from my own way of reacting (speaking harshly when upset), to God's way (speaking kindly). This is how we renew our mind. We line it up with God's Word, die to our natural physical reactions and align our souls and bodies with the Spirit of God. I literally had to deprive myself of my old reactions and words and replace them with God's. This is something I must work on continuously. It's not a one-time deal! I believe that's why Paul said he died daily!

For Abraham, human reasoning was beyond hope, but he hoped in faith!

- If we have no hope of changing or seeing our circumstances change we've allowed unbelief to stop and squelch our faith. Thus, we are living a carnal life that is controlled by our own human reasoning and physical senses. That kind of life brings forth death, and our God seems very small and unable.

Abraham did not weaken in faith when he saw the truth about his body and Sarah's.

- These people were old! Physically, they had no human reason to believe that their bodies even could produce a baby. But, with God's power coupled with their belief in His power, even an old couple could have a baby! We must learn to think and speak like God does about our circumstances. When we do this we see our God for how big and able He really is! He does things supernaturally, and nothing is impossible for Him!

No unbelief or distrust made him waver!

- Do you think Abraham and Sarah went through periods of doubt? Absolutely! I am positive the enemy constantly tried to give them reason to doubt. After all if their unbelief would have prevailed, the promise would not have occurred. But they chose not to *remain* in doubt or unbelief. Every time we live in unbelief we neutralize and eventually deaden our faith. It's like taking one step forward and three steps backward, getting nowhere fast.

But he grew strong and was empowered by faith as he gave praise and glory to God!

- It is impossible to remain in doubt and unbelief when we choose to renew our minds with the Word and interrupt negative thoughts with praise to God instead. Make it your practice to speak His Word back to Him! Regardless of what the circumstances seem to dictate, you are capable of changing.

Because he gave praise and glory to God, he was fully satisfied and assured that God was able and mighty to keep His Word and do what He had promised.

- When we praise God we encourage ourselves. When we believe God we will enter into His rest. (See Hebrews 4:3.) In this case entering God's rest means we stop trying to make something happen in the natural, with self effort, and rely on the supernatural-something that only *He* can do.

That's why faith was credited to him as righteousness (right standing with God).

- When we use our mouths to speak the truth of God's ability and we truly believe God gives us right standing with Him, He moves on our behalf. God loves to raise "dead" circumstances to life to show people His glory. Don't let unbelief mix in with your faith and squelch God's plans for your life.

God's top priority with His people is to build His character within each of us. It takes focus to think and speak as God does. This is the process of sanctification. He transforms us with His Word and His Spirit, by aligning our souls (mind, will, mouths, attitudes, and emotions) with His. It's our job to continue to renew our minds daily with the Word and then act on what it says. We are called to speak out and release by faith what the Holy Spirit has already deposited in our spirits and in His Word.

We must be friends and students of God's Word. We cannot speak the Word of God if we don't know it. His Word is a mirror that reveals the reflections of our hearts. It shows us where we need to be changed within. We must be willing to totally relearn how to think and speak if we want to live an abundantly full life and be effective in our world.

**God's top priority with His people
is to build His character within each of us.**

Kingdom Principle: We cannot expect our circumstances to change without first asking God to change us. It's as if we're a house, and God wants to "gut it and clean it" so that His power and character can be shown to the world. This is the process we read about in Romans 4:17-24 concerning Abraham. It's the process we are also called to.

Hebrews 11:1 describes what real faith looks like, "Now faith is the assurance (the confirmation, the title deed) of things [we] do not see and the conviction of their reality [faith perceived as real fact what is not revealed to the senses]." Similarly, in Romans 12:1-2 we're told to sacrifice ourselves to God and not be conformed to this world, but to be transformed by the entire renewal of our minds. Why? So we can prove to our physical senses and the rest of the world the life and power that God has deposited in our spirits. He did this by His grace, through our faith. And now, we live lives led by the Spirit of God rather than our physical, impulsive, and dictating senses of our carnal nature, which is human instincts and reasoning's void of Christ. (See Galatians 2:20).

Questions for Study
1. How should we talk the talk of faith?
2. Finish this sentence: The truth is, God's Word and our situations are subject to change if _____. Do you believe that?
3. How does a faith-filled mouth speak words of life into seemingly dead situations?
4. How are we to view ourselves and other people?
5. What natural tendencies do you have that do not match the character of Christ? Find a relevant Scripture and make it your prayer.
6. If the truth be known, what is the real reason we get upset?
7. What are some seemingly "dead" circumstances in your life that God would have you pray His Word over?
8. How did Abraham grow strong and empowered by faith? What squelches our faith?
9. Write out the Kingdom Principle in this chapter and make it your prayer.
10. According to Hebrews 11:1 what is faith?

Personal Prayer

Lord, help me to have a faith-filled mouth at all times. Forgive me for the times that I have failed in this area. You, Lord, give life to dead things by speaking of the nonexistent things as if they already exist (Romans 4:17). Help me to do the same thing in my seemingly "dead" circumstances and relationships. Help me not to focus on where I may be at this moment, but where I could be by Your grace. Help me to cooperate with Your Holy Spirit in this most important area. I desire to speak words of faith, giving hope to all those with whom I come in contact. Please build Your faith-filled character and speech in me. I desire the law of kindness to be on my tongue. I want my mouth to be filled with godly wisdom and speech (Proverbs 31:26). I realize that I will reap what I sow; therefore, help me to sow seeds of life with my speech, reaping the harvest You desire for me to have on this earth (Galatians 6:7). Thank You, for allowing me to partner with You on this great journey of faith and truly believing in the things that I cannot see with my physical eyes!

Chapter 30

Renewing of the
Mind and Mouth

faith-filled mind produces a faith-filled mouth, which results in a faith-filled life—a life led by God's Spirit, reflecting the character of Jesus Himself. God's objective is to make us like Christ from the inside out. We live on this earth as His personal representatives, just as Christ represented the Father. (See Romans 8:28-29 and John 17:18.) If we are to become "children of the Light," our minds and mouths need to be uprooted from the old nature and reprogrammed with the new nature of Christ. The life of a believer must be characterized by righteousness and holiness in thoughts, words, attitudes, and deeds. The grace God grants us when we receive Christ as our Savior puts us in right standing with Him. This is our starting point. We are to live from this position rather than trying to earn it through appropriate behaviors. Our progressive sanctification comes as we separate from the ways of the world and cooperate with God in every area of our lives. This is why we need to renew our minds every day with God's Word and align our thoughts, words, attitudes, and deeds with His.

**The grace God grants us when we receive Christ as our Savior
puts us in right standing before Him. This is our starting point.**

Ephesians chapters four and five are wonderful chapters that connect the workings of the mind and mouth. These chapters teach us about areas where growth and maturity are needed. They tell us about the things that stops the Spirit of God from flowing into our lives and out to others. Verse 15 of chapter four says, "Rather, let our lives lovingly express truth [in all things, speaking truly, dealing truly, living truly]. Enfolded in love, let us *grow up in every way and in all things into Him Who is the Head [even] Christ (the Messiah, the Anointed One)."* If we are enfolded (rooted) in God (who is love), He will grow us up and empower us to live our lives. He will enable us to express His truth in all that we think, and speak, and do. This will be demonstrated in our attitudes, by how we live, and by how we treat others. This represents a life where we see more of Jesus than self.

144

First, however, we must learn to speak God's truth to ourselves. If we intend to teach and lead others to Christ we must be sure that we are true representatives of Christ's character. Would you be willing to follow you? If you're not sure, how can anyone else be sure of following you? Ephesians 4:22 tells us to, "Strip yourselves of your former nature [put off and discard your old un-renewed self] *which characterized your previous manner of life and becomes corrupt through lusts and desires that spring from delusion.*" According to this verse, our lives become corrupt through lusting after, hoping for, and desiring the things that spring from delusion and wrong thoughts. These thoughts oppose God's Word about us. If we have wrong thoughts (faithless thoughts) we will also speak wrong words (faithless words). "If it is not of faith it is sin." (See Romans 14:23.) Remember, it's important to keep our conversations in agreement with the prayers and declarations of faith that we pray and proclaim.

> **It's important to keep our conversations
> in agreement with the prayers and declarations
> of faith that we pray and proclaim.**

Proverbs 29:18 says, "Where there is no vision [no redemptive revelation of God] the people perish." When we don't allow God's Word to mold our thoughts, we leave the door wide open for the enemy to work in our lives. Many of us continue to live without a redemptive revelation stuck in hopeless unbelief. This is why we desperately need to renew our minds so that we can change the visions in our minds. We are called to take control of the thoughts and pictures that enter our minds, to be careful what we feed our eyes, and what we allow our ears to hear. We must learn to discern the source of our thoughts and mental images and take dominion over them rather than live with the enemy's bombarding images.

Ephesians 4:23 says, "And be constantly renewed in the spirit of your mind [having a fresh mental and spiritual attitude]." This is why we should live in God's Word. It is the only way to have a fresh mental and spiritual attitude which leads us to an overall healthy mindset. It enables us to desire the things of God and transforms our thoughts to agree with His will and ways.

Ephesians 4:24 says, "And put on the new nature (the regenerate self) created in God's image, [Godlike] *in true righteousness and holiness.*" A pure inner thought life is a major contributor to consistent personal righteousness and holiness. Healthy thoughts enable us to see ourselves as righteous (having right standing with God) because we are in Christ. This means that God sees you and me just as He sees Jesus. Most Christians are more aware of their sins and imperfections than they are of the perfect Lamb of God. This shouldn't be. This represents a life that will display a false form of righteousness and holiness—a life that is filled with guilt and condemnation yet continues to go through the motions of Christian acts minus true heart and mind transformation. Our focus should be on Jesus and what He has already provided for us, not on our own shortcomings. After all, it is His finished work on the cross that will get us through this life, not our own perfections. We will always "fall short" when we depend on our own self-efforts.

Ephesians 4:25 says, "Therefore, rejecting all falsity and being done with it, let everyone express the truth with his neighbor, for we are all parts of one body and members one of another." In order to do what this verse is saying we need to be willing to take off our masks of pretense and be honest with ourselves. We each need to deal with who we really are before God. What we think, speak, and do absolutely matters—especially toward yourself and those around you.

Before there can be real outreach to others, there must be serious in-reach with God. We need to allow the Spirit of God to heal and direct our souls with the Word of God.

Ephesians 4:26-28 tells us to quit sinning every time we get angry and stop allowing this anger to fester or take root in us. Unresolved sin in our lives leaves the door of opportunity open to the enemy. It allows him to steal from us and place us under the bondage of his control. *We have the authority to stop this from happening.* The enemy is constantly trying to steal the life Christ came to give us. (See John 10:10.) We must guard our hearts! As temples of the Holy Spirit, we contain the treasures of God's presence and His power, His gifts, His fruit of the Spirit, His grace, and His character. If Satan can steal these things from us by tempting us to give in to the dictates of our flesh, he will control our souls. Therefore, we must hold fast to our inheritance and the treasures that God has placed in us, by yielding to the Holy Spirit. We need to let Him exhibit His fruit through us as we continue to look to Him, no matter the circumstances.

Here is a Kingdom Principle: God is more concerned with what is going on *inside* of you than He is with what is going on *around* you. In everything, He wants us to have His perspective about life.

**God is more concerned with what is going on
inside of you than He is with what
is going on around you.**

Let's examine the things that quench righteousness and holiness in our lives.

Ephesians 4:29 and 31 speaks of all the things we must get rid of:

- worthless talk
- foul, polluting language
- evil words (words that belittle and spread gossip)
- bitterness
- indignation
- wrath (passion, rage, bad temper)
- resentment (anger, animosity)
- quarreling
- slander
- abusive blasphemous language
- spite, ill will, and baseness of any kind

When these things are left unattended, to float around inside of us, they become hazardous pollutants, spiritually, mentally, and physically.

Ephesians 5:3-5 says,

> But immorality (sexual vice) and all impurity [of lustful, rich wasteful living] or greediness must not even be named among you, as is fitting and proper among saints (God's consecrated people). Let there be no filthiness (obscenity, indecency) nor foolish and sinful (silly and corrupt) talk, nor course jesting, which are not fitting or becoming; but instead voice your

thankfulness [to God]. For be sure of this: that no person practicing sexual vice or impurity in thought or in life, or one who is covetous [who has lustful desire for the property of others and is greedy for gain]—for he [in effect] is an idolater—has any inheritance in the kingdom of Christ and God. Take no part in and have no fellowship with the fruitless deeds and enterprises of darkness, but instead [let your lives be so in contrast as to] expose and reprove and convict them.

Ephesians 4:30 tells us the reason we must rid ourselves of this unrighteousness: It grieves the Holy Spirit. It offends and saddens Him because He is the one who can untangle and deliver us from it. He won't deliver us, however, from what we continue to choose. We must stop thinking and saying, "Well, this is just the way I am," or "I'm just wired that way." The truth is that God wants to change inside of us what is not in agreement with Him. We must stop enabling ourselves and deal with the traits in our lives that keep us bound and defeated. These mindsets, emotions, attitudes, words, and actions render us useless as God's ambassadors. The Spirit of God does not empower us to manifest behaviors that do not match Christ's.

> **God won't deliver us from something**
> **that we continue to choose.**

Let's take a look at the things that enhance righteousness and holiness in our lives.

- Ephesians 4:32 tells us to, "become useful, helpful, and kind to one another, tender hearted (compassionate, understanding, loving-hearted), forgiving one another [readily and freely], as God in Christ forgave you."
- Ephesians 5:4 says, "…but instead *voice your thankfulness to God*." A thankful attitude works like weed killer on a negative attitude in a believer's life. If we want to upset and reject the ways of the enemy in our lives, we should do it by praising God no matter what. Then we can be like Jehoshaphat and watch the enemy slaughter himself.
- Ephesians 5:8-11 says, "For once you were darkness, but now you are light in the Lord; *walk as children of the Light* [lead the lives of those native-born to the Light]. For the fruit (the effect, the product) of the Light or the Spirit [consists] in every form of kindly goodness, uprightness of heart (and mind)* and trueness of life. And try to learn [in your experience] what is pleasing to the Lord [let your lives be constant proofs of what is most acceptable to Him]. Take no part in and have no fellowship with the fruitless deeds and enterprises of darkness, but instead [let your lives be so in contrast as to expose and reprove and convict them]."

These mindsets, attitudes, words, and actions make us sensitive to the Holy Spirit and useful to God. They transform us into vessels F.I.T. for His service.

So what does your inner clothing look like? Ephesians 5:15-17 says,

> *Look carefully then how you walk! Live purposefully and worthily and accu-*
> *rately,* not as unwise and witless, but as wise (sensible, intelligent people)
> *making the very most of the time* [buying up each opportunity], because the

days are evil. Therefore do not be vague and thoughtless and foolish, but *understanding and firmly grasping what the will of the Lord is*.

These verses instruct us to do the following:

1. Pay attention to how we live our lives in all areas.
2. Choose God's ways *on purpose!*
3. Make the most of our time refusing to live a slack and sloppy life.
4. Understand and firmly grasp that the Lord desires us to represent His character here on earth.
5. Get rid of every attitude, mindset, and word that does not righteously represent the person of Jesus Christ.

Questions for Study
1. What is the point of being a Christian?
2. Who is the first person to whom we must speak truth and why?
3. How does a person's life become corrupt?
4. Ask the Holy Spirit to reveal what past hurts and negative visions you carry in your mind about your identity. Now ask Him to empower you to change them and align them with His.
5. Why must we live in God's Word?
6. What is "false" righteousness and holiness?
7. On a small note card, personalize and write out the "Kingdom Principle" in this chapter and place it where you will see it often.
8. In what areas of your life do you need to purposely choose God's ways? (Look up Scriptures pertaining to this; write them out and repeat them to yourself often).

Personal Prayer
    Lord, forgive me for not taking this subject seriously. I know that I need to renew my mind and mouth daily according to Your Word. Let my life lovingly express the truth in all things. Thank You, for Your continual help to grow me up (Ephesians 4:15). Lord, strip me of my former nature and manner of life. Help me to be constantly renewed in the spirit of my mind, having a fresh mental attitude. Help me now, Lord, to put on the new nature, which is created in Your image, as I reject all falsity and consider myself done with it (Ephesians 4:22-25). Lord, I desire to be transformed in my mind. I know this is the desire of your heart, too (Romans 12:1-2). Help me not to sin with my mind or my mouth when I don't get my way. Let me not allow Satan any inroads into my heart by permitting anger, upset, and strife in my life. I know that when a root of bitterness is permitted to grow inside of me, it will grow up and defile many (Ephesians 4:26-31 and Hebrews 12:15).

Chapter 31

The Ways and Will
of God

———————————❖———————————

"What is God's will for my life?" It's one of the first questions most of us ask when we accept Christ as our Savior. This may seem harsh, but in reality, that's a self-centered question. We may not even realize it, but our first question ought to be more like, "God, who are You?," followed by, "I want to know You, and what You created me to be. Teach me Your ways." Please understand, although we are saved, we have yet to begin to know and understand the wonders and depth of God in a personal way. That comes as we spend time in His Word, renewing our minds.

People often feel overwhelmed and confused as they seek God's will for their lives. Consider this scenario: A person gets to know a group of other Christians. Eventually, the group discovers they share common interests and decipher gifts or areas of ministry that pique their interests. But what if that person hasn't taken the time to quiet himself before God and allow His Word to speak to his heart? When you take the time to do this, it allows *God* to place His passion within you. He is the Commander-in-Chief and He is the One we must go to first—always.

Many people end up serving in a ministry out of a false sense of duty, peer manipulation, obligation, or guilt rather than a sense of God's direction. It is never wrong to step out and try something, but serving for the wrong reasons often leads to burnout and frustration, which in no way helps anyone, and it is not God's will for you. When we take the time to listen to God, through His Word, we allow Him to place His passion within us. It's the perfect place to find God's will.

God has a perfect will for our lives. At the same time, each of us possesses a will of our own. Others also have a will for us. And, of course, the enemy desires something altogether different for us, as well. We open ourselves up for confusion when we permit something other than God's will to prevail. One of the enemy's greatest ploys is keeping God's people busy with "good" works. He likes it when we are so busy with those things that we have no time to spend quiet, quality time with Jesus in His Word. When our relationship with the Holy Spirit is strong, and we allow Him to direct us, however, we avoid becoming involved in things that will burn us out.

As Christians working within the church, we are good at sizing each other up. We look, and then we label. For instance, we look to the highly educated or successful people to lead the board or to teach in various classes. We look for the sweet elderly ladies to rock the babies in the nursery and for strong men to help lead the junior high games. We look to the middle-aged women to help provide meals for people. Certainly, all these functions are necessary and good. But isn't this exactly what we are told *not* to do? Second Samuel 16:7 says, "But the Lord said to Samuel, look not on his appearance or at the height of his stature, for I have rejected him. For the Lord sees not as man sees; for a man looks on the outward appearance, but the Lord looks on the heart."

When our spirits are connected solely to the Holy Spirit, we don't see race, gender, a social ladder, or a valedictorian. We only see people who want to be like Jesus, and we encourage them to do so. All these "things" of the world and of the flesh fall to the wayside, and we begin to see and value each other as members of one body. (See Galatians 3:28.) We become willing to yield, uplift, and encourage one another for the sake of showing God's character to the rest of the world, drawing them to Him. (See Romans 12:6-8.)

God wants to use the ordinary, simple people, and the least expected to confound the wise and the ways of the world. Perhaps Grandma or Grandpa is anointed to play card games with the teenagers. Maybe that single mom or dad is most equipped to share with others what faith and sacrifice are all about. Throughout the Scriptures, God used these types of ordinary "no-na-mers" *because* they have hearts for Him and His ways. Look at these Bible greats who had a heart for God: Joseph, David, Ruth, Deborah, Esther, Rahab, the twelve disciples, Mary the Mother of Jesus, Mary Magdalene, Paul, Phoebe, and more. On the other hand, according to the world's standards, the most "qualified" and educated person to help run Jesus' ministry was Judas, the man who betrayed Jesus. Like Jesus, we must live beyond the physical realm where the looking and the labeling will always exist. We need to start viewing all people through the eyes of God, ascribing worth and value to all.

Indeed, the will of God is so simple that many fail to recognize it. This happens when it doesn't look like we think it should. We are the complicated ones. Complication always finds an open door into our lives, when we think more highly of ourselves than we ought and more lowly of others than we should. When we realize that the Lord is the Commander-in-Chief, and we are merely the soldiers in His army, we start to see as He does. Ephesians 4:11-13 makes it very clear that God will place people within His body as He sees fit, not as we see fit because He knows what is best. As members of the body of Christ, we need to stop labeling each other and stop allowing labels to be stuck on us. Instead, we need to hear the call of God. Truly, we are to come to Him with unveiled faces; free of preconceived ideas and mindsets. We must continue in His Word if we are to be changed from one level of glory into another. This is how we are constantly being transfigured into His very own image! Remember, it is the pure in heart who shall see God.

First and foremost, God calls us into a relationship with Himself for the purpose of fel-lowshipping with Him. He wants us to become like His Son, Jesus, and live out our lives like He did—in thought, word, attitude, and deed. This is known as the *general* will of God for all people. In other words, this is absolutely part of God's will for each one of our lives. This means that every place we go, or every time we enter into a situation, God wants us to be so full of His character and power that His presence is known instantly! In all truth, most Christians miss the *specific* will of God for their lives because they have bypassed the *general* will of God. The general will of God for each of us is always about relationship—getting to know Him more, and letting the Holy Spirit develop His character in our lives.

Let's take a look at the general will of God for all believers. His will is His Word revealed within the pages of His book, the Bible. First Timothy 2:4 tells us that God's will is for all men to be saved and to grow and mature in His ways.

His salvation includes:

- Repentance and Forgiveness (1 John 1:9).
- Deliverance (Luke 4:18; Psalm 34:4,7).
- Rescue from sin (Romans 6:11, 18; 1 John 3:8).
- Righteousness (Isaiah 53:11).
- Healing (Psalm 103:3-7; Isaiah 53:5; 1 Peter 2:24).
- Preservation (Psalm 32:7; 36:6-11; 121:7-8).
- Soundness (2 Timothy 1:7; 1 Peter 5:8).
- Wholeness (1 Thessalonians 5:23-24; Isaiah 53:5).
- Prosperity (3 John 2; Genesis 1:28; Jeremiah 29:11).

God wills for His children is to grow and to know Him in each of these ways:

- To believe that He rewards those who seek Him (Hebrews 11:6).
- To be led by the Spirit of God, not the demands of our flesh (Romans 6:11, 8:14-16).
- To share in His inheritance (Romans 8:17).
- To live without guilt, shame, and condemnation (Romans 8:2).
- To receive His love because He willingly laid His life down for us (1 John 4:9-10, 19).
- To love Him with all our heart, soul, and mind and our neighbor as ourselves (Matthew 22:37-40).
- To seek first the Kingdom of God and His ways of thinking, speaking, being, and doing (Matthew 6:33).
- To partner with His Holy Spirit and experience His Kingdom of righteousness (moral and spiritual rectitude in every area and relationship), peace, and joy (Romans 14:17).
- To be holy because he is holy—pure in thought, word, attitude and deed (1 Peter 1:16).
- To treat other people as He would (Micah 6:6-8).
- To have and enjoy our lives according to His ways (John 10:10).
- To see ourselves as His masterpiece and to do the good works which He predestined for us to do (Ephesians 2:10).
- To be thankful, and therefore to be fruitful (1 Thessalonians 5:14-23; Proverbs 28:14).
- To admit, confess, and repent of our sins on an ongoing basis, being prepared to suffer as we die to the flesh (Proverbs 28:13; 1 Peter 4:1-2).
- To make it our determined purpose to know Him and experience His resurrected power within us (Philippians 3:10-12).
- To be imitators of God, walking in love, esteeming and delighting in one another (Ephesians 5:1-2).
- To be faithful; to let our yes be yes and our no be no. To actually do what we tell people we will do, despite the circumstances (1 Corinthians 1:9; Proverbs 28:20; James 5:12).
- To readily and willingly forgive others (Mark 11:25).
- To know how to possess our own bodies (1 Thessalonians 4:3-5).

- To make Him our standard in everything (Ephesians 4:12-13).
- To be renewed in our minds; to think, speak, and act as He does (Romans 12:2).
- To have His positive God-filled attitude about all things (Philippians 2:2-5).
- To abound in His love and extend it to its fullest development (Philippians 1:9).
- To be empowered through our union and commitment with Him (Ephesians 6:10).
- To be kind and gentle, extending grace to others, and praying for people to be released from Satan's chains (2 Timothy 2:24-26).

This list could go on and on. The key to this is based upon our *relationship* with Jesus Christ and our *submission* to His Spirit as He promises to guide us in all things. As our relationship grows with Him, these things become our nature and flow out to others. How much of you does the Holy Spirit govern and possess? Have you submitted all areas of your life over to His guidance?

How much of you does the Holy Spirit govern and possess?

Begin to seek Him about these things first. Focus your attention on developing an intimate relationship with Him. This is His way and His will for you and me. As your bond with the Holy Spirit strengthens, you will start to discern God's specific will for your life.

Continue to place the highest priorities on these main things:

- Learning to receive His love.
- Learning to love and seek Him.
- Spending time with Him and allowing His character—the fruit of the Spirit—to develop within you.
- Learning to see and hear and to be led by His Holy Spirit.
- Believing and putting your faith in Him at all times.
- Treating others the way He would.
- Becoming a person who keeps their word.

As we start to do these things regularly, God will lift us up in ways we could never imagine! We should not simply do these things when we feel like it or when the circumstances are right. Rather, they must become part of who we are, no matter what is happening around us. This is how God matures us, providing the inner strength to stand against any attack of the enemy even though we may feel like running! True victory over the enemy happens when we live above the physical realm of our circumstances and remain in the will of God—staring at Him, listening to Him, and doing what is right no matter what.

Questions for Study
1. How will you commit to spending time with God each day so that He can start changing you first from the inside out?
2. In what ways have you labeled people or allowed other people to label you?
3. Evaluate your life: how much of you does the Holy Spirit have under His direction? Submit any area of your life that you have yet to give Him.
4. What happens when your spirit is solely connected to the Holy Spirit?

5. What type of person does God choose to use? How does that differ from the world?
6. Write out Ephesians 4:11-13. Do you have a passion in any of these areas?
7. What is the key to finding the specific will of God for your life?
8. List the things that should be our highest priorities at all times. Are you doing them?

Personal Prayer

Lord, may Your will for my life prevail. Help me to learn how to follow Your Holy Spirit's leading. Forgive me for the times that I have listened to others without first getting quiet to hear Your voice. Place Your passion and heart within me and cause me to know You. Help me not to become involved in things out of obligation, guilt, manipulation, feelings, or emotions. I want to be involved because You have directed my heart. Help me to stop judging others, including myself, by appearance and help me to see others as You do, according to their hearts (1 Samuel 16:7). Race, gender, socioeconomic status—none of these things matter to You. May they not matter to me, either. I desire to value others as You do and to work together as one body, bringing glory to You. Your Word says that You will place people within Your body as You see fit (Ephesians 4:11-13). I know that You have a specific plan for my life, but first help me to develop the character I need to proceed with Your plan. Empower me to do so through Your Spirit. I know that You desire for all people to be saved and to mature in Your ways (1 Timothy 2:4). Help me to treat others as You would and to learn how to walk in love toward everyone (Ephesians 5:1-2), so that I may become an instrument fit for your service.

Chapter 32

Emotions:
How Did Jesus Manage His?

Our emotions can create a snowball effect if we let them. It requires discipline and self-control powered by God to handle them the way He desires. Satan often uses our emotions as a primary means of creating anxiety and chaos inside of us. The seat of our emotions is yet another part of our souls that needs God's healing touch. Even if you have been a Christian for a long time, if you choose to live your life apart from God's Word, the enemy will use your emotions to entangle you.

**Satan often uses our emotions as a primary means of
creating anxiety and chaos inside of us.**

Before we allow God to be the true Lord of our lives, we live based on what we think is right and wrong, and we walk accordingly. However, when we hand over the reins of our lives to the Holy Spirit, He begins to show us how we've followed our emotions rather than Him. Consider the following example. In the world, when somebody is wronged, he or she will seek revenge, expel the perpetrator from their life, or hold a grudge. But God's Word says Jesus is your vindicator. As such, we are called to love our enemies, to be kind to those who persecute us, to pray for those who use us, to give them our coats if they are cold, and to do unto them as we would have them do unto us. The upside-down emotions of our society is quite evident in this example. It takes a mature Christian to walk this path. To follow His way requires *discipline, self-control, and Holy Spirit-bridled emotions*.

To be sure, I'm not talking about letting people walk all over us and taking advantage of us. Jesus didn't let people do that to Him. Neither should we. That's not what this is about. Indeed, there are many times that we need to confront others. However, our hearts' motive should be for his or her restoration to Christ. When our hearts desire that, God Himself will vindicate us. Remember this: If God asks us to become like Christ, which He does (see Ephesians 5:1-2), He will also empower us to do so. Remember that we must be willing to do our part by cooperating with Him if we want to change. The Holy Spirit will not sprinkle magic dust over our heads and cause all our troubles to vanish. But He will deliver us, bit by bit, when we partner with Him.

Obey Him, whether you feel like it or not and never quit. It is we who abandon God. He does not abandon us. If things are not going your way, perhaps you have given up, have disobeyed, or have stopped spending time with Him. Or maybe you're doing all the right things; He may be teaching you faithfulness, or pulling you to a deeper level of dependence on Him. Remember, the Holy Spirit does not empower us to give up, disobey God, stop spending time with Him, or jumping ship. No, these tendencies are caused because we have fickle allegiance, and we're choosing to be led by our feelings, rather than the Word and Spirit of God.

If God asks us to become like Christ
He will also empower us to do so!

Let's take a look at the definition of "emotions." According to Webster's dictionary, emotions tell us how we feel. They cause us to become aware or aroused, and they cause various complex reactions such as love, hate, fear, anger, etc.[1]

I believe that God gave us emotions to be used for good things such as:

- Showing compassion toward others;
- Knowing when we are in danger;
- Expressing encouragement, love, care and concern;
- Developing healthy relationships;
- Maintaining balance and stability in our lives;
- Knowing when we need food, clothing or rest.

Yet look at how the enemy can pervert our emotions:

- Instead of showing compassion, we may develop self-pity, which is compassion turned inward.
- We might willingly walk into a situation, such as an extramarital affair, because it feels good, even though we recognize danger.
- We might develop a false sense of balance and stability in our lives—living in extremes and doing things to gratify ourselves.
- We may indulge in food even when we're full, buy clothing or other items we cannot afford to immediately gratify our flesh.
- We sometimes engage in slander or gossip to belittle another and make ourselves feel better.
- We sleep more than we should because we don't want to feel the pain of our problems.
- Maybe we become workaholics to avoid feeling the angst of dealing with personal issues or family problems.

The list could go on and on. You name it, we can come up with an excuse or a reason for anything. Satan will always come along and try to take what God gives for our good and use it for our harm. If we allow it, the enemy is a master at persuading us to feel a certain way one day, then totally different the next. He causes confusion and chaos in our lives whenever we give him the chance. Our carnal nature always wants to be led by what we see, think, want, and feel. However, the Word of God teaches and empowers us for something completely different. By God's grace the Bible directs us to live according to what He says. In fact, doing things God's way will not "feel" good to our flesh initially. But this is exactly what frees us from Satan's entanglements. It doesn't "feel" good because it goes against our natural tendencies. This is why we cannot live according to our physical senses: what we see, think, want or feel.

Honestly, do we really ever feel like forgiving someone who has hurt us? No. But we should choose to do it because God's Word says to. Remember, God always has our best interests at heart. So, if He tells us to forgive it's for our good! It's so He can bless us! Yet sometimes we'll choose to hold a grudge or live in unforgiveness for years, justifying our actions wondering why we don't "feel" close to God.

Doing things God's way will not "feel" good to our flesh initially, but it is exactly what frees us from Satan's entanglements.

Colossians 3:5 says,

> So kill (deaden, deprive of power) the evil desire lurking in your members [those animal impulses and all that is earthly in you that is employed to sin]; sexual vice, impurity, sensual appetites, unholy desires, and all greed and covetousness, for that is idolatry (the deifying of self and other created things instead of God).

Just three verses earlier, we see how: *"And set your minds and keep them set on what is above (the higher things), not on the things that are on the earth."*
Look again at what these verses tell us:

1. Deprive impulses of their power and don't give in to them.
2. These impulses and ways of the world will cause you to sin.
3. Set your mind on how God's Kingdom within you works.
4. Keep it there, no matter what!

Think of it like this: When we set a *thermostat* it doesn't matter what the conditions outside are. The temperature is set and will stay there. A *thermometer* changes according to the conditions of the moment. Based on this, how would you define yourself? Is your mind "set" on God's ways or your ways? Are you swayed by the conditions around you or your circumstances?

- Thermostat = stable and balanced despite the conditions.
- Thermometer = vulnerable to whatever the conditions may be.

The enemy will always try to lead us by our emotions and how we feel. It's then that we must meditate on the life of Jesus. Below is a short list of how Jesus acted:

- He was never in a hurry.
- He went about doing good for others.
- He was patient, kind, and generous.
- He was an encourager.

- He was never grouchy or in a bad mood.
- He never grumbled, complained, or found fault in others.
- He loved everybody.
- He spoke only the things that benefited others.
- He was always fixing somebody's mess.
- He never complained of being tired or hungry.
- He wasn't prejudice, sexist, snobby, or self-righteous.
- He was never rude or obnoxious.
- He never compared Himself to others.
- He never competed for the sake of status.
- He was never afraid of confrontation.

And this list could go on and on. Please stop and consider the life of Jesus:

- How could the son of God never be in a hurry? Look at all the demands that people placed on Him. How was this possible? *He was led by the Spirit of God, not by how He felt.*
- He went about doing good for others. How was this possible? *He was led by the Spirit of God, not by how He felt.*
- He was patient, kind and generous. How was this possible? *He was led by the Spirit of God, not by how He felt.*
- He was an encourager! Not grouchy or in a bad mood. How was this possible? *He was led by the Spirit of God, not by how He felt.*
- He never grumbled, complained or justified Himself by finding fault in others. How was this possible? *He was led by the Spirit of God, not by how He felt.*
- He never compared Himself to others. How was this possible? *He was led by the Spirit of God, not by how He felt.*

Jesus was most definitely a thermostat!

Let me ask you a few questions:

- Did people wrong Jesus? Yes. In fact on the night Judas betrayed Him, Jesus called Him friend.
- Did people use Him? Yes.
- Did people make fun of Him? Yes.
- Did people despise Him? Yes.
- Did people challenge His integrity? Yes.
- Did that change Him? No.
- Did that change who He was? No.
- Did that change His intentions? No.
- Did that change His mission? Not even a little bit!

Maybe you're thinking, "Well, sure, but He's God!" Look at Hebrews 4:15. It says, "For we do not have a High Priest Who is unable to understand and sympathize and have a shared feeling with our weaknesses and infirmities and liability to assaults of temptation, but One Who has been tempted in every respect as we are, yet without sinning!"

Jesus was also fully human. He felt hunger, exhaustion, loneliness, rejection, pain, sorrow, joy, and so on. He felt every emotion that we do, but He never allowed the enemy to twist or pervert His emotions and cause Him to sin. We are called to do the very same thing.

**Jesus felt every emotion that we feel, yet He never allowed
Satan to pervert His emotions and cause Him to sin.**

Hebrews 4:16 tells us how. It says,

> Let us then fearlessly and confidently and boldly draw near to the throne of grace (the throne of God's unmerited favor to us sinners), that we may *receive* mercy [for our failures] and *find grace* in good time for every need [appropriate help and well-timed help, coming just when we need it].

Submit your feelings and emotions to God and allow Him to show you exactly the areas in which you need to be healed.

1. He will cause you to become balanced in all aspects of your life.
2. He will teach you how to stop allowing the enemy to push and pull you in whichever direction he chooses.
3. He will retrain your reactions and help you manage your emotions.
4. He will make anxiety, worry, jealousy, unforgiveness, upset, and so forth stop controlling your life. He will make peace reign in your heart.
5. He will empower you to trust Him.

Honestly, who doesn't need this?

Jesus came to free us from Satan's control. He came to set the captives free, to make the blind see, the lame walk, and to release those that are oppressed by Satan. If we remain blind to the ways of the enemy, especially in regard to our emotions, we remain under his control—oppressed, lame, and unable to walk according to the Spirit. Jesus tells us that in the world we will have troubles. But He also tells us to not be afraid for He has overcome the world! (See John 16:33.)

I believe the paraphrase of 1 John 1:7 says it best: If we choose to walk in the Light of God's love in all areas of our lives as He is in the Light (the way Jesus did when He was on earth), our souls will be cleansed. We will have healthy fellowship with each other, because we're living in the power of Christ's shed blood.

Remember, 2 Corinthians 3:17 tells us that "where the Spirit of the Lord is, there is liberty." That means freedom from the evil, perverted, manipulating, and binding ways of the enemy.

Next time you find yourself ready to devalue someone, disrespect a boss, parent, or spouse, enter into conflict for selfish reasons, or speak ill of someone, think of this verse: "But I say, walk and live [habitually] in (partnership)* with the [Holy] Spirit [responsive to and controlled and guided by the Spirit]; then you will certainly not gratify (give in to)* the cravings and desires of the flesh [of human nature without God]." (See Galatians 5:16.)

Questions for Study

1. Ask the Holy Spirit to help you see and live this life as Jesus did. Are you doing your part and studying the life of Christ?

2. Finish this sentence: If God asks us to be a certain way, He will also _____.

3. What are God's intentions for our emotions and what are Satan's?

4. If you've felt like exploding and telling someone off, what does Colossians 3:5 say to do? (On a side note—if you have a tendency to "stuff" things, pray for God to give you the courage to confront).

5. Are you going through life as a thermostat or a thermometer? What is the difference between the two?

6. How was Jesus able to be so stable and consistent in all of His ways?

7. What are the five things that happen when you submit your feelings and emotions to God?

8. Write out Galatians 5:16.

Personal Prayer

Lord, help me to become stable in my emotions. Heal any wounded emotions that exist in me. Forgive me for the times I use my emotions for self-pity instead of compassion and for grumbling and complaining about my situation rather than casting my care on You and believing Your good report (Philippians 4:6-8). Thank You that I have a High Priest who is able to understand and sympathize with my weaknesses, infirmities, and assaults of temptation, and has been tempted Himself in every respect as I am, yet without sin (Hebrews 4:15). Lord, cause my emotions to become like a thermostat which doesn't consider the conditions that surround it but remains constant. Help me to fix my mind on the things above and keep it there (Colossians 3:5). Help me to continue to do what is right, especially when I don't feel like it. This is exactly what will free me from the control that Satan exerts over me. Lord, as I look over the details of Your life and how You handled Yourself in every situation, I desire to become like You—never in a hurry, rude, grouchy, or complaining. Instead, You were always, kind, compassionate, and willing to lend a hand. Frustration didn't get the best of You because You were led by God's Spirit at all times, not by how You felt. Help me to become like that.

PART FIVE:

What Does It Look Like to Live Life God's Way?

Chapter 33

Establishing Godly Priorities in Our Lives

---

*I*f I took a survey within the body of Christ, asking people to list their priorities, I imagine it would look something like this:

1. God
2. My spouse
3. My family
4. My job
5. Myself

Definitely a noble list of priorities, but I wonder if it's actually what we do every day. For example: If you believe that God is first in your life yet fail to spend time with Him each day, He is not your first priority. If you are in the habit of running to a friend with a concern before running to God, He is not your first priority. If our spouse is on our list of top priorities, then why are there so many divorces? What would happen if we were to wake up each day, thank God for our marriage and consider how we might serve our spouse? Unfortunately, all too often, we wake up with our minds filled with to-do lists, and never consider what might be on our spouse's plate for that day.

How about your family? Why are so many children dealing with anxiety and stressed out by the time they're ten years old? Why do they need drugs to calm them down or help them stay focused? For sure, some children need medication due to chemical imbalances, but perhaps much of this is because of the parent's emotional instability which may have been inflicted on them. A pill will not love, spend time with, or teach a child how to think. Medication will not discipline him or her either. That's why God gave children parents. We need to teach our children how to think and react like Christ so they can be free of stress and reign in life as God intended. They need trained eyes of faith that enable them to see through their circumstances rather than the empty hopelessness that comes from disappointment and discouragement.

Is it a priority in your home to eat one meal together every day? Do you have uninterrupted family time for just being together? Remember, God established the family. Children are a gift from Him. Still, we find children sitting by the wayside (and expected to like it) while they watch their parents minister outside the home before meeting the needs of their own families. Maybe in some of these instances the parents are more concerned with performance than teaching their children how to maintain a proper heart attitude and follow the leading of the Holy Spirit. Unfortunately, these parents are teaching their children to wear the performance mask as well. At some time or another, we are all guilty of these things. But we must not be condemned. Instead, we must repent, draw near to God and move on.

Here is something else that plagues many families: Why do so many people sign their kids up for every possible activity yet fail to spend time playing with them? My husband and I laugh and say that we "home-sported" our children before we enrolled them in activities they knew nothing about. That was an awesome investment. Honestly, children just want to play with their parents anyway. As a family, we spent a lot of time playing ball together outside. By the grace of God, we waited until our kids were in second grade before we allowed them to participate in sports with other kids.

Unfortunately, many have bought into the world's system, which says that if we don't enroll our children at age three to play t-ball or sign them up for tumbling, they're already behind. Here's something to think about. Those three-year-olds standing in the field spend more time picking dandelions than watching the batter! How much fun can it be to have three tries to hit a ball off the tee then wait your turn for the other ninety kids to have their three swings? Seriously, have you tried doing this? It's boring! Why not stay at home and teach your children how to play ball? When they're bored go pick dandelions with them. Get to know your children through play. Then you will know their interests and be able to encourage them accordingly.

What about the priority of our jobs? Does your job own you? Have you achieved balance between work, family, and time for yourself? Do you keep trying to climb the corporate ladder to receive that three-hundred-dollar-a-month pay raise? Why is it that we see the dollar amount very clearly, but we don't count the cost? How can we ignore the effect an increase in pay will have on our families? Perhaps your desire is for the job that offers the office with multiple windows. Is it worth it if you find yourself watching the sun both rise and set from those windows?

Finally, what about making time for yourself? Many, many Christians live believing they must serve, serve, and serve some more. We can easily forget that God cares about us as individuals, too! Believe this: it is not godly to be out of balance when it comes to taking care of your own needs. The truth is, if we're not getting enough sleep, eating a proper diet, getting good exercise, and seeing to it that our children are, too, then our families are going to suffer. We can expect to become sick if this is how we live day in and day out.

The saying, "it's not about me," is a great saying and true in many cases, but anything taken to the extreme is out of balance. Remember, the devil wants us to operate in the extremes. It's one of his inroads into our lives. So if all we do is work, work, work, then serve, serve, serve, never considering ourselves or the effect it has on our families, we will become burnt out, stressed out, and totally out of the will of God. As a result, all facets of our lives will suffer. Consider this: If we put so much on our plates that we become stressed out, we leave no room for the fruit of the Spirit to flow through us.

Are we not forsaking God? . . .

- Every time we become involved in a new project which He never called us to in the first place?
- When we accept a job promotion before even considering His desires?
- When we work or serve in such a way that our spouses and children are left unattended and abandoned?
- When we enter our children in all sorts of events, rather than spending time with them ourselves?

How godly are these examples to a dying world? Granted, none of these things are "bad" things. However, they become bad or bitter when we don't first consult with our Lord and Savior. He will teach and lead each of us into the proper balance for our lives. This includes our spouses, our children, our friends, ourselves, our jobs, our finances, and much more.

The fruit of God's Spirit cannot flow freely through constant stress. As the saying goes, "If there's no peace in you, you certainly do not have any to give away."

If there's no peace in you,
you certainly do not have any
to give away.

A lot of families are spinning out of control, leaving demolished lives in their wake. This was never intended to be the will of God for your life or your family. Jeremiah 2:13 says, "For my people have committed two evils; they have forsaken (to leave, abandon, omit) Me the Fountain of living waters, and they have hewn (dug) for themselves cisterns, (projects, formulas and methods) broken cisterns which cannot hold (living) water." In verses 17-19 of that same chapter, Jeremiah says,

> Have you not brought this upon yourself by forsaking the Lord your God when He led you in the way? And now what have you to gain by allying yourself with Egypt (the ways of the world)* and going her way, to drink [the black roiled] waters of the Nile? Or what have you to gain in going the way of Assyria, to drink the waters of the Euphrates? Your own wickedness (doing your own thing)* shall chasten and correct you, and your backslidings and desertion of faith shall reprove you. Know therefore and recognize that this is an evil and bitter thing: [first,] you have forsaken the Lord your God; [second], you are indifferent to Me and the fear of Me is not in you, says the Lord of hosts

The Lord is asking a question of each of us, "What have you to gain by allying yourself with Egypt?" In other words, what could you possibly gain by aligning yourself and your family with the system of the world and following its ways? It is wickedness when we forget the One who made us and become indifferent to His concerns for our lives.

Do we really realize that when we align our priorities with the ways of the world, those "good" things we intended (job promotions, t-ball, serving, etc.), actually become bitter things to us. They end up souring our lives as well as the lives of our children.

Apply Galatians 5:1 to the previous scenario. It says, "In [this] freedom Christ has made us free [and completely liberated us] (from the system of the world);* stand fast then, and do not be hampered and held ensnared and submit again to the yoke of slavery [which you have once put off]." The truth is Jesus freed us from the ways of the world. Therefore, we need to stop being enslaved by the world's expectations for ourselves and our families. When we leave Him out of any areas of our lives, it is considered wickedness and we are acting against God's way. Most people don't do this to their families on purpose. It can even be done out of ignorance. We were created to live life with Him at the center.

Many people call Psalm 23 a favorite psalm. I believe that's because it offers the peace and wholeness that we need. It's a peace and wholeness that only Jesus Christ can give:

> The Lord is my Shepherd, I shall not be in want. He makes me lie down in green pastures, he restores my soul. He guides me in the paths of righteousness for his name's sake. Even though I walk through the valley of the shadow of death, I will fear no evil, for you are with me; your rod and your staff, they comfort me. You prepare a table before me in the presence of my enemies. You will anoint my head with oil; my cup overflows. Surely goodness and love will follow me all the days of my life, and I will dwell in the house of the Lord forever.

God promises peace and blessing in this psalm. Its key, however lies in verse one. "The Lord is my Shepherd." He is the one who leads, feeds, guides, and shields us. If we will submit all of our ways and give all of our cares to Him, we too can say, "I shall not want (my own way).*"

We find the story of Mary and Martha, two sisters, in Luke 10:38-42. Martha was a woman overly occupied. She served much and found herself busy and distracted. Mary seated herself at the Lord's feet and listened to His teaching. When the Lord saw this, He said, "Martha, Martha, you are anxious and troubled about many things; but there is need of only one thing. Mary *has chosen* the good portion *(that which is to her advantage),* which shall not be taken from her." When we spend time at the feet of Jesus Christ, we will hear everything He asks of us. Furthermore, He will always provide the means for whatever He asks us to do.

Truly, in order for each of us to establish godly priorities for our lives we must:

1. Choose to spend time at His feet, listening, studying and reading His Word; receiving His nourishment for our souls.
2. Choose to trust Him with every concern and every area of our lives to His care.

As a result He will:

1. Cause our paths to be straight,
2. Give balance to our lives,
3. Restore our souls, and
4. Cause us to live fruit-filled lives in accordance with His will.

Questions for Study

1. Make a list of your priorities. Do you really carry them out in the order you listed them?
2. Have you ever asked God what His priority list for you would look like? Do you believe that He would show you? Are you willing to spend time with Him so He can show them to you?
3. Do you spend time enjoying your family?
4. Make a list of all your activities (including those with your children). Is the list out of balance? What activities are good but might need to go in order to establish balance in your home and lives?
5. Do you spend time each day enjoying yourself? Do you laugh at the thought of that? God wants you to spend some time each day enjoying yourself. Are you able to spend any time at home just *being?* Or do you feel like you should be *doing* something all the time?
6. Do you want Psalm 23 to be the attitude of your heart?
7. Are you willing to become like Mary?

Personal Prayer

Lord, forgive me for not including You in every area of my life. Help me to create a priority list that is actually true, not just one that simply looks good. I desire for You to be at the center of every area of my life. Lord, You are my Shepherd, and I truly desire to be led and guided by You (Psalm 23). Forgive me for forsaking You, the Fountain of living waters, and for engaging in my own projects, formulas, and methods that You never led me to. I admit this as sin, and the consequences that have resulted are my own fault. I admit that I have aligned my ways with the world's system. I recognize it now as an evil thing. Forgive me for being indifferent to spending time with You, and for foolishly thinking that I could do anything apart from You (Jeremiah 2:13; 17-19; John 15:5). Lord, I am choosing to fear You. I choose to make You my Shepherd from here on out (Psalm 23). Help me not to be enslaved again to the ways of the world (Galatians 5:1) and to the system that causes people to spin out of control. Please keep me and my family in proper balance. I know that when I operate in extremes, I am opening the door for an attack from the enemy (1 Peter 5:8). Help me to think of ways to bless my spouse, spend time with my family, and keep my job in its proper place. I know that if I spend time at Your feet as Mary did, You will cause my priorities to be in order (Luke 10:38-42).

Chapter 34

Living a Disciplined Life

⁂

Although not the most popular subject these days, discipline is absolutely necessary in the life of every believer. It helps put the flesh to death and establish Christ-like character in our lives. Romans 13:13-14 tells us,

> Let us live and conduct ourselves honorably and becomingly as in the [open light of] day, not in reveling (carousing) and drunkenness, not in immorality and debauchery (sensuality and licentiousness, [moral unrestraint*]), not in quarreling and jealousy. But clothe yourself with the Lord Jesus Christ (the Messiah), and make no provision for [indulging] the flesh [put a stop to thinking about the evil cravings of your physical nature] to [gratify its] desires (lusts).

Those verses clearly instruct us to take off one type of behavior and put on another. Doing so requires certain effort on our part. God, in His perfect practicality, uses our everyday physical lives to discipline and teach us His spiritual ways. The way we live out our physical lives is the direct result of our spiritual beliefs. The two cannot be separated. What we do in our everyday lives, whether publicly or in the privacy of our homes, really *does* matter.

The way we live out our physical lives
is the direct result of our spiritual beliefs.

Let me share with you how God uses the often mundane, everyday activities of life to teach discipline to me, a stay-at-home mom. Before I married, I was a teacher and coach. Structure, goals, and competition were ingrained in my nature. One year after my husband and I married, we quit our jobs and went into business for ourselves. (That could be an entire book all of its own.). Two years later, I gave birth to twins! There is no doubt in my mind that God used my marriage, our business, pregnancy, and our children to draw me closer to Him.

I am closer to my husband and children because of the work He has done in me through all this change. I went from doing "my thing" to doing "their thing." I also realized the need for a healthy balance between my spouse, my children, and myself. I quickly realized how selfish my life really was. I learned to see the false and oftentimes unrealistic expectations I had for "family living." I would cry out to God for help, asking Him for the desire and the strength to be the wife and mother He wanted me to become. I asked Him to keep me from growing embittered about giving up my "career life." Ironically, God used that time to teach me first how to be the daughter He wanted me to be. Then, from the intimacy of my relationship with Him, He continues to transform me into the godly wife and mother that both He and I desire. Indeed, He drew me to Himself, set me apart to be consecrated, pure, and blameless before Him in word, thought, attitude, and deed in my everyday life—not just in my church life on Sundays.

During this time in my life, I started waking up early, on purpose, in order to start my day with the Lord before my family was up. It is a practice and discipline that has truly changed my life. During those quiet morning hours, God's Spirit prepared me and taught me from the Word. He showed me how to think, how to live, how to put off the old nature, how to stare at Him and what He accomplished for me at the cross, while His Spirit weaved His nature into my very being. Discipline is something I desire naturally. My personality prefers structure and order. My days were planned accordingly:

- Wake up early.
- Meet with God.
- Get the children breakfast.

On certain days I would:

- Run the sweeper.
- Do the laundry.
- Cut the grass.
- And once a week I would clean the house—bathrooms, dust, and mop.
- While my kids took their afternoon nap, I would prepare dinner and hopefully have enough time to collapse in a chair before they awoke!

While all these things are good and necessary, God showed me that in the midst of my scheduled routine and disciplined life, I had become very legalistic. I lived by the laws and demands that *I* had placed on myself. I had completely left out His law of grace for me and my family. By God's empowerment, the Holy Spirit began to show me some very important things. While I was doing a good job of tending to my family's needs, I was not doing a good job of enjoying them. I had used up all my energy caring for them. All I could see was what I had to get done that day! If I met all the demands, I felt good about myself and my family. But, oh mercy, if I didn't accomplish all of the tasks on the to-do-list, I felt horrible. During that time, God showed me some verses. Matthew 11:28-30 says,

> Come to Me all you who labor and are heavy-laden and overburdened, and I
> will cause you to rest. [I will ease and relieve and refresh your souls]. Take
> My yoke upon you and learn of Me, for I am gentle (meek) and humble
> (lowly) in heart, and you will find rest (relief and ease and refreshment and

recreation and blessed quiet) for your souls. For my yoke is wholesome (useful, good—not harsh, hard, sharp, and pressing, but comfortable, gracious, and pleasant), and My burden is light and easy to be borne.

This was exactly what I wanted, but I was striving to "get" it instead of "receiving" it. I was harsh, hard, sharp, and pressing forward all day long because of the pressure I had placed on myself. My house may have been clean and dinner prepared, but it was at the expense of my relationship with my family. This truth applies to stay-at-home or working moms and dads alike. If we have nothing left for our families, we are out of balance. The verses in Matthew convicted me. God used His Word to convince me that I needed to be gentle, comfortable, gracious, and pleasant, just like Jesus. I didn't like that I was more willing to be pleasant to strangers, acquaintances, and friends than with my own family. I knew that was not the will of God for me, and it is not for you, either. Our first and greatest ministry starts right in our own home.

Our first and greatest ministry
starts right in our own home.

James 4:1-2 provided some necessary answers. It says,

> What leads to strife (discord and feuds) and how do conflicts (quarrels and fighting) originate among you? *Do they not arise from your sensual desires that are ever warring in your bodily members?* You are jealous and covet [what others have] and your desires go unfulfilled; [so] you become murderers. [To hate is to murder as far as your hearts are concerned.] You burn with envy and anger and are not able to obtain [the gratification, the contentment, and the happiness that you seek], so you fight and war. You *do not have because you do not ask!*

As I consistently spent time with God, the Holy Spirit showed me that I was not seeking His help in the everyday, mundane details of my life. Suddenly, I put aside "my" priority list, and asked God to show me His priority list. I started receiving His empowering grace to help me instead of striving in my own strength. Yes, I still cleaned my house and took care of the tasks that needed to be done, but I began to notice my family and their personal needs first. I started sitting on the floor and playing with my children. I would sometimes read them a book first, before I started my demanding list of "to do's."

I hadn't realized before that I was actually partnering with the enemy, giving him the freedom to set me up for a downfall. Satan had me working against the clock all day long, completely focused on how much I could get accomplished. The Holy Spirit showed me, however, that I'd been warring with myself and my family any time I didn't live up to my expectations or complete what I had in mind for the day. This, in turn, caused me to be harsh, hard, and impatient toward the people I was supposed to love the most! As I laid down my expectations, priorities, irritations, and impatience toward my family, the Holy Spirit was able to fill me with Himself and His ways.

The truth is, God is always more concerned with our inner turmoil and how we're treating our families, than He is with our daily check lists. Slowly, He taught me my need for discipline in what mattered most to Him—how I treated other people. The more I submitted my ways to Him, the more He revealed to me the devil's tactics—to kill, steal, and destroy me and my family. God wanted me to receive the abundant life that He came to give me. He wanted me to live above pressure and circumstances. It didn't happen, though, until I humbled myself before God and asked Him for His grace and empowerment to help me. I no longer wanted to be upset over the uncompleted tasks on my agenda. I wanted to become more concerned with my attitude and love towards my family.

Perhaps some of you struggle with this as well, or maybe you're the complete opposite. Maybe your house is a wreck, and you need to make a list and follow through with it in order to establish some structure and routine. Maybe you need discipline to pay your bills on time, to not spend all your money, or to establish a healthy meal plan. Whatever the case may be, understand that your flesh, (what you see, want, think, and feel) is either very lazy or very controlling, and it wants to rule in its most comfortable realm. Despite which end of the spectrum you find yourself—lazy or controlling—it is out of balance. Take on the yoke of the Lord, and partner with Him. He will help you establish the proper priorities for your life and your home. He is the One who invented family. If you're married, He came to give you a wonderful marriage where two people really become one, not simply where the two become roommates or end in divorce. He also desires to help you rear and discipline your children. First receive His discipline and grace for yourself. He is able to make His grace abound to you. Then you will be able to instill these values into your home, children, workplace, and so forth.

This is something to always remember: nobody in your home, or elsewhere for that matter, is responsible for your happiness or for your reactions except you. This comes about only as you discipline yourself by partnering with and submitting your ways to God's Spirit. As your relationship with God develops and becomes stronger, so will all the other relationships in your life.

**No one else is responsible for your happiness
or your reactions except you.**

The words in Hebrews 12:11-14 sum it up best. They say,

> For the time being no discipline brings joy, but seems grievous and painful; *but afterwards it yields a peaceable fruit of righteousness to those who have been trained by it* [a harvest of fruit which consists in righteousness—in conformity to God's will in purpose, thought and action, resulting in right living and right standing with God]. So then, brace up and reinvigorate and set right your slackened and weakened and drooping hands and strengthen your feeble and palsied and tottering knees. And cut through and make firm and plain and smooth, straight paths for your feet [yes, make them safe and upright and happy *paths that go in the right direction*], so that the lame and halting (limbs) may not be put out of joint, but rather may be cured. *Strive to live in peace with everybody and pursue that consecration and holiness without which no one will [ever] see the Lord.*

Discipline is painful, but the rewards are great—health, happiness, and life for you and for your entire family. We must be trained in order to yield the peaceable fruit of righteousness. We must continuously practice doing the right things in our lives if we want to establish real change. Look how long I practiced doing the wrong thing. Change didn't come about because I chose to be different just one time. Rather, I had to make a series of adjustments to do things God's way. I had to do them over and over until they became my "natural" reactions. This process of discipline will continue either until I die, or until Jesus comes back to get me.

It is so awesome to have fun with my family and live in a home full of peace—because Peace Himself lives in me. This is the resurrected power of God working in the everyday activities of life. If we will embrace Him and cooperate with Him, He will set us free, especially from ourselves.

Questions for Study

1. In Romans 13:13-14, what area of your life is God desiring for you to "take off"?
2. Because God is so practical, what does He use to discipline and teach us His ways?
3. What discipline would God have you practice that will change your life? Have you asked Him?
4. Balance is a vital necessity in our lives. Ask the Holy Spirit to tell you specific areas in which He desires for you to become balanced.
5. How do you treat the people in your home, at work, or at school? How do you treat people when you don't get your way?
6. Who is the only one responsible for your happiness and reactions?

Personal Prayer

Lord, I know that with discipline comes the peaceable fruit of righteousness for those who have been trained by it (Hebrews 12:11-14). Help me to take off the dictates of the flesh and put on the Lord Jesus Christ in every circumstance (Romans 13:13-14). Forgive me for running from the "hard" places in my life, and cause me to stand still. I want to walk through these valleys holding Your hand. I know that You desire to use the difficulties in my life to draw me close to You. Help me to respond accordingly. I realize that the way I live my physical life is a direct result of my spiritual condition. I cannot separate the two. Your Word says that strife arises from not getting my way (James 4:1-2). I know that this attitude is sin. I am choosing to come to You, for You will give me rest. Help me to become gentle just as You are, and refresh my soul for Your burden is light and easy to bear (Matthew 11:28-30). Thank You for caring about the everyday, mundane activities of my life. I invite You to be in them, and I ask for Your guidance and help. Forgive me for placing my personal happiness on the shoulders of others. Forgive me for blaming everyone else for my negative reactions. I desire to take responsibility for my attitudes in every area of my life. I choose to do this despite what others have done to me or said about me. Please establish balance in my life in the area of discipline.

Chapter 35

Living a Self-Controlled Life

———————————◦◦———————————

*D*iscipline and self-control go hand in hand. It's an important truth. First, we become disciplined in the things of God. He wants to change us into vessels through which His fruit can be displayed. Second, we must develop the practice of *self*-control. As followers of Christ, we are held to a new standard in which excuses such as, "That's just how I'm wired," have no merit. They simply pretend to justify our natural inclination to remain bound to our flesh, our physical senses, and dictating passions. When we allow this, we let our feelings govern us instead of God's Spirit. When the Holy Spirit came to live inside of us, He deposited the seed of self-control as one of His fruits. However, until we personally "activate" this fruit, it will lie dormant within us. Actually, until we purposely cooperate and align our minds with God's Word the Holy Spirit's power and His fruit will lie dormant within us. This is why so many Christians live spiritually bankrupt lives.

In the previous chapter, I described my struggle with being disciplined in the ways of God. Yes, I was a disciplined person in general, but I was disciplined according to what I deemed necessary. In my lack of knowledge, much of my discipline was geared toward the external and physical things in my life. God wants us to be disciplined according to His desires. This starts with internal change. In order for us to conform to His will, God wants us to become more concerned with our hearts' attitudes than we are about applying external rules. Truthfully, each of us can tack on the appropriate behavior when necessary, or when trying to impress somebody. But God sees our hearts and motives. He knows our very thoughts and feelings. Proverbs 17:3 tells us that the Lord tries our hearts. In other words, He allows us to face certain situations so He might test us. Our responses reveal to us our hearts' conditions. They show "what we are made of."

God tests us to refine us. He wants to find us persevering and faithful to His Word regardless of our circumstances. Satan uses these tests to tempt us to give up our confidence in Christ and rely on our physical senses rather than the Word of God.

God wants us to be disciplined
according to His desires.
This starts with internal change.

173

When we are self-controlled, through Holy Spirit empowerment, we are not swayed by our circumstances or by what others think and say of us. There will always be situations and people in our lives that will annoy or rattle us. Rather than running from them, however, when we use our self-control, we are allowing God into these situations to mature us. He is peeling off and smoothing over our rough spots.

A great first step toward self-control is prayer. We should start by praying for God to change us. Now that's something He's very interested in doing! We become strong inwardly through our constant union and communion with Christ. Ephesians 6:10 tells us to "become strong in the Lord." Many people think this is an outward act or application. It actually begins with an inward decision, a commitment to partner with Him. Philippians 4:13, tells us the same thing. It says, "I can do all things through Christ Who gives me strength." He gives us the inner strength and empowerment to model His character in difficult situations. That character is then manifested in our reactions and behaviors toward others.

Consider this: How was Jesus able to endure the abuse that He did? The religious leaders spit in His face. They made false accusations about Him. Yet, despite what they thought about Him or did to Him, He was not swayed. They could not touch His inner life or His strength. Jesus was able to withstand this abuse because He knew who He was, why He was here, and where He was headed. Their treatment of Him didn't change Him. He was focused on the things above and doing the will of the Father. God desires to grow that kind of inner strength in all of us.

God once used a friend to create a life-changing realization for me. I had sent him an email expressing my dissatisfaction with some things that were going on in my life. I sincerely desired to see God work change within other people. The life-change came when I read his reply. He said, "*Lisa, don't expect God to change everyone and everything around you, if you haven't first asked Him to change you!*" Perhaps those words had been said to me before, but this time I actually *heard* them.

It had not occurred to me that I needed to change, because I didn't feel that I was in the wrong. All too often, this is a common mistake that we all make. I claimed an attitude of justification toward these people. Because I respected this friend and heard his words, I asked the Lord to change me. I told God that I was willing to follow any method He deemed appropriate because I wanted to be like Him. God, in His infinite wisdom and total practicality, had been faithful to teach me about myself through the everyday activities of my life, starting in my home. That day however, God began to teach me that my problem with other people was really a result of the problem I had within myself. Have you ever noticed that the things that annoy us about others are often the very things we ourselves are guilty of doing?

I had been allowing what other people had thought about me to determine my level of joy and contentment. And, unfortunately, I let them determine my identity too. This is not the will of the Lord for any of us. He desires to help us over this self-destructive trap.

God began to teach me that my problem
with other people was really a result
of the problem I had within myself.

In the last chapter, I wrote about feeling good about myself and my family when I completed all of my planned tasks, but feeling bad about myself and family when I didn't. My life was like a "rollercoaster" that was led by my physical accomplishments and unstable emotions.

Unfortunately, many Christians live like this. We don't face adversity well. We fall apart when things don't go as we have planned. The devil is thrilled when he sees this kind of Christian. After all, it requires very little effort on his part to create a disturbance in this person's life. Remember, the devil wants to steal our faith and the power Jesus Christ has placed inside of us. He wants to make the fruit of the Spirit within us useless. If we surrender our joy to him, we will have no peace, patience, kindness, and so forth, and this will end with us literally handing him our self-control. If we have no self-control, there is no way we can walk in love or in agreement with the Spirit. As a result, rather than living the life that Jesus came to give us, we live powerless and depleted lives.

Take a look at the downward spiral I set myself up for every day with my "to do" list. Keep in mind that I had two-year-old twins. Here is exactly what would happen if one thing caused a hiccup in my list:

- I was mad, irritated, and impatient.
- I would grumble and complain about the inconvenience.
- I would feel overwhelmed and behind schedule.
- I would take it out on my family by being annoyed with them (sometimes quietly and sometimes loudly).
- I would start to see myself as an inadequate wife and mother and feel bad.
- I would feel guilty and start to condemn myself for being annoyed.

Wow! Here I was, a Christian, thinking and behaving like this — all because I wasn't getting my way. I was basing all of my self-worth and value on my daily accomplishments. I had no confidence in God, in His love for me, or in His resurrected power working in me. The truth is, until I started spending time in God's Word renewing my mind every day, I could not see that He cared about every detail of my life. I was more concerned with the physical conditions of my life than I was with my heart attitude. I did not realize the truth of His Word regarding my worth and value.

Even though I was a Christian and would have gone to Heaven, the enemy's power was working in me, in the form of pride, fear, doubt, and unbelief. Until the Holy Spirit brought it to my attention, I was incapable of recognizing this. I believed the lie that my family was the problem, seeing them as obstacles that stood between my work and me. Believing the enemy made everything else negative as well. The devil will always be the negative force in your life. By the end of each day, guilt would set in because I had treated everyone so badly. That is exactly what the enemy wanted. The devil will rope us in and control us if we give our thoughts over to him. As we allow him to influence our thoughts, we will slowly give in to his ways, and ultimately find ourselves stuck in his trap. Then he tops it all off with the sting of guilt and condemnation over how we acted!

**The devil will rope us in and control us if
we give our thoughts over to him.**

Indeed, my mind needed renewal with God's Word. I needed to gain an understanding of His true expectations for me. My will and my ways needed to be conformed to His. My emotions needed to be healed and led by His Spirit rather than by my physical senses, surroundings, and circumstances. And most of all, my mouth needed to come into agreement with His Word rather than how I felt or what circumstances dictated. Romans 14:17 tells us that the Kingdom of God is within us. It says that He has given us the power to be like Him. Even though the Kingdom of God was within me at the time, I was ignorantly choosing not to reflect Christ's character because I was too busy looking at my circumstances and "to do" lists rather than looking to Jesus. We truly become what we fix our minds on.

The Holy Spirit started to show me that neither my family, nor my surrounding conditions, nor personal circumstances were the problem. Rather, I was the problem! My reactions, expectations, my grumbling and my complaining were the problem. They were way out of balance, and they opposed His will for me. The Holy Spirit had to teach me that I was the only one responsible for myself, my reactions, my words, and my behavior before Him. Here are some of the verses He used to help me change and to align my mind to His. I believe they will do the same for you.

- Psalm 32:8-9—He will instruct me and guide me in the way I should go. But I must not be like the horse or the mule, which lack understanding, which must have their mouths held firm with bit and bridle, or else they will not come with you.
- Proverbs 3:5-8—When I acknowledge Him in all my ways, trust Him and lean on Him, He will direct me, and will provide health for my nerves.
- Ephesians 6:12—I am not wrestling with flesh and blood, but with the enemy. Therefore, people are not my real problem.
- Colossians 3:15—Peace is meant to rule in my heart and act as the umpire in my life to inform me of right and wrong heart attitudes, words, and behaviors.
- Proverbs 16:32—Being slow to anger is better than being mighty. Ruling my own mind, mouth, attitude, and actions is better than conquering a city.
- Proverbs 17:4—I need to stop contention as its onset because it's just like the first trickle of water in the crack of a dam—ready to burst forth.
- Romans 8:1-2—There is no more guilt and condemnation for me because I am in Christ.

It is important to remember the Holy Spirit's job is to convict us of sin, not to condemn us. Satan, however, uses guilt and condemnation to push people down in order to manipulate and control them. The Holy Spirit uses conviction to bring us up higher, to make us aware of our sin so that we might confess it, repent of it, and immediately move on.

In order to walk in discipline and self-control, we must learn to talk to ourselves the way the Holy Spirit talks to us through God's Word. He will guide us according to His path (Psalm 32:8). He will warn us when we head down the wrong path. When we get upset with others or ourselves, we need to remember that people are not the real enemy (Ephesians 6:12). If we start to lose our joy and peace (Colossians 3:15), we need the discipline to stop, get control of ourselves (Proverbs 16:32), and stop the fighting before it even begins (Proverbs 17:14). The Holy Spirit will nudge us when we are walking on that slippery slope. Next time the devil tries to derail you, stop, ask for help, and submit your mind, mouth, attitudes, and actions to God's ways.

**In order to walk in discipline and self-control,
we must learn to talk to ourselves the way
the Holy Spirit talks to us.**

Something that is really hard for me to do when things don't go my way is to resist complaining about it. Thankfully, the Holy Spirit has an answer for that as well. Philippians 2:14 tells us to do all things without grumbling and faultfinding and complaining—and verse 15 tells us why: so that we may show ourselves to be blameless and guileless, innocent and uncontaminated children of God. When we use our mouths to grumble, complain, and find fault with others, we contaminate our inner selves and neutralize our faith. We literally shut out God's peace and His blessings. Satan is thrilled when we choose this method.

Second Timothy 1:7 describes the kind of spirit God gave us. It tells us it is not one of timidity, but one full of power and love. It says the spirit God has given us is one of a calm and well-balanced mind, with discipline and self-control. Notice that the Holy Spirit doesn't empower us to control others, nor does He want us to remain helplessly stuck in our fleshly carnal ways. The Lord showed me this truth as I realized how I would try to control my family through various moods or outbursts of anger when I didn't get my way. This especially happened when I couldn't complete my "to do" list.

Consider again the promises in 2 Timothy 1:7. He has given us a spirit of:

- *Power*—The ability to not fall prey to the devil's tactics, but to submit to God and resist the enemy's temptation to give in to our lower nature, physical senses, conditions, circumstances and surroundings.
- *Love*—The ability to choose life and His love, and to be led by the Holy Spirit.
- *A calm and well-balanced mind*—As God's children, we have the right to this blessing. If you are a person who gets easily wound up by the enemy, recognize his tactics and refuse to grant him the permission any longer to come into your thoughts. Actively stop allowing the enemy to have control of your thoughts by renewing and aligning your mind with God's Word. Exercise your faith to take your thoughts and words captive. Then, line them up and make them obedient to the Word of God, placing your faith in what He wants you to think and speak (2 Corinthians 10:5; Philippians 4:8).
- *Discipline and self-control*—The ability to develop discipline and self-control in order to stop believing the devil's lies. Understand that Satan wants to use our minds to dump his lies (garbage) and our mouths to speak them so he can gain an entrance into our lives. We must retire from our demanding ways and exchange them for God's so that we can have the life that He died to give us.

I was amazed at how God helped me through my day once I started *asking* and *obeying* Him. When I would take the time to play with my kids and enjoy my family, I *always* completed everything that I had intended to do that day. And I was able to complete it with peace, ease, and energy to spare. Yes, "His grace is sufficient, and if we ask Him He will do immeasurably more than we could dare ask, think or imagine!" (Ephesians 3:20). Indeed, He is waiting to show all of us how involved He wants to be in our everyday lives. Invite His help!

Questions for Study
1. Are you using excuses and remaining in bondage to ungodly attitudes and behaviors?
2. How do we activate the fruit of the Spirit in our lives?
3. Why was Jesus able to withstand the religious leaders spitting in His face and making false accusations against Him?

4. Have you ever asked God to change something or someone without first asking Him to change you? Do you want Him to change you?
5. My problem with others was actually a problem with _____. Do you believe that about yourself?
6. Why is it important not to grumble, complain, or find fault?
7. Do you try to control others through moods, words, or even looks?

Personal Prayer

Lord, I realize that discipline and self-control go hand-in-hand. Thank You for giving me the fruit of self-control. Forgive me for the times I have desired to control others instead of myself. Lord, I am asking You to give me inner strength and to empower me to model Your character in difficult situations (Mark 14:60-65). I know that I can do all things through You because you give me the inner strength to do so (Philippians 4:13). Forgive me for being short with others, and show me what is causing me to react this way. Thank You for Your forgiveness. Bring change, Lord, to me and my attitude. Help me to "get the plank out of my own eye," and repent, before I try to "remove the speck" from my brother's (Matthew 7:3-5). Help me to recognize the tools that Satan uses to cause upset and strife within me, and teach me how to conquer his attacks through your Word (1 Peter 5:8-10). I realize that I am not wrestling with flesh and blood, but with the enemy (Ephesians 6:12). Let peace rule as the umpire of my heart (Colossians 3:15). Help me to be quick to listen, slow to speak, and slow to become angry (James 1:19).

Chapter 36

Spirit-Led Living
and Moving Mountains

———————◦——————

When we live according to the Holy Spirit's leading, we will see mountains begin to move in our lives. Renewing our minds daily and learning to speak like God are two crucial elements and the key to the process God uses to transform us. Literally, our soul moves from death to life when we learn how to think and speak like Jesus. The Lord wants to move the mountains in our lives, but He needs our cooperation. So He waits. Often times, the biggest mountain in our way is our unwillingness to cooperate with God's Word and Spirit— an unwillingness caused by the flesh (what we see, want, think, and feel). The flesh wants to believe its physical senses and surrounding circumstances over God's Word. In order to build "spiritual muscles" of faith, however, we cannot let its sensualities and physical impulses dictate our desires, our thoughts, and our feelings. We must learn to line our minds and mouths up with the Word of God. We must allow the Word and the Spirit to lead the mind, mouth, and body.

When God told Joshua in the Old Testament, "Every place upon which the sole of your foot shall tread, *that have I given to you,* as I promised Moses," He meant it for us as well. (See Joshua 1:3.) Ephesians 1:3 says, "May blessing (praise, laudation, and eulogy) be to the God and Father of our Lord Jesus Christ (the Messiah) *Who has blessed us in Christ with every spiritual* (given by the Holy Spirit) *blessing in the heavenly realm!*" Similarly, 2 Peter 1:3 says, "For His divine power *has bestowed upon us all things that [are requisite and suited] to life and godliness,* through the [full, personal] knowledge of Him Who called us by and to His own glory and excellence (virtue)."

When we accept Christ as our Savior He deposits His power and everything we need for this life as well as for the next, into our spirit. As we develop our personal relationship with Jesus, renew our minds with the Word and believe what it says, pray, and speak as if these blessings really exist, we release those blessings throughout our souls and bodies. The blessings pertaining to life and godliness, include:

- *Salvation* from eternal damnation,
- *Forgiveness* of our sins,
- *Rescue* from Satan, sin, selfishness, and the system of this world,

- *Deliverance* from fears, bitterness, resentment, unforgiveness, and agitating passions,
- *Healing* for our spirit, soul, and body,
- *Wholeness* in our spirit, soul, and body,
- *Soundness of mind* which includes the ability to focus and to think like Jesus in order to be imitators of God on this earth,
- *Prosperity* in spirit, soul, and body, and *general well-being*.

The blessings that pertain to godliness include the fruit of the Spirit, which are:

- Love,
- Joy,
- Peace,
- Patience,
- Kindness,
- Goodness,
- Gentleness,
- Faithfulness, and
- Self-control.

Imagine, all of these things have been given to you and me when we accept and receive Christ into our inner most being. "Christ in me the hope of glory!" ... The hope of making Him obvious to the world.

Take a look at verses 4-10 in 2 Peter chapter 1. It says,

> By means of these *He has bestowed on us His precious and exceedingly great promises,* so that through them you may escape [by flight] from the moral decay (rottenness and corruption) that is in the world because of covetousness (lust and greed), and *become sharers (partakers) of the divine nature.* For this very reason, adding your diligence [to the divine promises], *employ every effort in exercising your faith to develop* virtue (excellence, resolution, Christian energy), and in [*exercising*] virtue [develop] knowledge (intelligence), and in [*exercising*] knowledge [develop] self-control, and in [*exercising*] self-control [develop] steadfastness (patience, endurance), and in [*exercising*] steadfastness [develop] godliness (piety), and in [*exercising*] godliness [develop] brotherly affection, and in [*exercising*] brotherly affection [develop] Christian love. *For these qualities are yours and increasingly abound in you,* they will keep [you] from being idle or unfruitful unto the [full personal] knowledge of our Lord Jesus Christ (the Messiah, the Anointed One). For whoever lacks these qualities is blind, [spiritually] shortsighted, seeing only what is near to him, and has become oblivious [to the fact] that he was cleansed from his old sins. Because of this, brethren, be all the more solicitous and eager to make sure (to ratify, to strengthen, to make steadfast) your calling and election; for if you do this, you will never stumble or fall.

We find in these verses all of the things we already have because Christ lives in us. In order to develop them, however, *we must learn to exercise our faith.*

Maybe right now you're thinking, "How can I exercise my faith to develop the things that I already have inside of me?" Here's how:

1. Believe that you actually have them. (Remember, everything that God has given you is in seed form; it needs to mature).
2. Water your seeds with the Word by praying and saying. Acknowledge and believe that you have them. Speak the truth that they are growing inside of you right now.

For example, pray back the verses in 2 Peter 1:3-10 as if you possess these things. Your prayer might sound like this:

> Lord, thank You, that Your divine power has bestowed upon me all things that are requisite and suited to life and godliness, through the full, personal knowledge of You Who called me to Your own glory and excellence. Thank You for giving me the things pertaining to life such as my salvation, forgiveness, rescue, deliverance, healing, wholeness, soundness, prosperity and general well being. Thank you for the things that pertain to godliness such as the fruit of the Spirit, which lives in my spirit. Thank You that I possess love, joy, peace, patience, kindness, goodness, gentleness, faithfulness, and self-control. By means of these, You have bestowed on me Your precious and exceedingly great promises. Through them I have escaped moral decay, and I can share and partake of Your divine nature. For this very reason I will be diligent and employ every effort to exercise my faith to develop virtue, knowledge, self-control, steadfastness, godliness, brotherly affection, and Christ-like love towards others. For these qualities are mine and increasingly abound in me. They will keep me from being idle and unfruitful.

Do you realize that it takes faith to develop all of these things? You and I can't possibly try hard enough to accomplish these things in our lives. We are told to exercise our faith, believing that we already possess them. Romans 4:17 says that God, "gives life to the dead and speaks of the nonexistent things that [He has foretold and promised] as if they [already] existed." As imitators and ambassadors of God, we are to do the same thing. God has already given to us many promises which are made real to us as we believe, as we water them with the Word through prayer, and as we continually study and renew our minds with the Word. Our increasing personal knowledge of Jesus, our personal experiences, and our cooperation with God's Spirit will enable us to let go of anything that would hinder the development and growth of these seeds.

The process of renewing our minds to think like Jesus takes focus, work, diligence, and persistence. Truly, most of us want a "miracle"—God's work without any effort on our part. Many times, though, He wants us to learn to "walk through" our situations holding His hand. This requires time and responsibility on our part, and the ability to consistently respond as Jesus would.

Second Peter 1:10 sums this up wonderfully by saying, "Because of this, brethren, be all the more solicitous and eager to make sure (to ratify, strengthen, to make steadfast) your calling and election; for if you do this, you will never stumble or fall."

Wow! Learning to live like this—like Jesus—is God's will for all of us! He promises if we are faithful to do these things, we will never stumble or fall. That's an amazing concept.

Look at the promises God gives us in Psalm 91:2-4.

> *I will say* of the Lord, He is my Refuge and my Fortress, my God; on Him
> I lean and rely, and in Him I (confidently) trust. For *(then) He will deliver*
> *you* from the snare of the fowler and from the deadly pestilence. *(Then) He*
> *will cover you* with His pinions, and under His wings shall you trust and find
> refuge; His truth and His faithfulness are a shield and buckler.

Speaking God's truths is a means of expressing our faith which leads to believing. Second Corinthians 4:13 says, "Yet we have the same spirit of faith as he had who wrote, 'I have *believed,* and *therefore have I spoken.*' We too believe and therefore we speak."

We will surely speak what we believe. Look at the promises of Jesus in Mark 11:22-24,

> And Jesus, replying, said to them, Have faith in God [constantly]. Truly I tell
> you, *whoever says* to this mountain, Be lifted up and thrown into the sea!
> And does not doubt at all in his heart but *believes* that what he says will take
> place, it will be done for him. For this reason I am telling you, whatever you
> ask for in prayer, believe (trust and be confident) that it is granted to you,
> and you will [get it].

These are extremely powerful and hope-filled words! Let's sift through these verses closely to remove any confusion.

1. We cannot simply speak our will into a situation; we are to speak God's will. Remember, God's Word is His will! This is how it looks: We have to live in God's Word daily, not just visit it occasionally, in order to understand His heart's desires. Then the Holy Spirit will teach us what to speak in accordance with His Word to bring about the manifestation of His will in our lives.
2. Believe God's Word over your feelings. That is in spite of a doctor's report, in spite of your circumstances, and in spite of your situations. (A hard task indeed, but one that proves our faith).
3. Believe that what you say is true and will take place. Remember, God's Word gives life into our lives and situations and does not return void, but accomplishes that which He pleases and for which it was sent. (See Isaiah 55:11.) As ambassadors and imitators of God, we must learn to speak as God speaks. (This is another hard task that builds our faith. Undoubtedly, it's much easier to speak about what we see, what we think, and how we feel).
4. Do not doubt at all, but believe that *what you say* will take place and it will be done for you. To continuously doubt God is to deny His power to work in our lives. James 1:5-8 explains that if we are lacking in wisdom regarding a situation, we are to ask and God will give it to us. But we must ask in faith without wavering or doubting. For when we waver or doubt we are like the billowing surge out at sea that is blown and tossed every which way by the wind. This person, it says, shouldn't even imagine that God will answer Him, because he is a man of two minds—unstable and unreliable about everything he thinks, feels, and decides.

God's Word is His will!

Continuous doubt is a result of the enemy's influence and of a mind that struggles to believe what the Word says. It comes from a mind that remains lined up with the physical senses, natural impulses, and dictating passions of the flesh rather than with God's Word and the Holy Spirit. The mind that continues to doubt allows Satan to dominate and even control its thoughts, discrediting God's Word. Satan desires for you to bow to human reasoning rather than to God's Word. When what we ask for isn't done instantly, we tend to use this human reasoning. But we need to remember, miracles and answered prayer usually takes a lot longer than we'd like. God often uses times like this to transform us to see according to His Spirit, trusting Him when we do not know how long His answer will take. Really trusting God means living according to what we believe (faith), not by what we can see—for however long it takes. Mark 11:25-26 gives light on our part of walking and speaking in faith-filled, Spirit-led living.

> And whenever you stand praying, if you have anything against anyone, forgive him and let it drop (leave it, let it go), in order that your Father Who is in heaven may also forgive you your [own] failings and shortcomings and *let them drop. But if you do not forgive, neither will your Father in heaven forgive your failings and shortcomings.*

Here are some key points from this Scripture:

1. We can't expect God to move our mountains if we harbor unforgiveness in our hearts. When we hold on to unforgiveness, we actively disobey God. If we love God, we will obey Him.
2. We are told three times in verse 25 to let it go and let it drop. Part of forgiving and walking in faith is letting offenses drop. We need to stop talking about the offenses and the offender and start speaking God's Word over our own hearts and the hearts of the offenders. Mature Christians observe a situation and remove self from the offense, refusing to speak their own opinions into the situation. Instead, they would choose to speak God's Word, through prayer, into the situation. This enables God to move on behalf of the people involved the way He wants to. This is what it means to look at situations from God's perspective or to "see" in the Spirit with our hearts.
3. If we choose not to forgive, God will not forgive us. Remember, a life without forgiveness ends in permanent death. Unforgiveness quenches the Spirit of God. We cannot ignore God's order, principles, or His structure in any area or relationship in our lives.

Sadly, many Christians remain powerless and frustrated because they refuse to forgive, whether it's themselves, someone else, or even a grudge they may have against God. Forgiveness is a choice, not a feeling. When you start to pray for people who have hurt or offended you, watch your feelings then catch up. The enemy wants to keep your mind focused on the offense so you speak *about* the offense rather than speaking *to* the offense. Please understand that people are not the "mountains" in our lives. The enemy is!

Forgiveness is a choice.
People are not the "mountains"

in our lives, the enemy is.

If you want to be led by the Holy Spirit and watch Him "move the mountains" in your life, then understand that you need to have right standing with God in these areas:

1. Forgiveness, that is, choosing to forgive others of faults and shortcomings. James 5:16 says, "Confess to one another therefore your faults (your slips, your false steps, your offenses, your sins) and pray [also] for one another, that you may be healed and restored [to a spiritual tone of mind and heart]. The earnest (heartfelt, continued) prayer of a righteous man makes tremendous power available [dynamic in its working!]." The word, "confess" in this passage also means to practice confessing what's right! Be sure to confess who you are in Christ and what the Word says about you.
2. A clear conscience before God—that is, as far as you know, you are not harboring anything that would quench God's Spirit or render Him unable to work in you. First John 3:21-22 says, "And, beloved, if our consciences (our hearts) do not accuse us [if they do not make us feel guilty and condemn us], we have confidence (complete assurance and boldness) before God, And we receive from Him whatever we ask, because we [watchfully] obey His orders [observe His suggestions and injunctions, follow His plan for us] and [habitually] practice what is pleasing to Him."
3. Forfeiting our opinions and words and speaking God's Word, rather, into our own lives, the lives of other people, and the situations in which we are involved.
4. Praising God and giving Him thanks despite the circumstances. Furthermore, believing in His ability, to intervene, heal, restore, and do whatever is necessary.
5. Learning how to speak to others. Ephesians 5:19-20 says, "Speak out to one another in *psalms* and *hymns* and *spiritual songs,* offering praise with voices [and instruments] and making melody with all your heart to the Lord, at all times and for everything *giving thanks* in the name of our Lord Jesus Christ to God the Father."

Let's look at the meanings of some of these words in Ephesians 5:19-20.

- Psalms—A psalm is a story of a man's deliverance or a commemoration of mercies received.[1]
- Hymns—A hymn is a magnificent proclaiming of how great someone or something is. It is a direct address of praise and glory to God.[2]
- Spiritual songs—Spiritual speaking that is assisted and inspired by the Holy Spirit.[3]
- Giving thanks—Praising God, expressing thanksgiving.[4]

Our faith is manifested and our confidence in God is boosted when we consistently practice these things. At no time does the Bible tell us, "If you *feel* like giving thanks . . . If you *feel* like forgiving someone . . . If you *feel* like forfeiting your opinion . . . If you *feel* like speaking well of someone . . . If you *feel* like having a clear conscience. . . ." No, we are told to *do* these things by faith in Christ because we no longer represent ourselves, but rather His Kingdom and His economy. Now the God of glory will move on our behalf in our lives, as well as in the lives of others for whom we are praying. This is how God's will is done on earth as it is in Heaven.

Questions for Study

1. What vital and crucial elements change in a person's life during the process of transformation?
2. What is our "flesh," and what must happen to it in order for the Spirit to be able to lead and guide us?
3. Is your mind more in agreement with your flesh or with God's Word and His Spirit?
4. What is God's will?
5. What is a major contributor to doubt?
6. Why is it so important to forgive?
7. If you want to be led by the Holy Spirit and watch Him move in your life, in what areas must you have right standing with God?

Personal Prayer

Lord, I know that my soul moves from death to life when I learn how to think and speak as You do. Forgive me for allowing my flesh to have control over me, causing me to sin. My desire is to cooperate with Your Holy Spirit as You lead and guide me to move the mountains in my life. Your Word says that I did not receive the spirit of the world, but the Spirit who is from God, so that I may know the things freely given to me by You. I am to speak these things, not in words taught by human wisdom, but in those taught by the Spirit, combining spiritual thoughts with spiritual words (1 Corinthians 2:12-13). Thank You that Your Word is Your will for me! Help me to live in it, to understand it with my heart, and to allow the Holy Spirit to teach me. Help me to believe in You constantly so that I may be pleasing to You (Hebrews 11:6). Lord, I choose to forgive those who have hurt me, and I forgive myself as well (Mark 11:25-26). I ask You to show me if there is any wicked way in me, and I pray for it to be removed (Psalm 139:23-24). I desire a clear conscience so that I can receive what You desire for me to have (1 John 3:21-22). Help me to ask for the things in accordance with Your will.

PART SIX:

Trials, Prayers, and Praising God

Chapter 37

The Purpose of Trials

———————•———————

We all struggle with trials. We also struggle to understand how or why joy can have anything to do with them, especially when we are in the middle of one. Trials are painful, and I doubt any of us cares to intentionally invoke pain upon ourselves. It's no secret: our flesh likes comfort! However, trials reveal a lot about us — our character, integrity, and loyalty, our willingness to forgive, and our spiritual level of maturity just to name a few. When facing a trial, Satan will encourage us to run from whatever we think is causing us the pain. But God wants us to face and embrace each trial and allow Him to use it for our good.

Many times the trials that we go through are brought about by a series of unwise, ungodly, or disobedient decisions we have made. Remember the law of sowing and reaping? Whether we like that fact or not, it will never change. The seeds, (thoughts, words, attitudes, and choices) we sow will produce a harvest for good or a harvest for bad. We choose. Even though we can't always control what happens (or happened) to us, we still get to choose how we will react. Proverbs 19:3 says, "The foolishness of man subverts his way [ruins his affairs]; then his heart is resentful and frets against the Lord." Unfortunately, this verse describes a lot of us. We go about thinking, saying, and doing our own thing, but when the consequences come about, we get upset with God.

In Luke 8:5-15, Jesus tells a parable about a seed. In it He explains that the Word of God is the seed. He says, "But as for that [seed] in the good soil, these are [the people] who hearing the Word, hold it fast in a just (noble, virtuous) and worthy heart, and steadily bring forth fruit with patience (v 15)." Jesus is explaining how to reap a harvest that brings forth fruit. In this case, the Word is heard, held onto, planted, and watered with prayer. So, if you or I are interested in reaping a harvest for good, we must take the Word of God into our hearts, obey it, believe it, and say it out loud as we hold it above any trial or circumstance we face. Remember the importance of praying God's Word? Isaiah 62:6 says, "Put the Lord in remembrance [of His promises], keep not silence." Likewise, John 15:7 says, "If you live in Me [abide vitally united to Me] and My words remain in you and continue to live in your hearts, ask whatever you will, and it shall be done for you."

Again, we can either reap a good harvest for our lives, or we can reap a not-so-good harvest for our lives. Regardless, we will reap something.

If we are interested in reaping a good harvest,
we must take the Word of God into our hearts,
obey it, believe it, and say it out loud
as we hold it above any trial or circumstance we face.

Let's consider those who go through trials and do not understand why. Maybe they are godly, and lead godly lives. What about them? What are these people supposed to do or think? Let's take a look at the life of Job. Other than Christ, he went through the most horrific trials endured by man. Job was a man of God. He feared Him, was blameless in His sight, and shunned evil. (See Job 1:1.) He was wealthy and obtained much land and animals. He was so wealthy, in fact, that he was viewed as the greatest man in all the land.

However, Satan accused Job of simply loving God because it was easy… because Job had acquired such great wealth. That's when God, in His infinite wisdom, allowed the enemy to wreak havoc on Job's life. Job lost his children and all his animals. He was covered from head to toe with grotesque and painful sores, and his wife told him to curse God and die! (See Job chapters 1-2). Yet Job responded to his wife with these words: "You *speak* as one of the impious and foolish women would speak. What? Shall we accept (only) good at the hand of God and shall we not accept (also) misfortune and what is of a bad nature?' *In (spite of) all this, Job did not sin with his lips* (Job 2:10)."

Oh yeah, then along came Job's three friends who accused him of harboring sin in his life! Truly, the man faced many trials of different kinds. Even so, he never blamed, or accused God. He never let his feelings cause him to act unbecomingly. Rather, Job remained faithful and full of praise all the days of his life. We find it in Job 19:25 when he said, "For I know that my Redeemer and Vindicator lives, and at last he will stand upon the earth!" Job believed that God would take care *of* him despite what was happening *to* him. He rested in God's hands and waited for His Redeemer and Vindicator! Finally, at the end of the book, (see chapter 42), Job got his vindication; he forgave his friends and was restored double of what was lost. God used Job's trial to bring him redemption, renewal, and restoration.

Job believed that God would take care *of* him
despite what was happening *to* him.

Just like Job, we need to:

- Believe that no matter what we are facing, God knows and understands.
- Keep believing in Him, by keeping our minds, mouths, attitudes, and actions in line with His.
- Continue going about our days overcoming evil and doing good.
- Wait on God's timing to redeem us from the trial.
- Watch God's blessings come.

First Peter 4:12-13 says,

> Beloved, do not be amazed and bewildered at the fiery ordeal which is taking
> place *to test your quality,* as though something strange (unusual and alien
> to you and your position) were befalling you. But insofar as you are sharing
> Christ's sufferings, *rejoice,* so that when His glory [full of radiance and
> splendor] is revealed, you may also rejoice with triumph [exultantly].

These verses tell us:

- We should not be surprised when we face trials.
- God uses the difficulties we face to reveal, test, and strengthen the quality of our characters.
- As we follow God's ways, we are going to suffer, so rejoice!
- His glory, (His excellence and provisions) will be revealed through us *if* we do not give up on Him during the trial.

When we are in the midst of a trial which seems to offer no way out, God's glory is revealed when He provides an open door! When others see it they believe because they understand there was no human way possible for rescue and deliverance apart from God's intervention. However, in the meantime, Satan will do everything he can to cause us to give up. Remember, John 10:10, tells us the thief comes only to kill, steal, and destroy. Therefore, if we give up during our times of trial, we are choosing to side with the enemy. *When we choose to give up, we renounce our belief in God.* We are essentially saying, "Devil, I guess you're right, God isn't big enough to handle this problem, I'm choosing to place no confidence in Him. I'll have to try and handle this situation myself." Of course, this sounds ridiculous, but it's exactly what many of us choose to do!

Remember, without the inspiration and help of the Holy Spirit combined together with the power of God's living Word, we are no match against Satan. Yes, there really are devils. Their job is to torment you and try to cause you to give up. They want to control you and steal the life and faith that God has given you. As believers, we must fight off any attack from Satan with God's Word just as Jesus did. When Satan tempted Him, Jesus replied, "It is written . . ." (See Luke chapter 4.) Truly, no matter what our circumstances may indicate, God is able. We must choose to place our confidence in Him! Let's do this! Let's choose to invite God's Holy Spirit into our situation. Let's allow Him to guide our thoughts, words, attitudes, and actions with His Word.

**Remember, without the inspiration and help of
the Holy Spirit combined together with the power
of God's living Word, we are no match against Satan.**

First Peter 1:5-7 tells us this,

> *You* Who are being guarded (garrisoned) by God's power through [your]
> faith [till you fully inherit that final] salvation that is ready to be revealed
> [for you] in the last time. [You should] be exceedingly glad on this account,*

though now for a little while you may be distressed by trials and suffer temptations, *so that [the genuineness] of your faith may be tested, [your faith] which is infinitely more precious than the perishable gold which is tested and purified by fire.* [This proving of your faith is intended] to redound to [your] praise and glory and honor when Jesus Christ (the Messiah, the Anointed One) is revealed.

These verses reveal some wonderful promises. We must realize that:

- We are guarded by God's power! He is our keeper!
- His power comes to us by His grace through our faith (belief) in Him!
- Because of the trial and our belief in God's ability, we should be glad.
- The reality of our belief in God is put to the test, and we are tempted to quit and give in. We will always be tempted to believe what we see and feel from our physical senses, instead of believing that God is able to rescue, deliver and bless us.
- Our belief in God is precious. Our blessings from God come through His grace and our belief that He has provided for us. Our faith—confidence and belief in God—becomes pure, genuine, and strong through trials.
- Our love and confidence in Christ grows because He shows Himself faithful.

God has put His resurrected power inside of us. Think about that! The power that God exerted when He raised Christ from the dead now lives in every believer. Wow!

God desires to save, heal, deliver, and bless us—always. As such, we need to learn how to align our minds, our wills, our emotions, our words, and our attitudes with these blessings that He has *already* provided for us through the finished work of the cross!

God intentionally uses trials to increase our faith. He desires for us to be faithful to Him in the good times as well as in the difficult times of our lives—just as Job did. And just like Job, we must not use our lips to sin against God or negate our faith. Instead, we must use our lips to proclaim the promises of God. When we do so, the blessings already deposited in our spirit become real to our physical bodies. On the other hand, Satan will try to use our trials to decrease our faith. He wants you to live according to what you see and how you feel. He tries to make you focus on your circumstances, a negative report, a negative friend, or whatever else he can find, so that you will look at your situation with your physical eyes and proclaim hopelessness.

God's Word says that our tongues hold the power of life or death. We are to choose life by aligning our souls (minds, wills, emotions, and attitudes) to God's Word and the Holy Spirit. (See Proverbs 18:21 and Deuteronomy 30:19.)

If our circumstances were always bearable and we never experienced trials and tests and temptations, we would never really know how to call on or trust in Jesus. We would not be able to know and witness firsthand His resurrected power alive in us. Don't buy into the devil's ways when you are in the midst of a fiery ordeal; instead, set your face like flint, dig in your heels, and verbally express your confidence in God. This will allow your confidence and faith in God to grow. It will help you realize that His grace (undeserved favor, kindness, mercy, and power) is sufficient.

Let's look at some verses that speak about God's purpose for grace and faith:

- Second Corinthians 12:9-10 says, "But He said to me, My grace (My favor and lov-ing-kindness and mercy) is enough for you [sufficient against any danger and enables you to bear the trouble manfully]; for *My* strength *and* power are made perfect (fulfilled and completed) *and* show themselves most effective in [your] weakness. Therefore, I will all the more gladly glory in my weaknesses and infirmities, that the strength and power of Christ (the Messiah) may rest (yes, may pitch a tent over and dwell) upon me! So for the sake of Christ, I am well pleased and take pleasure in infirmities, insults, hardships, persecutions, perplexities and distresses; for when I am weak [in human strength], then am I [truly] strong (able, powerful in divine strength)."
- Second Corinthians 8:9 says, "For you are becoming progressively acquainted with and recognizing more strongly and clearly the grace of our Lord Jesus Christ (His kindness, His gracious generosity, His undeserved favor and spiritual blessing), [in] that though He was [so very] rich, yet for your sakes He became [so very] poor, in order that by His poverty you might become enriched (abundantly supplied)."
- Second Corinthians 9:8 states, "And God is able to make all grace (every favor and earthly blessing) come to you in abundance, so that you may always under all circum-stances and whatever the need be self-sufficient [possessing enough to require no aid or support and furnished in abundance for every good work and charitable donation]."
- Romans 5:2 says, "Through Him, also we have [our] access (entrance, introduction) by faith into this grace (state of God's favor, empowerment, mercy and kindness*) in which we [firmly and safely] stand. And let us rejoice and exult in our hope of expe-riencing and enjoying the glory of God."
- Romans 10:17 tells us, "Faith comes by hearing [what is told] and what is heard comes by the preaching [of the message that came from the lips] of Christ (the Messiah Himself)."
- Romans 10:9 states, "Because if you acknowledge and confess with your lips that Jesus is Lord and in your heart believe (adhere to, trust in, and rely on the truth) that God raised Him from the dead, you will be saved, (rescued, forgiven, delivered, healed, and blessed)*"
- 2 Peter 1:5-8 says, "For this very reason, adding your diligence [to the divine prom-ises], *employ every effort in exercising your faith* to develop virtue (excellence, resolu-tion, Christian energy), and in [exercising] virtue [develop] knowledge (intelligence). And in [exercising] knowledge [develop] self-control, and in [exercising] self-con-trol [develop] steadfastness (patience, endurance), and in [exercising] steadfastness [develop] godliness (piety). And in [exercising] godliness [develop] brotherly affec-tion [develop] Christian love. For as these qualities are yours and increasingly abound in you they will keep [you] from being idle or unfruitful unto the [full personal] knowl-edge of our Lord Jesus Christ (the Messiah, the Anointed One)."

Our very lives, and the lives of others, depend on two things: God's grace, and our faith in God's ability to redeem, renew, and restore us to His original plan to rule and reign on earth.

This process is set in motion when we take the Holy Spirit's hand and allow Him to walk us *through* our trials. As He teaches us how to walk through adversity, He equips us to help others through the same kind of trials. He uses this to make us more like Jesus. And just like Jesus, the Spirit of God is upon us "to preach the good news to the poor; to announce release to the captives and recovery of sight to the blind, to send forth as delivered those who are oppressed who are downtrodden, bruised, crushed, and broken down by calamity, to proclaim the accepted and acceptable year of the Lord, the day when salvation and the free favors of God profusely abound." (See Luke 4:18.)

With the Spirit of God as our partner, we will always find the Promised Land. Partnering with the enemy, on the other hand, brings us to our demise.

Next time you're in a fiery trial and don't understand why, do this:

1. Believe that God is able . . . He said, "I Am!"
2. Partner with God's Spirit.
3. Pray, obey, and speak God's Word.
4. Hang on and wait on God's timing.
5. Go about overcoming evil with good while you wait for your deliverance.

Questions for Study
1. What does a trial reveal about a person?
2. When facing a trial the enemy encourages us to _____. God encourages us to _____ it.
3. What was the point of Job's trial?
4. When we are in a trial and there seems to be no way out, how is God's glory revealed?
5. According to 1 Peter 1:5-7, what do we need to realize?
6. What are God's intentions for our trials? What is the enemy's intention? Whose team are you on?
7. The next time you are in a fiery trial and don't understand why, what should you do?
8. Look up Hebrews 4:3 and write out the promise.

Personal Prayer
Lord, I know that You will test my faith in order to refine me (1 Peter 5:7). During times of trial, help me not to run or cower in fear, but to keep on doing what is right, and build endurance despite my circumstances. Enlarge my faith, and cause my love for others to grow even greater (2 Thessalonians 1:3-4). Job, whose circumstances were horrific, never sinned against You with his lips (Job 2:10). Let that be an example to me. As I walk through very trying circumstances, help me to keep my mind and mouth in harmony with You, the solution, while casting my problems to Your care. Forgive me for the times that I have worried instead of worshipping. Help me to remember that Satan uses the trials in my life to cause me to give up and quit, but You use trials to increase my faith. Lord, I will set my face like flint, dig in my heels, and express my confidence in You. Your Word says that faith comes by hearing, and what is heard comes by speaking the message (Romans 10:17). Cause me to speak Your Word in order to encourage myself, especially when I am faced with a trial (1 Samuel 30:6). Thank You that Your grace (favor, kindness, mercy, and empowerment) is sufficient for me; 2 Corinthians 9:8).

Chapter 38

The Purpose
and Power of Prayer

❧

W hy is praying the last thing we do instead of the first? Perhaps the answer stems
from one of many misconceptions regarding prayer. In essence, the proper role of
prayer is widely misunderstood. Believers often view prayer as something we *must do* instead
of something we *get to do!* When we feel as if prayer is a duty or obligation, we show that we
really don't understand all that is available to us and others through prayer. We need God's
Word to renew our minds regarding prayer. As His ambassadors on earth, we have the privilege
of inviting Almighty God into our own situations, and into the circumstances of other people's
lives. Think about that!

Many times, however, we choose to grumble, complain, and let our emotions lead us rather
than going straight to the Source and Giver of all life. It seems that we, the body of Christ,
understand that we are the hands and feet of God on earth. Still we struggle with becoming His
mind, mouth, eyes, and ears as well. This is the purpose of prayer. How can we be the effective hands and feet of God, going about doing His work, if we do not understand how He sees,
hears, thinks, and speaks? The Word of God tells us that we have the mind of Christ. (See 1
Corinthians 2:16.) Therefore, we have the ability to view situations as He does, empowered by
God's grace, and the leading of the Holy Spirit, *if* we believe it's available to us.

The Bible tells us that our thoughts will be revealed through our words (Matthew 12:34).
Just think what would happen if more of us spoke the truth about having the mind of Christ and
possessing His power on earth to go and do greater things than He did. How can we expect to
do the work of the Great Commission if we don't believe we can? (See Mark 16:15-18.) How
can we do His work if we're not praying God's Word that empowers us with His grace to do so?

**As His ambassadors on earth,
we have the privilege of inviting
Almighty God into our own situations,
and into the circumstances of other people's lives.
Think about that.**

More than anything, I believe that we pray out of ignorance to God's Word and all that He has *already* placed inside of us. Many times we pray for God to work in us, another person, or situation, but we fail to do our part, believing and tapping into the grace He has given us through His Word and Spirit. Perhaps we pray to God and then speak negatively about everything we just prayed for. With words as our seeds, oftentimes we go about planting life seeds through prayer. Then, we walk behind these seeds and spray them with poison through our grumbling, complaining, faultfinding, negative thoughts, and conversations about the situation. If we are to become effective ambassadors on this earth, we must learn to remain focused on and connected to our Heavenly Father through prayer. All too often, though, we focus on our personhood and all of our inadequacies instead of God's grace, favor, ability, efficiency, might, and power. This is the power He has made available to us through His grace and His Holy Spirit.

Let's take a look at the definition of prayer: According to Vine's dictionary, *prayer* means to ask, to request a desire, or a need.[1] Prayer is open communication with God; constantly *speaking* and *listening* to God. Picture a refrigerator. Without an electrical outlet, it is worthless. We all know that refrigerators need to be plugged into a power source if they are to work effectively and keep food fresh. In like manner, we operate just as refrigerators do. We need to:

1. Be plugged into the Holy Spirit—our power source.
2. Tap into God's grace, His readymade power that's available to us through prayer, faith, and His Word. This is how the fruit of the Spirit and everything that God has placed inside of us pertaining to life and godliness remains fresh and usable.

Consider this thought: What would happen to us (as refrigerators) if we were plugged into an outlet three days a week? Obviously, that doesn't make sense because a refrigerator needs to be plugged in at all times. Otherwise, it won't take long for the food in the refrigerator to spoil. Why then, should we think that we can only be plugged into God when we go to church once or twice a week? James 5:16 says this very thing.

> Confess to one another therefore your faults (your slips, your false steps, your offenses, your sins) and pray [also] for one another, that you may be healed and restored [to a spiritual tone of mind and heart]. The earnest (heartfelt, continued) prayer of a righteous man makes tremendous power available [dynamic in its working].

What is this verse saying to us?

- *Confess* your sins to one another (starting with God). Be willing to share your sins and struggles with others *as God so leads you*. It's not necessary to reveal all of your personal sins to whomever. If you simply start with God, He will direct you from there. Confession is a big part of prayer. It allows us to unload our sins by admitting them.
- It's also important to *confess what's "right"* about us and about God's greatness. For example, after you confess your sins, you need to shut the door on guilt and condemnation, because Christ's sacrifice on the cross and His shed blood has cleansed you of your sin. Now, you must confess your righteousness. That is your "right" standing with God. You say what God says about you; "God, I believe that I'm Your child; I have right standing with You; when You look at me You see Jesus! I'm covered by You.

I'm approved and accepted by You. I live in You; I'm one with You. Thank You for choosing me. Thank You for Your forgiveness, rescue, deliverance, healing, wholeness, prosperity, and blessings for me. And thank You that there is no more guilt, shame, and condemnation for me because I am in Christ." Wow! Isn't it uplifting to remind yourself what God says about you?!

- *Pray* for one another, that we may be healed and restored (to a spiritual tone of mind and heart). We must pray God's Word over other people (whether they are present with us or not). This brings healing and restoration to our minds, hearts, thoughts, words, attitudes, and actions. It aligns us to Christ rather than on our own inadequacies.

When we harbor sin in our lives, our relationship with God is out of whack. Therefore, we cut off and block the flow of the Holy Spirit into and out of our lives. Notice that the prayer that God wants is for the healing and restoration of our minds and hearts. It's not about begging God to return us to our own comfort zones. God wants to heal and transform our eyes, ears, minds, mouths, and hearts and make them like His. He wants to show us His perspective regarding a situation and then use us to bring His grace, mercy, and power to the aid of those needing rescue.

Quite often we are more concerned with "getting on with our life" than we are with God's revelation of Himself to us. This makes our communication with God one-sided and selfish. When we treat Him like our personal "genie," we forget that we are actually *His* servants. As harsh as this may sound, this kind of attitude does not reveal the heart of a person desiring relationship. To be sure, we need to make our requests known to Him, but I believe many times we are making the wrong requests. We should be asking for eyes, ears, hearts, minds, and mouths that will portray the beauty of His character in us. Truthfully, God desires to heal the inner man, and as we receive and release that healing inside of us, the outer portion will naturally follow.

The earnest, heartfelt, continuous prayer of a righteous man makes tremendous power available that is dynamic in its working. Affective, fervent, and earnest prayer is not about *begging* God. Rather, it's about *believing* that He is able to rescue and deliver us—no matter what, when He so chooses. Our first prayer to God should always be, "God, how do you desire to change me through this situation?" Unfortunately, we don't like this process of changing and waiting—we want God to change everything else except us. Remember, the spirit is willing, but the flesh is weak. (See Mark 14:38.)

Our first prayer to God should always be, "God how do you desire to change me through this situation?"

A righteous man is one who enjoys right standing with God in all areas of life, and lives as such. That is why it is so extremely important to know all that you possess in Christ and to remain constantly connected to Him. This allows Him to clean out and align our souls with His. It prevents us from blocking the flow of His power into and out of our lives. When we harbor the "crud" of unforgiveness, bitterness, resentment, bad attitudes, negative mindsets, and words apart from God's, we eliminate His grace (power, kindness, and favor) from working in our lives. We find ourselves in agreement with the enemy instead. As partners with Christ, He chooses to work through grace, faith, holiness, and purity. Therefore, truly good works come from clean thoughts, words, attitudes, and behaviors.

Remember the refrigerator? Every time we choose to harbor the previously mentioned "crud" in our lives, we literally unplug ourselves from God's power, and we will soon spoil and stink. That's hardly what we want to show to a world that is in desperate need of Jesus. When we're living "unplugged" lives, we're choosing to be branches separated from the Vine and we sever our very lifeline, hindering others from seeing God in us.

Ephesians 6:18 says, "Pray at all times (on every occasion, in every season) in the Spirit, with all [manner of] prayer and entreaty. To that end keep alert and watch with strong purpose and perseverance, interceding in behalf of all the saints (God's consecrated people)."

The concept of praying at all times confuses many Christians. Obviously, God knows that we cannot be literally praying all the time, so what does it mean? I believe that as God's ambassadors on earth, we are to always be mindful of our role and as such, are to live in a constant attitude of prayer. This means that when we see a situation, our first response is to invite God's power to intervene. Instead of analyzing the situation only with our eyes and minds, we need to ask the Holy Spirit for His help as we pray about it. Then as we begin to pray, He will utter His desires through us. This is how we bring God's will to earth. We must align our hearts, minds, eyes, ears and speech with Christ's so we can go about doing what the Spirit leads us to do. As we team up with Him in this way, supernatural power (grace) is released through our unity with Him (faith). As branches are resting and connected to its Vine, and a refrigerator is connected to an outlet, so must our faith be resting in and connected to Christ's ability and grace.

We are told to "keep alert and watch with strong purpose and perseverance," especially for other believers. It's easy to become complacent and lazy in our prayer lives. Such laziness, however makes us and others vulnerable to Satan's attacks. Remember, we are called to be alert and to watch out for our brothers. But the kind of alertness and watch that we are asked to keep comes only through our power source—the Holy Spirit. This is why we must remain constantly plugged into Him—so that we are available for God's use. Persevering in prayer and never giving up on a person or situation is the key to living victoriously here on earth. As believers, it is necessary to stand in the gap and pray for others to come through any ordeal.

Prayer is not limited to the position of the believer on his knees. Assuredly, this is an appropriate position and one we should assume regularly, but prayer is simply an open conversation with God regarding all things. The words we pray don't have to be fancy, long, or religious sounding. They just need to be simple and sincere. Be sure to set time apart and become available to listen to God's heart through His communicated Word, the Bible. This is how we have a two-sided conversation with the Lord Jesus Christ, both parties speaking and listening.

Questions for Study
1. After reading this lesson, have you come to realize some of your misconceptions regarding prayer?
2. Do you understand that, as a believer, you are not only the hands and feet of the Lord, but also the mind, mouth, eyes, and ears of the Lord? Where have you struggled in this area?
3. How "plugged in" to communicating with God are you?
4. Ask God to renew, change and enlighten your mind and to reveal His mind and heart to you. Then spend time listening by reading and studying His Word. (Remember, the thought and measure that you give to the studying the Word is the measure that will come back to you. See Mark 4:24.)
5. Explain in your own words what effective, fervent, and earnest prayer is.
6. When we see a situation or become involved in one, what should our first response be?

Personal Prayer

Lord, forgive me for the times that I have not prayed for Your intervention in a situation. Forgive me for the times I have chosen to speak my own words of criticism, judgment, and complaint instead. I realize, as Your ambassador on this earth, I have the privilege of inviting You into every situation; please remind me of this! I don't want to hinder Your work on earth I want to help it! Please remove any sin in my life that may be cutting off the flow of the Holy Spirit into and out of my life. Your Word says that the earnest, heartfelt, continued prayer of a righteous person makes tremendous power available and is dynamic in its working (James 5:16). Lord, I desire this power in my life. Thank You that I have right standing with You! Help me, Lord, to be prepared to pray in the Spirit at all times, as the occasion arises (Ephesians 6:18). Teach me how to remain in Your presence all day long, as I go about my life. I know that I am not only the hands and feet of Christ, but the mind, mouth, eyes, and ears of Christ as well. Let that be developed and seen in my life. Please strengthen my union and communion with You, Lord, and let my life become a constant prayer (Ephesians 6:10).

Chapter 39

The Lord's Prayer
—Our Example

⁕

When we pray, we open the door for God to work in a given situation on someone's behalf—whether our own or someone else's. As ambassadors and partners with God, we represent Him on this earth. I mentioned in the previous chapter, that many believers understand that we are God's hands and feet, but we struggle to see ourselves as ambassadors of His mind, mouth, eyes, and ears. It's a principle we don't often consider.

In order to see God execute His will on earth as He does in Heaven, however, we must treat Jesus as the Commander in Chief that He is, the King of our lives. Far too often as Christians, we express our own opinions, our own feelings, and our own desires rather than seeking the thoughts and intentions of God's heart. How can we go about seeing, thinking, hearing, speaking, and doing good deeds all day when we have not met with our Commander? We certainly wouldn't walk into our job each day and do our own thing. If we did, we probably wouldn't be there for long. Obviously, at work we do what our boss requires whether we feel like it or not. We should have this same attitude about doing the will of our loving Father in Heaven.

Yet, if we are going to do God's will, we must spend time with Him first so that we understand His heart and His mission for us each day. Why is it that we think nothing of breaking our commitment with our Commander in Chief each morning, but we would never think of failing to fulfill a requirement at work? I believe this shows our true heart's condition before God. It's something of which we need to repent of if we are to carry out His will. We must start approaching Jesus as if He is our true lifeline. The more we understand about His coming to earth and showing us how to live our lives through His life by crucifying our old nature and rising into our new nature, the more we will understand our purpose to imitate not only His actions, but to grasp the intentions of His heart and meaning of His words. Prayer does exactly that: it crucifies our thoughts, words, attitudes, and actions that don't agree with His. It makes known His thoughts and intentions. As we pray God's Word, we invite His grace, empowerment, mercy, kindness, gifts, and favor into our daily lives and into the lives of others. His purpose is to fill everyone and everything with Himself!

In Matthew 6:9-13, Jesus teaches us how we are to pray.

> Pray, therefore, like this: Our Father Who is in heaven, hallowed (kept holy) be your name. Your kingdom come, your will be done on earth as it is in heaven. Give us this day our daily bread, and forgive us our debts, as we also have forgiven (left, remitted, and let go of the debts, and have given up resentment against) our debtors. And lead (bring) us not into temptation, but deliver us from the evil one. *For yours is the kingdom and the power and the glory forever.*

Within these few verses, Jesus teaches us many things. Here are a few observations:

1. Simple prayer is the best prayer. In fact, in verse 7, Jesus tells us not to heap on phrases thinking that we will be heard because of our lengthy speaking.
2. Praise and adoration are an important part of prayer. It causes us to focus on Christ. Jesus starts out His prayer by praising God His Father, recognizing His greatness and authority in all things.
3. God's will is the ultimate good. Jesus says, "Your kingdom come, your will be done on earth as it is in Heaven." When He says, "*Your kingdom come,*" Jesus expresses His desire for God's way and His economy to come and rule. As believers, we have the kingdom of God living inside of us to rule over our entire being—spirit, soul, and body. I believe Jesus' next phrase states this truth. He says, "*Your will be done on earth as it is in Heaven.*" Jesus is teaching us to pray that God's will, and God's ways, be done on earth, just as they are in Heaven. If God's will is to be done on earth, it must occur through us since we are His ambassadors and the representatives of His kingdom. God's economy and His ways will be accomplished through us as we partner with His Holy Spirit, submit our wills, ways, eyes, ears, hearts, minds, attitudes, actions, and strength to His, and acknowledge our belief in Him, what He has done, and His ability to bring it to pass.
4. God wants us to express our needs. When Jesus says, "*Give us this day our daily bread,*" He, of course, knows what we need before we even ask. But as His partners, we need to have constant and direct communication with Him in order for the relationship to grow. Hebrews 4:16 reminds us that we have a partner who wants us to come boldly to His throne of grace (empowerment, favor, mercy, and kindness) and ask for His help. It says we are to do this understanding and believing that He is able to provide whatever we need. This means spiritually, physically, emotionally, financially—in every area. In the physical realm, if we do not feed our bodies food over an extended period of time, we will die. The same is true with our spiritual lives.

Most people eat at least three times a day; just think what our lives would be if we "ate" the fruit and life of God's Word three times a day. Unfortunately, many Christians think they can eat from God's Word once a week at church on Sunday and expect to make it. If this describes you, you are in danger of starving your spirit to death. It will affect the health of your soul and body, and ultimately those around you. The harsh reality is this: if we don't renew our minds with God's Word, letting Him change how we think, we won't change and our circumstances won't either. In fact, things will only worsen. We all must be purposeful to make an appointment every day to meet with God and to eat of His bread—the life of Jesus—just as we physically partake of a meal.

5. Confession is critical to prayer. *"And forgive us our debts,"* tells us that we must admit our sins and ask for forgiveness. It's a daily releasing and cleansing that we get to participate in. As we meet with Jesus each day, we ask the Holy Spirit to reveal any hidden sin in our lives. Remember that sin and pride hide. Quite often, if we do not ask the Holy Spirit for His help with this, we will remain blind to our sin. If sin is lodged within us, we block the flow of God's grace from coming into and out of our lives. Sin also prevents us from hearing God's voice. It clogs our souls, hindering us from receiving the light coming from within our spirits.

> **Sin prevents us from hearing God's voice.**
> **It clogs our souls, hindering us from receiving**
> **the light coming from within our spirits.**

6. Forgiving is a key! *"As we have forgiven our debtors."* Forgiving people who have offended or wronged us is one of the most important acts we can do for ourselves and for others. It is also one of the hardest because our flesh wants to hang on to offenses and keep the offender(s) indebted to us. This attitude opposes God's Word. Jesus tells us to forgive, let go of, and give up resentment. Remember this: when God asks us to give something up, it's because He wants to bless us. He cannot bless a person who is harboring unforgiveness and resentment in their life. We cannot be "in faith" if we're constantly "in strife" with others. Faith works through love, and love is the force connected to the power of God's grace. Forgiveness keeps our "pipeline" of God's empowerment into our lives open. Forgiveness is a choice. We are told to forgive whether we feel like it or not. It's especially difficult when we feel justified in hanging on to the offense. However, this is a very dangerous mindset, one that lies in agreement with the enemy rather than God. If we harbor unforgiveness in our lives, we become focused on the wrong that was committed against us instead of on Christ living in us and our hope of seeing His glory.

7. Prayer and fasting allows us to seek God's help in exercising self-control. Jesus tells us to get control of our souls when He says, *"lead us not into temptation."* For when we are governed by our soul (what we want, think, and feel) and our physical senses (what we see, hear, touch, smell, and taste), we are not allowing God's Spirit to govern us. Each time we face a situation, and we are tempted to handle it on our own rather than with the Holy Spirit's help, Jesus wants us to get control of ourselves and submit our way to the Father's. It amazes me that Jesus never speaks of His own accord; but only that which the Father tells Him. (See John 14:10.) Wow . . . can you imagine that?! As believers, we are called to that kind of obedience, too. Now think of Jesus when He was led by the Spirit into the desert, and the devil tempted Him several times. Satan used food as one of the temptations because Jesus was fasting and was obviously hungry. Jesus could have given in to the temptation to turn the stones into bread in order to fulfill His physical need, but Jesus did not. In fact, every time the devil tempted Jesus to fill a legitimate physical need, Jesus answered him with, three words

followed by Scripture. "It is written . . .," He said as He attacked the devil with a verse from the Bible.

In like manner, when we are tempted to give in to our flesh, we are to fight the temptation with God's Word. Remember, God's Word, rooted in our hearts and coming out of our mouths, is the two-edged sword that defeats the enemy every time he attempts to derail us. Fasting, on the other hand, is designed to deny our physical senses the authority to rule over our emotions and actions. Jesus did this perfectly. Once again, when we are asked to give up our way for His, it is always so He can bless us. Part of that blessing will cause us to rise above the situation at hand.

> **When we are asked by God to give up our way for His,**
> **it is always so He can bless us. Part of that blessing**
> **will cause us to rise above the situation at hand.**

8. God's glory is the goal! *"For yours is the kingdom and the power and the glory forever."* This is a confession that God's ways are the best. It's a statement that the Father's ways should have dominion in our hearts. Then our entire beings will display who Jesus is. Starting with the entire renewing of our minds and mouths, we can literally exchange our thoughts and words for His, opening the eyes and ears of our hearts and working out His grace to our hands and feet. When we allow Him to reign in our lives, others around us can see the power, ability, efficiency, and might that He placed inside of us. It will in turn, cause them to hunger and thirst for Him. This is the glory and purpose of our being. Period.

9. Finally, Jesus says in verse six, "But when you pray, go into your [most] private room, and, closing the door, pray to your Father, Who is in secret; and your Father, Who sees in secret, will reward you *in the open*." It is so important to close out the noise of the world before we enter into the world each day. Jesus had to practice this, too. In Mark 5:39-42, Jesus was asked to heal a sick girl, but the girl dies while He was on His way to her house. When the news reached Jesus and His fellow travelers, He said, "the little girl is not dead but is sleeping." (See verse 39.) The very next verse says, "And they laughed and jeered at Him. *But He put them all out.*" When you and I pray and dare to believe Jesus, we will be laughed and jeered at by the world. We too, must "put them all out." Truly, if you are a believer, prayer is neither an option nor a duty. Rather it's a privilege to invite the all-knowing, all-empowering God of the universe into our own personal lives. As we pray, we close the door on the enemy and choose to shut out his ways. We submit to God as we speak forth His Word into our situations. Prayer is designed for us to *consult with Him* before we reason with our futile minds in an attempt to "do" something. Unfortunately, many times we choose to go ahead and reason, do, and then consult. Remember, Mathew 6:6 says, *"When you pray . . ."* not, *"If you pray."*

I'd like to share a personal and practical experience that happened to me a few years ago. Believe me when I say that I've failed many times by expressing my own thoughts instead of God's. On this particular day, however, I (we) got it right. My family and I, along with my sister and niece, were headed to the beach for vacation. We spent the night in a hotel before reaching our destination. The following morning, as we approached our car, we noticed that one of the windows had been smashed in. Needless to say, we had been robbed. Our kids were upset about losing some of their favorite things. We all were. But I had spent time with God that morning, and because of that, I believe His love took over my mind and actions. He caused me not to give in to my anger or to express it through my words. I told the children that things could be replaced, but that we should pray for the people or person who had done this harmful deed.

Then I started cleaning up the shattered glass. As I did so, however, I saw our children and my niece out of the corner of my eye. They were standing in the grass, holding hands, and praying for the people or person who committed this crime. I couldn't help but stop what I was doing and go over to them. I remembered the verse in Isaiah 55:11. It says that God's Word does not return void but goes out and accomplishes that which it was sent forth. The children and I talked about how awesome it will be when they get to heaven. We imagined Jesus ushering over the person that did this to us hearing him say, "Thanks, for praying for me. I was the one who broke into your car that day, and because you prayed for me, God began to work in my life—and now I'm here!" Our anger quickly turned into an opportunity to plant seeds of life into whoever had broken into our car. We praised God for counting us faithful that day to think and speak His will, rather than our own. Believe me, in the natural, I would have had a few choice words for this person.

The same can be true in our everyday lives. We can stop and pray for the mom in the grocery store with the unruly child, or for the man who looks depressed. Whatever the case may be, we can be sure that only God knows the full story behind the face. We can know that He is moved with mercy and compassion. God is more concerned with the consequences and the bondage caused by the sin, than He is with the actual sin. So, rather than speaking about or judging a situation from our own perspectives, we need to put on mercy and compassion. We can take the high road and pray! . . . Just like Jesus.

**Rather than speaking about or judging a situation from
our own perspective, we need to put on mercy and compassion.
We can take the high road and pray!**

What a privilege we have to pray God's Word. Think about it. *His Word does not return void*. It may take a while for change to occur, but it goes forth and accomplishes that which it was sent forth. Praying God's Word should always be our first choice, whether we feel like it or not. Don't pass up the blessing!

Questions for Study
1. If we desire to do God's will, what must be the first thing we really need to do?
2. What is your true heart's condition before God regarding prayer?
3. Do you treat Jesus as your daily lifeline? If not, what can you do to change this?
4. After reading Matthew 6:9-13, write down any new revelations you received regarding prayer and fasting and why you should pray.
5. Why does Jesus tell us to go into our most private room and close the door when we pray?
6. If you were in a situation similar to ours, headed to the beach for vacation and your things were stolen, how would you have responded? Do you need to ask the Holy Spirit to change you?
7. List some simple ways you can incorporate prayer into your daily life even while at the grocery store!

Personal Prayer

Thank You, Lord, for prayer and for showing me how to pray through Your example (Matthew 6:9-13). Forgive me for the times when I have been more concerned about expressing my own will through prayer, rather than Yours. Help me to get quiet before You, to seek Your heart, then to use Your Word to pray and speak Your heart. I realize that in my life, Your will cannot be done "on earth as it is in Heaven" if I insist on my way of doing things, rather than seeking Yours. Please help me not to be tempted or disobedient in this area, for I know that Your will is absolutely the best. Thank You for giving me the mind of Christ (1 Corinthians 2:16); please help me to be discerning in my prayers. Your Word says that I am to be anxious for nothing, but in everything by prayer and supplication with thanksgiving, I am to make my requests known to You (Philippians 4:6). Help me to rejoice in You always, and may my spirit be gentle (reasonable, fair-minded, and charitable) so that all people may see You in me. Thank You for being near to this kind of behavior (Philippians 4:4-5). I realize that You desire for me to come boldly to Your throne with great reverence, and to ask for Your help (Hebrews 4:16). Lord, I ask Your Holy Spirit to remind me to do so at all times throughout the day. Cause me to become completely connected to You through simple, prayerful conversation all day long. For Yours is the kingdom and the power and the glory forever! (Matthew 6:13).

Chapter 40

Praising God,
No Matter What!

A mazing things happen when we praise God. When we praise Him, He blesses and uplifts us. When we truly praise God, we also encourage others. As with prayer, however, many Christians hold misconceptions about how and when we are to praise God. It's more than merely singing songs in church once a week. We need to incorporate praising God into our everyday lives. It doesn't matter what we're doing or what is happening to us, we can choose to praise God anywhere! It's up to us, though, to take the time to praise Him. Whether we're walking down a hallway at work or school, or doing laundry at home, we can choose to praise Him!

When we worship God, we open the door for Him. We need to make worship the ongoing attitude of our hearts regardless of the situations and problems we encounter. For many of us, the Holy Spirit has a lot of work to do when it comes to praising God. Unfortunately, all too often, we choose to grumble and complain, opening the door for Satan to work. We absolutely need the help and the gentle nudging of the Holy Spirit in this area, and we need to listen to Him when He speaks to us.

**We need to make worship the ongoing attitude
of our hearts regardless of the situations
and problems we encounter.**

Partnering with God's Spirit is the only thing that will usher in this change. Zechariah 4:6 says, "For it is not by might nor by power, but by My Spirit, says the Lord." I am reminded again of Jesus only speaking that which His Father told Him to speak. (See John 14:10.) Without a doubt, when we pause and praise God, we reaffirm our belief in Him, and we shut out Satan's noise, especially when our situations might lead us to think otherwise.

Let's take a look at some of the things that happens when we praise God despite our circumstances:

Praising God releases power in our inner being. When we praise God, His glory and His presence emanates from us, strengthening and reinforcing His mighty power within us. Ephesians 3:16 says, "May He grant you out of the rich treasury of His glory to be strengthened and reinforced with mighty power in the inner man by the [Holy] Spirit [Himself indwelling your innermost being and personality]." When we praise God, we shut out the enemy. Our willingness to praise God affects how we establish the mind and mouth of Jesus Christ here on earth. Psalm 100:1 says this, "Make a joyful noise to the Lord, all you lands!"

Praising God releases joy into our lives. Nehemiah 8:10 says the joy of the Lord is our strength! Not a complaint or a grumble, but a joyful noise. Verse two of Psalm 100 tells us to, "Serve the Lord with gladness! Come before His presence with singing!" I admit, many times I have come before Him with my complaining instead of with singing. As a parent, if my children only came to me to complain, I'm not sure how often I'd want them to come around! Isaiah 61:3 says, "Put on the garment of praise for the spirit of heaviness!" Psalm 66:13-14 says, "I will come into your house with burnt offerings [of entire consecration]; *I will* pay you my vows, which my lips uttered and my mouth promised *when I was in distress*."

Praising God eliminates depression and fills us with gratitude. When we have grateful hearts, depression lifts from our face and from our lives. Gratitude and depression live at opposite ends of the spectrum. Truthfully, we don't feel like praising God in the midst of a trial. But, *we must deprive our flesh of doing what if feels like and submit our way to the Holy Spirit! We do this by obeying the Word and saying it, too.*

When we obey God's Word, we praise Him. It is the right thing to do, *especially* when we don't "feel" like it! Doing what the Word says is the will of God. He promises to empower us, when we *ask* for His grace and then actually choose to *obey* His Word. Look at what Jesus said in Luke 6:46. "Why do you call Me, Lord, Lord, and *do not [practice] what I tell you?*" Pause and calmly think about that! Psalm 101:1-2 says this, "I will sing of mercy and loving-kindness and justice; to you, O Lord will I sing. *I will behave myself wisely and give heed to the blameless way*—O when will you come to me? *I will walk within my house in integrity and with a blameless heart*." Gratitude, integrity and obedience always open the door for God to work and they close the door on the enemy! Psalm 100:3 says, "Know (perceive, recognize, and understand with approval) that the Lord is God! It is He Who has made us, not we ourselves [and we are His]! We are His people and the sheep of His pasture."

Praising God releases us from our ability and entrusts us to His. This is why it is so important to speak God's Word. In Psalm 2:7, King David said, "I will declare the decree of the Lord!" As we speak His Word, it settles within our inner being, and causes us to believe it. This is also the picture 1 Peter 5:6-7 paints when it says,

> Therefore, humble yourselves [demote, lower yourselves in your own estimation] under the mighty hand of God, that in due time He may exalt you, casting the whole of your care [all your anxieties, all your worries, all your concerns, once and for all] on Him, for He cares for you affectionately and cares about you watchfully.

When we choose to praise God no matter what, we humble ourselves before Him. We entrust our entire situations at hand, to Him. *We cast our cares on Him by praising Him and believing that He is working behind the scenes.* When we do this, we display 1 Peter 5:8-9 which says, "Be well balanced, (temperate, sober of mind) be vigilant and cautious at all times; for that enemy of yours, the devil roams about like a lion roaring [in fierce hunger], seeking someone to seize upon and devour. *Withstand him; be firm in faith . . .*" Praising God not only builds faith, but it releases it, too.

**We cast our cares on Him by praising Him
and believing that He is working behind the scenes.**

Praising God through the storms of life establishes us and creates balance and stability in us. The devil wants the storms in our lives to defeat us. They will if we continue to utter complaints and grumble. Complaining reveals our doubt about God's ability to help. We shut the door to this nonsense by being firm in our faith. Declare your trust in God, and choose to use your lips to praise Him. We must stop uttering what we see and what we feel like talking about and start praising God for the fact that He is able and working in our situations. Romans 8:28 testifies to this fact; "We are *assured* and *know* that [God being a partner in their labor] all things work together and are [fitting into a plan] *for good* to and for those who *love* God and are called according to [His] design and purpose." (Remember, to love God is to obey Him and His ways). As we renew our minds and fill our mouths with God's faith-filled Word, we begin to believe that He is working everything out for our good. Our part is to keep praising Him while we wait for Him to accomplish His work in us and in the situation at hand. First Peter 5:10 attests to this. It says, "And after you have suffered a little while, the God of all grace [Who imparts all blessing and favor], Who has called you to His [own] eternal glory in Christ Jesus, will Himself complete and make you what you ought to be, establish and ground you securely and strengthen, and settle you." When we surrender to Him, He transforms us from complainers into creatures of praise. God is always more concerned with what is going on inside of us than around us! Psalm 100:4 says, "Enter into His gates with thanksgiving and a thank offering and into His courts with praise! Be thankful and say so to Him, bless and affectionately praise His name!"

Praising God blesses the Lord and takes us into His presence. By shutting the door on the enemy and praising God with our mouths, which comes about from a mind set on God's ways, we literally move ourselves into position to receive the blessings that God intends for us. I am certain that if we could see how many times our complaining has closed the door to God's blessings we would be utterly astonished. We must be determined to reverse this course of action in our lives! As His ambassadors, we are not only the hands and feet of Jesus, but we also represent His mind and mouth! Let's determine to use all our faculties for the purpose of His good will in our lives as well as in the lives of others. We must stop focusing on the problems and start talking about and praising God, the Solution!

**We must stop focusing on the problems and
start talking about and praising God, the Solution!**

Praising God opens our hearts to see and experience His goodness, mercy, loving-kindness, faithfulness, and truth. Psalm 100:5 says, "For the Lord is good; His mercy and loving-kindness are everlasting, His faithfulness and truth endure to all generations." When we choose to praise God, we are telling Him we want His way and not our own. At that moment, all of His attributes—and His very presence—start to become very real to us. He Himself empowers us and causes us to overcome the situation and problems we face.

Praising God gives us peace that we cannot possibly understand. Philippians 4:7 says, "And God's peace [shall be yours, that tranquil state of soul assured of its salvation through Christ, and so fearing nothing from God and being content with its earthly lot of whatever sort that is, that peace] which transcends all understanding shall garrison and mount guard over your hearts and minds in Christ Jesus." When we use our lips for God's praise rather than complaining, we activate God's peace in our lives. God's grace does not flow through grumbling and complaining. Ever. His grace flows through faith, trust, kindness, mercy, and compassion.

**When we use our lips for God's praise rather than
complaining, we activate God's peace in our lives.
God's grace will not flow through grumbling and complaining.
Ever.**

Praising God cleanses our inner beings and brings clarity to our lives. Praising God is like taking a hot shower and washing off the day's "scum." 1 Corinthians 14:33 tells us that God is not the author of confusion. When we complain, confusion enters and when we praise, confusion exits. The enemy is the author of confusion. When we choose to praise God, though, we actually create confusion for the enemy, and we thwart his plans for our lives. We distance our minds from the enemy's voice as we praise God and place our trust in Christ. This in turn enables us to see as God sees and hear His direction.

I'll end this chapter with another personal story. I used to dread going to the grocery store, but God has turned my complaining into gratefulness. He has taught me to be thankful for a place where everything I need waits for me on a shelf, and that He's given me the means to buy it! There are many for whom preparing a meal is literally an all-day project, particularly people in Third-World countries. I started using my time in the grocery store to praise God for His wonderful provisions.

You can do the same thing, no matter where you are or what you're doing. Praising God through the things that you dread and fear is the means to overcoming them. Praise God for what He has done for you. Thank Him for what He's given you. Praise Him by focusing on the good. It will change your attitude and ultimately, your life. Let the habit of praise uproot that of complaining. Just think of the power that would be unleashed if we would choose to look at the good and to praise God instead.

Questions for Study

1. How can you incorporate praising God into your everyday life?
2. What is your automatic response when you encounter a difficult or trying situation? Ask God what you might need to alter.
3. When you use your lips to praise, who are you partnering with? When you use your lips to complain, who are you partnering with? Who do you partner with the most?
4. Look over the list of things that praising God does for us. Which one(s) do you need the most? Now ask God–and receive them.
5. Do you have a negative attitude regarding any situation(s) or person(s) in your life right now? In what ways can you choose to look at the good and praise God instead?

Personal Prayer

Lord, help me to incorporate praising You into my everyday life. Whether I'm working, cleaning, cooking, enjoying my husband, playing with the children, coaching, having fun, or struggling with an issue, help me to keep a praising-heart attitude. I know that complaining opens the door for Satan to work, and that praising You opens the door for You to work. Lord, out of the rich treasury of Your glory, and through the Holy Spirit, grant me strength, with might and power in my innermost being and personality (Ephesians 3:16). Lord, as Your Word says, help me to make a joyful noise to You, for the joy of the Lord is my strength! (Psalm 100:1; Nehemiah 8:10). I will trade the spirit of heaviness for the garment of praise. I will come into Your house with the burnt offering of entire consecration to You. I will pay You my vows, which my lips utter and my mouth promises even when I am in distress (Isaiah 61:3; Psalm 66:13-14). Lord, I cast my cares on You, praising You and believing that You are working behind the scenes (1 Peter 5:7; Romans 8:28). Lord, I trust You to establish me as I praise You throughout the storms of life (Romans 5:2-5). Thank You for this peace which surpasses all of my understanding and guards my heart and mind (Philippians 4:7).

Chapter 41

Holiness, Purity,
and
Spiritual Insight

As we develop the habit of praising God, we start to rise to the top, like cream being separated from butter. The closer we come to God and the more we choose to praise Him in our circumstances, the more He reveals Himself to us. Before long, we discover how desperate we really are for His help and how much grace He has already extended to us. Throughout this process, our focus shifts from our impurities to His holiness. The Holy Spirit separates us from our old nature and consecrates us to Christ. Proverbs 27:21 says, "As the refining pot for silver and the furnace for gold [bring forth all the impurities of the metal], so let a man be in his trial of praise [ridding himself of all that is base or insincere; for a man is judged by what he praises and of what he boasts]."

We also begin to realize that we are truly nothing without Him. God never intended for us to manage our own lives. We are called to partner with Him and honor Him in our thoughts, words, and deeds. Our God desires for us to become like Him – holy, pure, and righteous – in your spirit, soul, and body. We can't "work" to obtain what God has already given us. When we partner with God's Spirit and believe what the Word tells us about our identity in Christ and cooperate with Him, He changes us from the inside out. Christ's character and power is manifested in us. When we first come to Christ, He meets us wherever He finds us, even in the middle of our pits. But He loves us too much to let us stay there. He gives us the choice. The Bible tells us to "Be Holy, because I am Holy." (See Leviticus 11:44 and 1 Peter 1:16.) I like to think of this as *becoming* progressively holy in our thoughts, words, attitudes, and actions. Since God told us to be holy, we can be assured that He has provided a way for us to be holy. Our part is to believe in His finished work on the cross, and be in agreement with His Word.

Satan has lied to many people, making them think that holiness is boring and eliminates everything fun. Becoming holy in spirit, soul, and body actually frees us, moving us into large and open places *in this life*. At conversion, God makes our spirit holy because Jesus has come to live there. As such, He has placed everything that we will *ever* need pertaining to life and godliness in our spirit. (See 2 Peter 1:3). This includes the character, nature, and power of God as well as every spiritual blessing. However, the second and third layers of our being, the soul (mind, will, emotions, and attitudes) and our physical bodies desperately need God's help. As part of the body of Christ, we should be as concerned about becoming holy in our thoughts, words, attitudes and deeds as we are about seeing nonbelievers accept Christ as their Savior. Both aspects lead to lives that bear continuous, wholesome fruit.

**As part of the body of Christ, we should be as concerned
about becoming holy in our thoughts, words, attitudes, and deeds
as we are about seeing nonbelievers accept Christ as their Savior.**

What is Holiness and Purity?

- *Holiness* is also called sanctification. It signifies the separation from sin to God, followed by the faith and behavior that represents the character of Christ. Vine's Dictionary says, "Sanctification is thus the state predetermined by God for believers, into which in grace He calls them, and in which they begin their Christian course and so pursue it. Hence they are called saints."[1]
- *Purity* is defined in Vine's Dictionary as, "Pure from defilement, not contaminated; being cleansed.[2] As we partner with the Holy Spirit, He desires to cleanse our entire vessel—spirit, soul, and body. Many times we stop at the spirit level without ever realizing our need for the total cleansing of our minds and bodies. We must be changed from the inside out in order to see the manifestation of all the great things God has placed in our spirits.

There are many, many verses describing what sanctification looks like in the life of the believer. The choice is ours—will we partner with God and let Him work out this path of sanctification in our lives or not? God has great plans for us, but in order to obtain His promises, we need to deal with many of the impurities in our thoughts, motives, and attitudes. The amount of time this takes is partially up to us. The Israelites spent forty years in the wilderness making a trip that could have taken eleven days. The question then, is how long are you willing to spend in the "wilderness"? The longer we refuse to deal with the issues and sins of our hearts, the longer we will "wander" about doing our own thing. Truly, the depth of our hunger for God and obedience to Him will determine the length of our "wandering" time. He is ready, and willing, but walking through this journey requires that we grab His hand and let Him lead.

**Truly, the depth of our hunger for God and obedience
to Him will determine the length of our "wandering" time.**

Let's examine how to incorporate holiness and purity into our lives. Second Timothy 2:20-24 says,

> But in a great house there are not only vessels of gold and silver, but also [utensils] of wood and earthenware, and some for honorable and noble [use] and some for menial and ignoble [use]. *So whoever cleanses himself* [from

what is ignoble and unclean, who separates himself from contact with contaminating and corrupting influences] will [then himself] be a vessel set apart and useful for honorable and noble purposes, consecrated and profitable to the Master, *fit* and *ready* for any good work. *Shun youthful lusts* and flee from them, and *aim at and pursue righteousness* (all that is virtuous and good, right living, conformity to the will of God in thought, word, and deed); [and *aim at and pursue*] *faith, love, [and] peace* (harmony and concord with others) in fellowship with all [Christians], who call upon the Lord out of a pure heart. But refuse (*shut your mind against, have nothing to with*) trifling (ill-informed, unedifying, stupid) *controversies over ignorant questionings,* for you know that they foster strife and breed quarrels. *And the servant of the Lord must not be quarrelsome (fighting and contending). Instead, he must be kindly to everyone and mild-tempered [preserving the bond of peace]; he must be a skilled and suitable teacher, patient and forbearing and willing to suffer wrong.*

These verses tell us:

- Cleanse and separate yourself from sin—in thought, word, and deed.
- Shun and run from immature and sinful lusts.
- Aim at and pursue right standing with God in thought, word, and deed because He is now our standard.
- Aim at and pursue faith—placing your confidence in God's ability. Love God by honoring His Word and obeying Him, and His peace will come—that peace which enables you to remain stable even when your circumstances are not. Be responsible for yourself and the attitudes of your heart before Him.
- Shut your mind off against controversies over ignorant questionings. Do you realize how many silly arguments are started because of our desire to be right? We must leave behind this type of controversy, and allow God to be our vindicator.
- Do not be quarrelsome—going around looking for an argument.
- Be kind to everyone, especially those who have wronged you.
- Be mild tempered. Search for peace rather than trying to prove you're right.
- Become a skilled and suitable teacher. Be ready to help solve problems. Focus on Jesus, His Word, and prayer.
- Be forbearing and willing to suffer a wrong. Be willing to put up with people who are not like you, loving them in spite of your differences.

This is how we become holy and win people to Christ. As believers, we are not setting as good of an example as we ought to be. We deal with divorce, road rage, bad attitudes, and evil hearts just like the world does. Jesus wants to cleanse us of all that He sees that is impure and repulsive.

First Peter 2:1-2, 5, 11-12, 15 says,

So be done with every trace of wickedness (depravity, malignity) and all deceit and insincerity (pretense, hypocrisy) and grudges (envy, jealousy) and slander and evil speaking of every kind. Like newborn babies you should crave (thirst for, earnestly desire) the pure (unadulterated) spiritual milk, that by it you may be nurtured and grow unto [completed] salvation. [Come] and, like living stones, *be yourselves built [into] a spiritual house, for a holy (dedicated, consecrated) priesthood,* to offer up [those] spiritual sacrifices [that are] acceptable and pleasing to God through Jesus Christ. Beloved, I implore you *as aliens and strangers and exiles [in this world] to abstain from the sensual urges* (the evil desires, the passions of the flesh, your lower nature) *that wage war against the soul. Conduct yourselves properly (honorably, righteously) among the Gentiles,* so that, although they may slander you as evildoers, [yet] they may be witnessing your good deeds [come to] glorify God in the day of inspection [when God shall look upon you wanderers as a pastor or shepherd looks over his flock]. *For it is God's will and intention that by doing right [your good and honest lives] should silence (muzzle, gag) the ignorant charges and ill-informed criticisms of foolish persons.*

These verses tell us to:

- Be done with every trace of wickedness: deception, insincerity, hypocrisy, envy, jealously, slander, and evil-speaking of all kinds. God wants us to be done with these things because they pollute us and those around us. Which one do you struggle with the most? Ask the Holy Spirit to deliver you and help you to put an end to this debauchery that cuts Him out of your life and *choose* to obey and do things His way. Pollution clouds our view in the ways of God, thus hindering and eventually eliminating our spiritual insight.
- Instead, crave the things of God. As we crave Him and require Him, He is faithful to fill us with Himself, and lead us in His ways—how He thinks, speaks, and does things.
- Come and be built into a spiritual house. Building anything takes time, effort, and diligence. Are you willing to be built up into a spiritual house where every room of your heart is filled with Jesus? God desires this more than anything we could "do" for Him. He simply wants all of you and all of me! Then He can accomplish His purposes through us.
- Be aliens and strangers in this world. We live in this world, but we are not to be governed by how the world operates. It promotes self-centeredness. We are to be God-centered and promote God-centeredness. A self-centered life wages war against your mind, will, and emotions, while a God-centered life frees the soul.
- Conduct yourself properly in the world, just as Jesus did. Even though He suffered great pain, Jesus continued to entrust Himself to God. In the end, Jesus was exalted. We will be too! By going about conducting ourselves properly, we show the world what it is to live like Jesus did.
- Our good and honest lives will muzzle the mouths of the critical and foolish people. Oh what a glorious day that will be!

Consider the words of 1 Corinthians 6:17-20.

But the person who is united to the Lord *becomes one spirit with Him.* Shun immorality and all sexual looseness [flee from impurity in thought, word, or deed]. Any other sin which a man commits is one outside the body, but he who commits sexual immorality sins against his own body. Do you not know that your body is the temple (the very sanctuary) of the Holy Spirit Who lives within you, Whom you have received [as a Gift] from God? You are not your own, you were bought with a price [purchased with a preciousness and paid for, made His own]. So then, honor God and bring glory to Him in your body.

Basically, we all come to this one question in the sanctification process: Will we choose to walk in our own way, or will we choose to walk in God's ways as revealed to us in His Word, through His Spirit? Taking the time to become holy and pure pleases the Lord and He delights in revealing His ways to us. (See Psalm 25:14). In that way the world will be changed. Let's become more devoted to Him. Keep knocking, keep asking, and keep seeking! Keep your eyes fixed on Jesus and He will change you and me from one level of glory to another! (See 2 Corinthians 3:18).

Questions for Study

1. Do you spend as much time in God's presence—praying, reading, and studying the Word—as you do serving Him? Which does He desire more? Which do you desire more?
2. In your own words, define holiness and purity.
3. Are you as concerned about being holy as you are about winning people to Christ? Do you see that being holy is what attracts the lost world to Christ?
4. What part of this world, and the way it operates do you need to overcome in your own life?
5. Read Ephesians 5:3-11, 18-21, Philippians 2:2-5, and Colossians 3:1-17. What do these verses say to you about holiness and purity?
6. Do you view your body as the temple of the Holy Spirit? How "at home" is the Spirit of God in you? Is He confined to only your spirit, or have you opened up your entire being to Him? If not, do so now—it's time to clean out the clutter.
7. If we really want to live the lives that God intended and planned for us to live, what must we do first?
8. Determine a specific time each day that you will meet with Jesus and commit to it.

Personal Prayer

Lord, help me to crave and drink deeply of Your kindness. I am being built into a spiritual house to be a holy priesthood, offering spiritual sacrifices acceptable to You through Jesus Christ (1 Peter 2:1-2, 9). Cause me to live a good life that is blameless before You, silencing the ignorant talk of foolish people (1 Peter 2:5, 15). Cleanse and separate me from all sin in thought, word, and deed. Thank You that I have right standing with You; therefore, I want to run from immature and sinful lusts. I desire to pursue faith and love and to shut my mind against ignorant controversy. I do not want to be quarrelsome, but kind to everyone, especially to those who have wronged me. Cause me to become mild tempered, in search of peace with all people. Help me to be a skilled and suitable teacher, ready to help solve problems by focusing on You. Help me to be forbearing and willing to suffer when wronged (2 Timothy 2:20-25). Cause me to love others in spite of our differences, and may I always speak the truth in love (Ephesians

4:15). Your Word says that You confide and make Your covenant known to those who fear You (Psalm 25:14). Let that be me, for I desire holiness, purity, and spiritual insight in my life. Help me, Lord, to know You in my heart and not just in my head.

PART SEVEN:

Daily Maintenance and Spiritual Growth

Chapter 42

The Wiles of the Enemy: Part I

---

*T*he enemy's ways always involve craftiness, trickery, and deceit. The devil patiently and relentlessly spends his time attacking our thoughts. He is always working to get us focused on the problems at hand so that we will stop believing the Word of God. Satan bombards our minds with questions that often make us doubt, for he knows that continual doubt will eventually give birth to spiritual death. Then God's plans and purposes for our lives will not manifest in the physical realm.

When situations occur, we have two options. We can take the high road and choose God's ways, or we can take the low road, the ways of the enemy. We would like to think that we always choose the moral and upright road. I am amazed at how easy it is to advise others to do the right thing, but I believe we struggle greatly when the incident involves us. Many times we know the right thing to do, but I wonder how often we actually choose it *consistently* throughout an entire ordeal. Perhaps our intentions are good, but if we give way to our emotions and the enemy's voice, we will fall. I believe that is why God warns us to be on guard, to be alert, and pay attention, especially to the condition of our hearts because when we fall prey to the enemy's ways, we fall under his control and head straight for bondage.

I have personally struggled in this area when the decisions involve me. It's easy for me to expect others to hold the standard, but I can always justify my own reasons to compromise. I believe that many of us do this. Perhaps we can blame some of it on ignorance and the veils of deception. However, when we look into the Word of God and see ourselves within the pages of Scripture, we gain a better understanding of how to come against Satan. The enemy is a crafty, masterful deceiver.

I believe four main areas exist in which we tend to fall prey to the enemy and "eat the forbidden fruit." In this chapter, we will discuss two of them: a negative mindset and self-righteousness. The next chapter will then move on to unforgiveness and guilt. Let's look at these two topics. They trigger many unhealthy emotions and cause upset and sickness. They can even bring death if we don't address and handle them properly, according to the Word of God.

Negative mindset—This is a mindset that constantly notices what's wrong and fails to see what's right about any given situation. I wonder how many marriages might be saved if more people focused on the one hundred good qualities in their spouses rather than their five or ten faults.

It is impossible to be encouragers when our minds constantly acknowledge the negative. Jesus always has His good plan for us in the front of His mind, focusing on our potential. He waits for us to get into agreement with Him, even as we partner with Him. Satan, on the other hand, tries to switch our focus to our pasts and to our present overwhelming circumstances. Jesus wants us to be hope-filled; Satan wants us to be hope-less.

**Jesus always has His good plan for us
in the front of His mind, focusing on our potential.**

The person with the negative mind constantly discovers things to complain about. This is absolutely the enemy's deceit and trickery. We must recognize that a negative mindset will cause us to miss out on God's blessings. It was the Israelites' negative mindset which kept them out of the Promised Land. Out of the original one million people Moses led, only two people actually made it to the Promised Land. They were named Joshua and Caleb. Remember when Moses sent twelve spies to check out the land of Canaan before they went to battle? Ten spies came back with negative reports, but two came back with an altogether different one. Numbers 13:28-33 tells us the story.

> But the people who dwell there are strong, and the cities are fortified and very large; moreover, there we saw the sons of Anak [of great stature and courage]. Amalek dwells in the land of the South (the Negeb); the Hittite, the Jebusite, and the Amorite dwell in the hill country; and the Canaanite dwells by the sea and along by the side of the Jordan [River]. *Caleb quieted the people before Moses, and said, Let us go up at once and possess it; we are well able to conquer it.* But his fellow scouts said, *We are not able to go up against the people [of Canaan], for they are stronger than we are.* So they brought the Israelites an evil report of the land which they had scouted out, saying, The land through which we went to spy it out is a land that devours its inhabitants. And all the people that we saw in it are men of great stature. *There we saw the Nephilim [or giants] and we were in our own sight as grasshoppers, and so we were in their sight.*

These verses paint a true picture of what happens when we lose sight of God. Instead of focusing on Him and His ability, we choose to focus on the situation at hand and everything that is against us. We look at our "man-hood" instead of our "God-hood." Joshua and Caleb were well aware of the facts. However, they were the only two men willing to trust the might and power of God over the physical greatness of the giants in the land.

Let's take a look at how the enemy uses his wiles in the mind of negativity.

1. Fear—Negative minds are fearful minds, constantly comparing themselves to something or someone else. The first thing the ten spies reported to Moses and the group was how big, strong, and courageous the enemies were compared to their own smallness.
2. Excuses—Negative, fearful minds make reasons why they can't or shouldn't move forward when the situation doesn't clearly favor them.
3. Murmuring, complaining, and accusing—Negative minds produce negative mouths with words of destruction and seeds of death.
4. Justification—Fear causes us to refuse responsibility for our actions before God. Negative minds justify their actions because they focus on self-protection. It would have been easy for Joshua and Caleb to just agree with the ten spies. The people were many, they were courageous, and they were giants. However, their negative focus made them forget God's ability! Keep in mind that this is the same God who had parted the Red Sea so they could cross through. The truth is, in the physical realm, they were exactly correct regarding their view of themselves as grasshoppers. Without God, we are as grasshoppers in comparison to our enemy, the devil. The Israelites were no different.
5. Unbelief—A negative mind destroys faith. When faith collides with fear, a struggle will ensue and we will be forced to choose a path. Truthfully, the flesh will always choose the path of least resistance. The right choice however, will usually involve some uncomfortable effort on our part.

**When faith collides with fear, a struggle will ensue,
and we will be forced to choose a path.**

As we continue to read Numbers chapter 14, we find the Israelites ready to stone Joshua and Caleb. How often do we as Christians want to "stone" people for believing God is able? We have to be willing to get out of our boat of comfort and take action. At first, change will make us uncomfortable, like speaking positively about a situation when we want to focus on the negative. However, such positivity in God's ability strengthens both the inner man and our belief in God. If we choose to be positive throughout, we will see God do the impossible in our lives and in our circumstance.

Self-righteousness—This is another area that many Christians stumble through. Self-righteousness causes us to look down on others. It makes it easy to forget the depth of sin from which we came from and how God has delivered us. We need to remember that all Christians are in different places as they walk with Christ. When we start making right choices and obeying God, we might start to view others who are not doing these things as unworthy, selfish, and out of the will of God. This puts us at odds with each other, causing division and strife. If this continues, people start to fulfill the fleshly desires that spring from their lower nature. Self-righteousness disrespects and disregards another person's opinion whether it's correct or not. Remember, Jesus gives us the freedom to choose, even if it's the wrong choice. First Corinthians 8:1-3 says,

> Now about food offered to idols: of course we know that all of us possess knowledge [concerning these matters. *Yet mere] knowledge causes people to be puffed up (to bear themselves loftily and be proud), but love (affection*

and goodwill and benevolence) edifies and builds up and encourages one to grow [to his full stature]. If anyone imagines that he has come to know and understand much [of divine things, without *love*], he does not yet perceive and recognize and understand as strongly and clearly, nor has he become intimately acquainted with anything as he ought or as is necessary. But if one loves God truly [with affectionate reverence, prompt obedience, and grateful recognition of His blessing], he is known by God [recognized as worthy of His intimacy and love, and is owned by Him].

Look at the contrast in these verses! We mustn't let the discussion about food distract us from the point of the teaching. Consider what these verses teach us about the enemy's wiles regarding self-righteousness:

1. The enemy desires for us to continuously compare ourselves and our deeds with each other.
2. Self-righteous people tend to mind the business of others, instead of viewing their own situations, and heart attitudes.
3. Self-righteousness makes us critically judge others who are not like us. It causes prejudice, division, and strife, putting people at odds with each other. Why do you think there are so many denominations in the world?
4. Self-righteousness says, "My way is better!" It is rooted in pride. When given the opportunity, it belittles others through haughty eyes, looks of disgust, and words of resentment.
5. Self-righteous people are not concerned with someone else's restoration into right relationship with God. Usually, these people are more concerned about vindicating themselves and belittling another, but would likely never admit to that.

When we become self-righteous and critical toward someone else and feel justified, quite often we are expressing back to them the very things they are doing to us. And the merry-go-round continues. I'm not suggesting that we compromise God's Word and buy into the ways of the world. Certainly not! However, we can still choose to love others and show them God's grace despite their personal beliefs. God spoke very directly to me about this issue. He revealed to me that He was not showing me things about people so that I would judge them and count them as unworthy, but that I would pray for them. *He always wants us to invite Him into the situation in order to restore the person back to Himself!*

How many times do we see a person becoming upset and disengage ourselves? Do you realize that every time we choose that, we are agreeing with the enemy? There are certainly times when grace means space, but that doesn't excuse us from praying for the person or people involved.

> **There are certainly times when grace means space,**
> **but that doesn't excuse us from praying for**
> **the person or people involved.**

If we would just stop and analyze our hearts every time we choose negativity or self-righteousness, we would realize the negative emotions that we are permitting to operate in our own lives. I know because I was that way and those characteristics still like to rear their ugly heads now and then. I was good at seeing the cup half empty and wondered why others couldn't. But in reality that's a small and pathetic way to live life, especially when Christ came to give us life in abundance and to the full.

If you struggle with the faults described in this chapter, pray for God to set you free and heal you from these life-stealing emotions. Remember, the devil comes to steal, kill, and destroy—especially the fruit of the Spirit living inside of you. (See John 10:10.) Let's take a moment and consider the emotions that the enemy uses to entice the negative and self-righteous person. Here are just a few:

- Envy
- Jealousy
- Bitterness
- Resentment
- Hatred
- Discontentment

The results of these emotions are:

- Strife
- Division
- Competition
- Comparison
- Complaints

Seriously, how can the Spirit of God work in us if we are controlled by negativity and self-righteousness? Plain and simple, He cannot. It's against His nature and character, plus it hinders His power. The deeds of the flesh must be crucified so the light of Christ's nature, character, and power can shine through us.

Questions for Study
1. Define the term "wiles of the enemy."
2. What does it mean to have a negative mindset?
3. Do any of the characteristics of a negative mindset describe you?
4. Does your attitude resemble that of Joshua's and Caleb's—or the ten other spies?
5. Do you view your problems completely without God or do you believe that your God is able, no matter what the situation?
6. To answer #5 correctly, think about what your mind is focused on in these situations, and what comes out of your mouth.
7. Do you spend as much time praying as you do murmuring, complaining, and faultfinding?
8. Do you look down on others who act or believe differently than you do? Do you pray for these people or only talk about them?
9. Look over the list regarding the wiles of the enemy toward self-righteousness. Do you struggle with any of these?

10. Take the time to ask the Holy Spirit to reveal any displeasing ways within you that may be blocking His work. Repent, change your mind, and move on.

Personal Prayer

Lord, deliver me from any negative mindsets and self-righteous attitudes. Forgive me for always seeing what is wrong instead of taking note of all that is right. Help me to focus on those things which are of good report, praiseworthy, noble, true, reputable, authentic, compelling, and gracious; things which are the best, not the worst; the beautiful, not the ugly; things to praise, not things to curse; for this is Your Word (Philippians 4:8). Thank You, Lord, that You always focus on what I can become. I bind the work of Satan from trying to get me focused on my past. Instead, I choose to fill my mind with positive thoughts from Your Word. I am approved and accepted by You. (John 15:16; 2 Corinthians 7:11). You have a good plan for my future, a plan to prosper me and not to harm me (Jeremiah 29:11). I am more than a conqueror in Christ (Romans 8:37). Lord, I know that You consider it sin and wickedness when I choose a different report other than Your Word for my life. Help me to keep and guard my heart and mind by renewing it every day in Your Word (Ephesians 4:22-24). Forgive me for any self-righteousness that may lurk within my heart. I do not want to be disrespectful to others, compare myself to others, or look down on others. Love does not do this, therefore neither should I. You desire me to have Your attitude in my heart and consider others as better than myself (Philippians 2:3-5). Forgive me, for wanting to prove myself right more than desiring to see someone restored to You. Lord, I know it's Your kindness that leads others to repentance (Romans 2:4). Help me to be kind and compassionate, not negative and self-righteous. I desire the Holy Spirit to flow in me and out of me, with no hindrances in my soul.

Chapter 43

The Wiles of the Enemy: Part II

---

*I*n this chapter we will discuss the unforgiveness and guilt the enemy uses against us. We must understand how the enemy works so we do not fall into his entanglements. The devil constantly bombards our minds to keep us focused on situations rather than on the Solution. For example, the enemy might repeat an offense on the "movie screen" of our minds until the situation at hand gets bigger and bigger. This is how we gradually become entangled in his web of deception regarding the incident. By keeping our minds focused on an offense, Satan is able to keep us from forgiving and forgetting. Then he uses guilt about how we've responded to keep us even more entangled. In other words, Satan entices us to think about a situation over and over then hammers us with guilt for doing so. Truthfully, when it comes to unforgiveness and guilt, he doesn't have to work very hard or long on many of us. Being prone to selfishness and constantly wondering, "What's in this for me?" or, "How dare you treat me like that!" and, "You're going to pay for this one!" makes us easy targets.

**By keeping our minds focused on an offense,
Satan is able to keep us from forgiving and forgetting.**

In the last chapter we discussed Satan's use of the negative mindset and self-righteousness. It is no surprise that if we struggle in these areas, unforgiveness and guilt follow closely behind. One fosters the other, causing a snowball effect, and both are used for our demise. If we're going to be true disciples of Jesus, these negative and destructive mindsets must be removed from our lives—no more excuses, no more compromises. They simply must be removed. The Holy Spirit will not sprinkle magic dust on us to rid us of our unhealthy mindsets and emotions. We must determine to do our part and close the door against the devil's wiles of entanglement and enslavement. Let's take a look at unforgiveness and guilt within a believer's life.

Unforgiveness—When a person harbors unforgiveness in his heart toward another person, whether consciously or unconsciously, he closes the door to the Holy Spirit in this area of his life, leaving it under the enemy's control.

Forgiveness is a choice that does not rely on how we feel. Please re-read that phrase and let it sink into your heart. It often takes time for our feelings to catch up when we choose to forgive someone. Throughout the process of forgiveness we will have to be determined to hang on to our choice and depend on God's grace in order to remain strong. The enemy will not ease his grip simply because we've decided to forgive someone. In fact he will increase his ammo, working harder to persuade us and remind us of the offense. But remember, we can control what we let our minds think about. (See Philippians 4:8.) The best way to interrupt Satan's attacks on our thoughts is to interrupt him with the Word of God.

**The best way to interrupt Satan's attacks on our
thoughts is to interrupt him with the Word of God.**

Let's see if we can discern the heart of God by looking at the following verses:

- Second Corinthians 2:10-11 says, "If you forgive anyone anything, I too forgive that one; and what I have forgiven, if I have forgiven anything, has been for your sakes in the presence [and with the approval] of Christ, *to keep Satan from getting the advantage over us; for we are not ignorant of his wiles and intentions.*"
- Mark 11:24-25 says, "For this reason I am telling you, whatever you ask for in prayer, believe (trust and be confident) that it is granted to you, and you will [get it]. And whenever you stand praying, if you have anything against anyone, *forgive him and let it drop (leave it, let it go), in order that your Father Who is in heaven may also forgive you your [own] failings and shortcomings and let them drop.*"
- Matthew 18:21-22 says, "Then Peter came up to Him and said, Lord how many times may my brother sin against me and I forgive him and let it go? [As many as] up to seven times? *Jesus answered Him, I tell you, not up to seven times, but seventy times seven!*"

Notice the truths within these verses:

1. When we submit to God's ways by partnering with the Holy Spirit and choosing to forgive, we release ourselves from the enemy's intended entanglement and give the Holy Spirit free reign in our lives.
2. When we choose to forgive, we walk by faith and release God's blessings into our lives.
3. When we choose to forgive, we prevent Satan from controlling us with the negative emotions that come from unforgiveness (such as bitterness, resentment, hatred, envy, jealousy, etc.). Initially this is hard on our flesh, but dying to the flesh—our earthly desires, lower nature, and our feelings—will always give us freedom and power over our flesh and Satan.
4. When we choose to forgive, we must also choose to let it drop, forget it, let it go, and be done with it! This means we no longer habitually think or talk about the offense. This causes us to die to self even more. Our flesh wants to think about it and talk about

it. However, if we give in to it, we are neither forgiving nor forgetting. We're actually re-living the offense every time we bring it up. Seriously consider . . . when you decide to forgive, with whom are you choosing to agree? Similarly, with whom are you agreeing with when you decide *not* to forgive? I believe the body of Christ struggles desperately with this issue of unforgiveness, and it greatly depletes our witness for Christ.

5. When we choose to forgive, we must also be willing to forgive over and over again if necessary. I believe we all want and appreciate God's mercy and grace for ourselves, but we want to hold others accountable when they offend us. Jesus tells us to willingly forgive someone as many times as it takes. (See Matthew 18:23-35 for an explanation of this very thing.) He asks us to forgive others so He can forgive and bless us.

**Jesus asks us to forgive others
so He can forgive and bless us!**

Remember, when we live in agreement with Satan, we will reap those consequences which lead to death. When we live in agreement with the Holy Spirit, we will reap those consequences which lead to life.

Trying to forgive in our own strength is impossible. Many hurting people are stuck in a terrible cycle, continuing to hurt others. Even if you experience awful things or have been terribly victimized, you must believe that God's grace (His empowerment, mercy, favor, and kindness) is what enables you to forgive. It's not to be confused with how you feel. Focus and believe that God's grace is the only thing that is sufficient for you and me. After all, that's why we need a Savior in the first place! We can't do things in our own strength.

**Even if you experience awful things or have been terribly victimized,
you must believe that God's grace is what enables you to forgive.
It's not to be confused with how you feel.**

Guilt — We live under the cloud of condemnation when we let guilt into our lives. The cycle of guilt looks something like this:

*   We do something wrong.
*   We feel bad about the offense.
*   Guilt grows inside of us.
*   We develop a feeling of reproach against ourselves.
*   This guilt becomes rooted inside of us to the point of shame and self-hatred.
*   The devil reminds us how "guilty" we are.
*   The cycle continues.

Satan loves to beat Christians up whenever we sin. It's a way for him to keep our souls under his control. But look at what the Holy Spirit wrote through Paul in Romans in chapter 8, verses 1-2;

> Therefore, *[there is now no condemnation (no adjudging guilty of wrong) for
> those who are in Christ Jesus, who live [and] walk not after the dictates of
> the flesh, but after the dictates of the Spirit.* For the law of the Spirit of life

[which is] in Christ Jesus [the law of our new being] has freed me from the
law of sin and of death.

We learn from these verses to not take guilt, condemnation, and shame into our being. It's
funny how we Christians seem to forget that Christ paid for our sins. He forgives our sins when
we repent. Yet, somehow even after we repent, we hold on to remorse and guilt instead of just
moving on with our lives in right relationship with Christ.

Let me ask you these questions: "Who do you think wants you to hang on to guilt? And
who do you think wants you to feel like you owe something?" Truly, we struggle with not
having to "pay" for our sins. Remember, Jesus already paid sin's price for you and me. To try
and pay it again by feeling guilty is both a waste of time and an insult to Jesus' sacrifice. You
must believe that when you repent, change your mind and heart, and then move in the opposite direction, you are justified. Yes, that means, "Just as if you never sinned." That's freedom!
We can remind ourselves and Satan that we are justified! Then we can live like we are saved,
believing that Christ paid the price, being grateful and very confident in Christ's all sufficient
grace, and knowing that we have right-standing with Him!

Spiritual maturity means moving to repentance quickly and then moving on quickly. You
must not dwell on your sins when Jesus has already forgiven you and removed them as far as
the east is from the west! We either believe it or we don't.

**Spiritual maturity means moving to repentance quickly
and then moving on quickly. You must not dwell on your sins
when Jesus has already forgiven you and removed them
as far as the east is from the west!**

As we walk and partner with the Holy Spirit, we recognize the desires of the flesh. However,
when we commit an offense, the Holy Spirit will *convict* us, and we will feel *godly sorrow* and
move on to *repentance*. This is God's way of leading us back to Him. Please don't choose to
run from Him! I believe there are many Christians who struggle with knowing the difference
between guilt and conviction. The enemy uses guilt to condemn us and to keep us in bondage,
while the Holy Spirit uses conviction to lift us up higher.

In my own personal life, I'm learning to not only confess and repent when I sin, but also
to confess what is right and true about me according to God's Word. Remember, the Holy
Spirit not only convicts of sin, *but He also convinces us of righteousness*. (See John 16:8.)
Therefore, I use my mouth and confess that I have right standing with God. I say out loud that
I have been cleansed and that my sin has been removed from me. I confess that I am God's
child, that He loves me and that His love has been poured into my heart. (See 1 Corinthians
6:11). If you want to give Satan a nervous breakdown, just start confessing who God says you
are! All I can say is *Wow!* It's an amazing way to overpower Satan's attacks of guilt, condemnation, and unforgiveness.

**If you want to give Satan a nervous breakdown,
just start confessing who God says you are!**

Consider Judas, the man who betrayed Jesus. Here are the steps of his demise:

- Satan entered Judas' thoughts.
- Judas responded and followed that lead.
- Judas betrayed Jesus.
- Satan used Judas's sin to further entangle him by bringing on guilt.
- The guilt he felt left Judas hopeless and in despair.
- Because of this guilt, condemnation, shame, and hopelessness, Judas cowered under the pressure and chose to hang himself.

Alternately, let's consider Peter:

- Satan used his fear tactic on Peter.
- Peter followed that lead and betrayed Jesus three times (not just once) in order to protect himself.
- Because we know how Satan works, we can assume that he then attempted to use Peter's betrayal to try and entrench him in guilt. Matthew 26:75 tells us, "Peter remembered Jesus's words, when He had said, 'Before a single rooster crows, you will deny and disown Me three times.' And he went outside and wept bitterly."
- Because Peter chose godly sorrow and repentance, God forgave him and then empowered him with His Holy Spirit to use him for His purposes. Peter's repentance kept his conviction from turning into condemnation.
- Peter received God's grace, peace, and forgiveness from Jesus after His resurrection. (See John 20:21-23.)

Both followed Jesus. Both committed sins against Him. But each ended with two very different outcomes.

- Judas chose guilt, condemnation, and shame.
- Peter chose godly sorrow, conviction, repentance, righteousness, and freedom.

Judas' decision resulted in a *fruitless* life which ended in death. Peter's decision, however, resulted in a *fruit-filled,* empowered life which produced even more life. Second Corinthians 7:10 says,

> For godly grief and pain God is permitted to direct, *produce a repentance that leads and contributes to salvation and deliverance from evil, and it never brings regret;* but worldly grief (hopeless sorrow that is characteristic of the pagan world) is deadly [breeding and ending in death].

Satan wants us to remain in unforgiveness and guilt, especially when it comes to forgiving ourselves. Then he can use all the accompanying deadly emotions and turn them inward, walling us in to our self-imposed prisons.

Jesus, on the other hand, wants us to quickly repent and accept God's forgiveness for ourselves. If we follow the Holy Spirit's lead when He convicts us of wrong, we will always rise to the top, empowered and enabled to do His will.

God's kindness leads us to repentance, and when we are willing to place God's ways above our own, our kindness towards others will lead them to repentance. As members of the body of Jesus Christ, we need to become well known for our willingness to forgive others, allowing the Holy Spirit's conviction to take us up higher and empower us.

**God's kindness leads us to repentance, and when
we are willing to place God's ways above our own, our
kindness towards others will lead them to repentance.**

Questions for Study

1. Ask the Holy Spirit if you are harboring any unforgiveness or guilt in your life at this time.
2. If so, repent and by grace (God's empowerment) through faith (your belief in God's empowerment), move on. Disregard your feelings; they will eventually catch up to your decision. It's important not to let the devil make you feel as if you haven't forgiven someone when in fact you have.
3. Do you believe it's possible to experience victory in your life and be a witness for Christ if you are living with unforgiveness and guilt? Having answered that question, who are you choosing to partner with when someone offends you?
4. Can you think of anyone who has offended you lately? Extend these two biblical acts of kindness at this time: Pray for the person(s) and ask God to bless and forgive them. And . . . do something nice for them. Practice speaking well of him or her. These godly acts will cause a hardened heart to repent, which is what God desires. Are you willing to do this God's way?
5. If you are suffering or have ever suffered with guilt and condemnation, reread and then write out Romans 8:1-2. Living with guilt is not godly.
6. What is the difference between condemnation and conviction?
7. When you offend someone do you respond as Judas did or as Peter did?

Personal Prayer

Lord, You desire for me to know how the enemy tries to keep me in bondage through unforgiveness and guilt. Lord, I know it is sin to constantly play an offense over and over in my mind. Help me to release others who have offended me and to entrust them to Your care. Specifically, I forgive _____ now. I realize that forgiveness is a choice and is not determined by how I feel. I also realize that forgiveness does not excuse what happened to me, but I am entrusting this person who wronged me to Your care. Now help me to walk in love toward him or her. You have said in Your Word that if we have anything against anyone, we are to forgive him or her and let it drop. I need to leave it and let it go, so that You, who are in heaven, may also forgive me of my own failings and shortcomings (Mark 11:24-25). Lord, I understand that You are asking me to forgive others so that You can also forgive and bless me (Matthew 18:23-35). Help me to do this by the power of Your Holy Spirit. Thank You, Lord, that there is now no condemnation for those who are in Christ (Romans 8:1-2). Thank You for paying for my sins. Thank You that I do not need to take shame, blame, and guilt into my being. Lord, even after I repent, help me not to feel remorse, instead, help me to move on in faith. Thank You that Your Holy Spirit convicts me of sin, not to condemn me but to bring me to repentance, (2 Corinthians 7:10). Thank You that Your Word teaches me the wiles of the enemy. I can choose either to believe them or reject them. Thank You, that Your Holy Spirit also convinces me of my right standing with You. Help me to practice admitting the good things about me, too. Help me to choose life, to choose to follow the Holy Spirit and to choose Your blessings (Deuteronomy 30:19).

Chapter 44

From Victim to Victor: Part I

———————⟡———————

or the last few chapters we've been discussing negative mindsets, self-righteousness, unforgiveness, and guilt—attitudes that lead to defeated and frustrating living. They keep us entangled inside self-imposed prison walls. Jesus did not die for us to remain entangled within these walls. The truth is, when we give in to the enemy's wiles, we allow him to entangle us. The slippery descent of deception begins when we let him influence our thoughts. Then we begin justifying our feelings and behavior instead of believing and trusting in God's Word.

Jesus tells us to do to others as we would have them do to us. (See Luke 6:31.) He commands us to pray for those who use us, bless those who curse us, and forgive those who hurt us. (See Matthew 5:44.) Why is it so difficult, then, for us to actually do these things? I believe it is because it's so much easier to follow our feelings and fleshly emotions, rather than follow the Holy Spirit, who resides in us.

Once again, we have a choice. We can choose to agree with God and His Word, or with the enemy and his word. When we choose the enemy's side and hang on to our negative thoughts, self-righteousness, unforgiveness, and guilt, we maintain the mentality of victims. We continue to believe everyone is out to "get us," and we will go to extreme measures to make sure no one will ever hurt or take advantage of us again.

Friend, this is no way to live. It's a very puny, small, miserable, and imprisoned life. When we determine to take care of ourselves and avenge our offenses, we disobey God by taking matters into our own hands. Choosing to disobey God's Word will never lead us to victory. It will keep us in bondage, guilt, hopelessness, and condemnation.

Let's look at Joseph and see how he went from victim to victor over the course of his life. Joseph's story reveals many applicable revelations for our own lives.

We find his story in Genesis chapters 37-50. Here is the account of Joseph's life:

- Joseph's father, Jacob, loved Joseph more than any of his other children.
- At the age of seventeen, Joseph was given a coat of many colors by his father.

- Joseph began having dreams which he shared with his brothers. In essence, his dreams were about his brothers bowing down to him. All these things led his brothers to envy, jealousy, and hatred toward him.
- One day, their father sent Joseph to check on his brothers who were shepherding Jacob's flock at Shechem. The brothers saw this as an opportunity to get rid of Joseph.
- The brothers tore Joseph's coat off of him and threw him into a pit to die.
- However, a band of Ishmaelites and Midianites came by on their way to Egypt, and the brothers decided to sell Joseph instead.

No doubt about it, the behavior of Joseph's father caused a lot of problems between Joseph and his brothers. Granted, Joseph couldn't help the fact that his father loved him more, but he sure didn't have to flaunt his dreams to his brothers. Joseph was young and full of energy, but he was not very wise at this stage of the game. However, the favor of God was with him, and God had a plan. He used Joseph's circumstances to develop character and integrity in him to fulfill the call He had on Joseph's life. Do you realize that as God's son or daughter, He has given you favor, too? Do you believe God is building His character and integrity in you through the circumstances in your life just like He did with Joseph?

Joseph's brothers schemed against Joseph, sold him as a slave, and lied to their father about it. Maybe you have been hurt by your own family. Do you go about with spite in your life like Joseph's brothers did? What are your own reactions toward the people who have hurt you? We need to remember that what Joseph's brothers intended for his harm, God intended for Joseph's good, but that would only happen *if* Joseph chose to remain with God in thought, word, and deed.

Do you believe that God will work out everything no matter what it is, for your good *if* you continue to walk with Him? Or are you trying to use God as your personal "Genie," hoping He will change all of your circumstances instead of allowing Him to use your circumstances to change you? These difficult questions that deal with our motives are necessary for us to face if we want to continue on with God.

**Do you believe that God will work out everything,
no matter what it is, for your good if you continue
to walk with Him?**

Let's follow Joseph's story further and see how he responded when faced with the most negative, depressing, lonely, and dismal situation possible.

- A man named Potiphar, the royal guard's captain and chief executioner, purchased Joseph from the Ishmaelites.
- But the Lord was with Joseph, and made him successful, even though he was a slave.
- Potipher saw the favor of God on Joseph's life. He was pleased with Joseph, and promoted him as supervisor over his household. He put Joseph in charge of all that he had.

Here was Joseph, in a foreign country, a slave to a man named Potiphar, the captain and chief executioner of the royal guard! After all Joseph had been through, he could have easily developed a negative attitude, feeling sorry for himself. Yet, Joseph chose to remain positive. Do you realize that when you choose God's ways and keep your mind fixed on Him, He will grant you His favor no matter the circumstances? Are you willing to be patient while you wait for God's hand to vindicate you?

One thing Joseph didn't expect, though, was the big character test approaching him through the wife of Potiphar.

- Joseph was a handsome man, and Potiphar's wife began to desire him.
- Joseph kept refusing her sexual advances because he didn't want to commit evil and sin against God.
- When Potiphar's wife physically grabbed Joseph one day, he refused and ran from her. But she held onto his garment as he ran. This, of course, made her angry and led her to cry rape to her husband. She used Joseph's garment to "prove" he had done it and cause massive trouble for Joseph.
- Ultimately, Potiphar believed his wife's story and threw Joseph in prison.

The good news is that Joseph passed this test with amazing grace! Here he was, in a foreign country, refusing to sleep with the boss's wife, all because he didn't want to sin against God. Honestly, all I can say to that is, "Wow!" How about you—when you're tempted, do you cave or do you run like Joseph, wanting to serve God more than your own fleshly desires? In all honesty, I've failed this test many times.

Joseph made all the right choices. Then someone lied about him, and he was put in prison for a crime he didn't even commit. I don't know about you, but I think this scenario would have made a great opportunity for Joseph to take offense at God and throw himself a grand ol' pity party. Yet, despite Joseph's dismal, negative and even depressing circumstances, he continued to remain positive. How about you? Do you get offended at God or others when things don't turn out as you had hoped even after you've made right choices? Again, I have failed this test many times. Even so, I've realized that God has continued to develop my character, and I have found that the sooner I partner with Him in my thoughts, my words, and my deeds, the sooner I will rise victorious. God is creating a pure heart and clean hands within every one of us each time we face adversity. So the question is, how will you respond to this opportunity the next time an injustice comes your way?

Back to Joseph's story . . .

- But the Lord was with Joseph while he was in prison. He showed him mercy and loving kindness. He gave him favor in the sight of the prison warden.
- The warden put Joseph in charge of all the prisoners.

Once again, God gave Joseph His favor. I believe Joseph enjoyed so much of God's favor because he let God be in control of his heart and his attitude. I'm sure there were times when Joseph questioned God or wondered why all of it was happening to him. I also believe that Joseph didn't dwell on those questions for long. He simply chose to trust God instead. Joseph knew that God would take care of Him just as He always had done.

Joseph enjoyed so much of God's favor because
he let God be in control of his heart and his attitude.

Do you have this same kind of faith that Joseph had? Do you realize that God is your Vindicator and is waiting for you to completely entrust yourself to Him, knowing that He will always come to your rescue? We'll continue on with the story of Joseph in the next chapter.

Questions for Study

1. What is the prescription for a frustrated and defeated life?
2. Are you in the habit of doing unto others as you would have them do to you—praying for those who use you, blessing those who curse you, and forgiving those who hurt you?
3. Are you giving your feelings more priority than you allow the Word of God?
4. Do you believe that you have the favor of God on your life? Do you realize that God's grace is His favor, along with His empowerment, mercy and kindness?
5. How is God using your circumstances to establish His character in you?
6. Do you despise people who hurt you? Do you realize this is disobedience?
7. Do you exhibit victim mentality or a victor mentality in your circumstances? In what ways?

Personal Prayer

Lord, forgive me for the times that I display a "victim" attitude, forgetting that You died, so that I might live victoriously in you. Teach me how to do this. I know as long as I hold on to negative mindsets, self-righteousness, unforgiveness, and guilt, I will keep a victim mentality. Lord, Your Word says that I am to do unto others as I would have them do unto me (Luke 6:31)—to pray for those who use me, to bless those who curse me, and to forgive those who have hurt me (Matthew 5:44). I realize in my own strength I do not have the ability to do this at all, let alone consistently. Cause me to ask for and rely on Your grace in order to do this. Thank You for Joseph's example (Genesis chapters 37-50). He could have easily had a victim mentality, but instead, he chose to walk in Your favor. Joseph had Your favor because You were in charge of his heart and his attitude. I give you my heart, Lord; mold me and make me into Your image. Help me to walk in Your favor by choosing to do what's right even when my circumstances seem dismal. Help me to realize that these types of trials are meant to be building blocks of Your character and integrity working and taking root in my own life. Help me not to run from that, but to endure and continue to walk through it.

Chapter 45

From Victim to Victor:
Part II

⸺⸺⸺◆⸺⸺⸺

*L*et's pick up the story of Joseph again and see how he went from victim to victor.

- Sometime later the king's butler and his baker offended the king, so he put them in the same prison where Joseph was confined. The captain of the guard placed Joseph in charge of them.
- Both the butler and the baker experienced disturbing dreams.
- Through God's power and wisdom Joseph interpreted their dreams—the butler would be released from prison and restored to his position, and the baker would be hanged within three days.
- Joseph asked the butler to tell Pharaoh about all the unlawful deeds that had been done to him, including his false imprisonment.
- Joseph had interpreted the dream correctly, and the butler was restored to his butlership and the baker was hanged.
- And the butler forgot all about Joseph.

God's favor and the gift He had given Joseph enabled him to interpret these dreams. God's Spirit working in Joseph made him aware of the baker's and the butler's depression that day in prison. Rather than focusing on and worrying about his own needs, Joseph concerned himself with the needs of others. When you face unfair circumstances are you like Joseph, concerned with what is happening in others' lives, or are you immersed in trying to solve your own problems through reasoning, worry, and anxiety? Joseph chose to go about his day as a servant and become more in sync with the needs of others than with his own problems.

Joseph tried to take care of himself by was asking the butler to think of him when he got released from prison. Had I been in his shoes, I'm certain I would have done the same. God, however, had a bigger lesson to teach him. Joseph needed to learn to trust God to care for him and vindicate him totally and completely without his help. Joseph's job was to believe, obey, and keep a good attitude while God worked on his behalf. In all honesty, after all those years Joseph spent waiting to be released from prison for something he didn't do, I think I might have felt forgotten, too! Like Joseph, though, we may well be forgotten by family and friends, but we will never be forgotten or forsaken by God. He makes promises, and He cannot lie. Our job is to believe, obey, and keep a good attitude while we wait, whether we're in difficult times or prosperous times.

Do you realize that if we humble ourselves by entrusting every difficult situation to God, and continue helping others, He will use all of it for our good and for the good of others?

Do you realize that if we humble ourselves by entrusting every difficult situation to God, and continue helping others, He will use all of it for our good and for the good of others?

- According to Genesis 41, two years later Pharaoh had a dream which he wanted interpreted.
- The butler then remembered Joseph and mentioned him to Pharaoh.
- Pharaoh sent for Joseph, who then interpreted the dream.
- Joseph's interpretation and plan seemed good to Pharaoh.
- Pharaoh recognized the Spirit of God within Joseph and praised his intelligence and understanding of the living God.
- Pharaoh put Joseph in charge of his house and over all the people. Joseph was second-in-command only to Pharaoh in the entire land of Egypt.
- God gave Joseph favor again!
- Pharaoh's dream came to pass just as Joseph had interpreted it. (See Genesis chapter 41.)

Joseph had much practice in the department of waiting! No doubt, he looked to God as his caregiver. Because Joseph kept a good attitude during his time of waiting, God developed him into the servant leader that He wanted him to be. Joseph was filled with humility, grace, and forgiveness—just like Jesus! Now Joseph's character and heart motives matched his gifts. God had a big job in mind for Joseph, but Joseph needed some work done in his soul. Joseph started out as an immature, arrogant boy, full of his own fleshly zeal and pride. We saw that in his dealings with his brothers when he revealed his dreams to them.

Just as God did for Joseph, He has important plans for our lives, too. And just like Joseph, oftentimes we can be immature, arrogant, and full of our own fleshly zeal and pride. When we feel forgotten by God, we can rest assured He has not forgotten us. In fact, He is likely using our current circumstances to change us. Usually, we are the ones who forget to keep our focus on Him. Are you in agreement with Him as He attempts to build His character and right heart motives in you or could you be walking around filled with spiritual immaturity, arrogance, fleshly zeal, and pride?

Guaranteed, it was no mistake that the butler forgot about Joseph. God had more refining to do in Joseph's life at that time. We can learn from this. *We should never resent where we are at this moment.* If we will adhere to God's ways, He will cause our day of recompense and vindication to come, too! He promises!

Do you think your friends, family, and co-workers can see God's Spirit in your life like Pharaoh was able to see Him in Joseph's life? Or does your attitude display bitterness, unforgiveness, resentment, hatred and jealousy? Do you have a victim's mentality or victor's mentality?

Joseph truly was a man with a victorious mindset. Because of this, he was given an even better position as second-in-command in all the land only to Pharaoh. Wow, that's how God works and only God can do such a thing!

Back to the story . . .

- Joseph's brothers came to Egypt in search of food.
- They didn't recognize Joseph, for it had been many years since they had last seen him.
- Joseph recognized them, and his mindset was to *bless* them. (W*ow!*)
- The dreams Joseph had as a seventeen-year-old boy were finally coming to pass.
- Joseph's brothers bowed down to him because Joseph spared their lives and gave them food.
- Joseph reunited with his father and brothers and moved his family close to him.
- Joseph told his brothers that what they intended for his harm, God intended for his good.

Famine had ravaged the land of Canaan where they lived, so Joseph's brothers came to Egypt to purchase food. It would have been a perfect opportunity for Joseph to repay his brothers for all they had done to Him. But, that was not his intention at all! Even when Joseph exposed his brother's past sins, he looked to bless his brothers—not seek revenge or vindication, but to *bless* them. It's a perfect picture of total forgiveness. This is exactly what Jesus does for us when we humble ourselves and come to Him. He gently exposes our sins, not in order to crush us or seek revenge, but to *bless and prosper* us. Do you believe that? Do you have this Christ-like forgiveness and grace within your heart? Or are you seeking revenge for what others have done to you? Are you building walls and never letting anyone in again? Or are you building bridges to bring about healing and restoration?

God brought Joseph's dreams to pass when God could trust him to display His own character. This trust put Joseph in a position to bless those who cursed, abused, and used him. Because Joseph stuck with God, God was able to use him to save a nation. Truly, what His brothers meant for his harm, God was able to use for his good. If we are willing to let the Holy Spirit develop and mature God's character inside of us He will use us for many great things, too. We will bear much fruit with lives that are willingly submitted to God. He is our Savior, Protector, Provider, Healer and Vindicator, and He will recompense us.

In Luke 9:23, Jesus said,

> If any person wills to come after Me, let him deny himself [disown himself, forget, lose sight of himself and his own interests, refuse and give up himself] and take up his cross daily and follow Me [cleave steadfastly to Me, conform wholly to My example in living and, if need be, in dying also].

The story of Joseph's life serves as a great example, of denying ourselves of pity parties, bad attitudes, negative mindsets, self-righteousness, unforgiveness, vengeance, self-vindication, guilt, and condemnation. The verse we just looked at in Luke is asking us to give these things up, too. Our journey with Christ is about giving up our spirit, soul (mind, will, attitudes and emotions), and body to the care of Jesus Christ.

Isaiah 61:7 says, "Instead of your [former] shame you shall have a twofold recompense; instead of dishonor and reproach [your people] shall rejoice in their portion. Therefore in their land they shall possess double [what they had forfeited]; everlasting joy shall be theirs." Because Joseph cooperated with God and never walked away from Him, God restored to him double for all the heartache and loss he had experienced. Joseph's mind was set on not offending God in any way, for he knew to whom he belonged.

> **Because Joseph cooperated with God and never walked away from Him, God restored to him double for all the heartache and loss he had experienced.**

Do you believe this promise for you? Are you willing to give up any bad attitudes, negative mindsets, vengeance, unforgiveness, and so forth, and entrust yourself totally to Christ? If your answer is yes and you cooperate with God, you can expect Him to fulfill His promises in your own life.

The path that both Joseph and Jesus walked is the path that took them from victim to victor. Are you willing to walk that path as well? All the great men and women of the Bible and each of God's consecrated people right now have walked and are walking that path. Remember, the road that leads to destruction is wide, and the path that leads to life is narrow. Few find it. Perhaps few find it because few want to *go through* this kind of consecration, sanctification, testing, and growing. We can become among those few if we don't give up and if we keep pressing on! We too will receive the victor's crown revealed in Christ when He comes in glory!

Questions for Study

1. Go back through the last two chapters, and consider the questions in relation to your own life.
2. When you have unfair circumstances in your life, how do you react? Do you believe that God is just?
3. How do you try to vindicate yourself? After studying the life of Joseph, how do you think God wants you to handle vindication? (See Romans 12:19.)
4. Do you wait with a good attitude, trusting God to handle your situations, or are you entangled in the wiles of the enemy with reasoning, worry, anxiety, and doubt?
5. In what ways might Jesus be asking you to deny yourself in order to follow Him?
6. Do you believe that God will recompense you if you cooperate with Him?
7. Think about and list the ways God would have you agree with Him in your thoughts, words, attitudes, and actions.
8. Do your heart motives match Christ's?

Personal Prayer

Lord, forgive me for being immersed in my own reasoning, worry, and anxiety while trying to figure out the solutions to my own problems. Instead, I should be casting my care on You and waiting for Your direction and timing (1 Peter 5:7; Philippians 4:6; Galatians 6:9). Lord, I believe that You are my Caregiver, and I am leaving my vindication up to You (Romans 12:19). Help me to see that You desire to expose my sins in order that I might repent. Thus You will bless me by restoring me to fellowship with You. I know, Lord, that You are also testing me to determine my level of faithfulness to You (Psalm 139:23-24). Please, Lord, help me to be faithful, steadfast, and enduring for Your Name's sake. Lord, You promise in Your Word to recompense me, to pay me back all that I have lost if I give myself to You completely (Isaiah 61:7). I know that You want me to pick up my cross and follow You (Luke 9:23). Help me, Lord, to deny myself of pity-parties, bad attitudes, negative mindsets, self-righteousness, unforgiveness, vengeance, self vindication, guilt, and condemnation. None of these things can cling to me if I am clinging to You! Cleanse me, Lord, from head to toe as I lay these things at Your feet and follow after You. Your Word says that I will reap what I sow (Galatians 6:7); help me to sow those things which are life-giving and to renounce as sin those things which bring death (Galatians 6:8). Your Word says that I am not to be overcome by evil, but to overcome evil with good (Romans 12:21; Galatians 6:9-10)! Please help me to do this.

Chapter 46

The Armor of God:
Part I

We've spent the last several chapters looking at Joseph's life and discussing how to move from victim to victor. Understanding and exposing Satan's ways is essential in order for us to recognize his lies and deception. Doing this enables us to avoid his snares and flee the temptations that lure us into his entanglements. Once we identify Satan's ways, each of us must learn how to arm ourselves with the spiritual armor of God. Just as we get dressed each morning before leaving the house, we must also dress ourselves spiritually from head to toe, with the weapons of warfare. God's grace supplies our spiritual weapons and our faith enables us to defeat the enemy warring against us throughout the day fighting off temptation, sin, selfishness, and the system of this world.

Ephesians 6:10-18 reveals how we as Christians must dress ourselves so that we are "F.I.T." for the journey and ready to serve in God's army. We cannot defeat our spiritual enemy with fleshly, man-made weapons from our own minds, mouths, hands, and feet. Spiritual warfare must be fought with spiritual weapons supplied to us by a Spiritual God. If we had the power to ward off the enemy on our own, Jesus would not have had to come to this earth to show us the way. Remember, becoming a F.I.T. Christian means being firm in our *Faith* (confident in God's ability), *Free* from the enemy's entanglements, and living *Fruit-filled* lives that please God, while *In* the process of *Transformation* (becoming more like Him).

Let's take a close look at what Ephesians 6:10-13 says:

> In conclusion, be strong in the Lord [be empowered through your union with Him]; draw your strength from Him [that strength which His boundless might provides]. Put on God's whole armor [the armor of a heavy-armed soldier which God supplies], that you may be able successfully to stand up against [all] the strategies and the deceits of the devil. For we are not wrestling with flesh and blood [contending only with physical opponents], but against the despotisms, against the powers against [the master spirits who are] the world

rulers of this present darkness, against the spirit forces of wickedness in the heavenly (supernatural) sphere. Therefore put on God's complete armor, that you may be able to resist and stand your ground on the evil day [of danger], and, having done all [the crises demands], to stand [firmly in your place].

As Christians, we must believe and understand that we are at war with the enemy. Spiritual warfare is real. More often than not, the enemy first wages his attack on our minds. Remember, if he can win our thoughts, he can direct our lives. Satan desires to steal the fruit of the Spirit within us. If he steals our joy, he steals our strength. He wants to keep God's light from shining through us and spreading his darkness instead.

I'm not sure how many Christians believe there is an actual enemy of their souls (mind, will, and emotions) who is trying to destroy us, our families, our friends, our co-workers, and our country every day of our lives. If we will look, we will see the physical manifestations of the warfare that is taking place in the spiritual realm. The selfish, greedy, and out-of-control behavior so many exhibit, (including Christians) is the result of an internal spiritual breakdown. If more Christ-followers actually grasped this concept and understood the real enemy—the devil—many of us would act differently.

Verses 10-13 reveal the following truths:

- Our power comes from our union with Christ, partnering with Him, and obeying Him.
- By His grace, God alone supplies the power we need. Our part is to live in agreement with Him and believing Him for it. John 15:5 says, "Apart from Me [cut off from vital union with Me] you can do nothing."
- Only the armor of God allows us to stand up against the strategies and deceits of the devil.
- We do not wrestle against other people, but against the devil. He is the real enemy.
- We wrestle against the spirit forces of wickedness in the heavenly (supernatural) sphere.
- We are to put on God's *complete armor* (from head to toe) that we may be able to resist the enemy and stand our ground every day.
- We are called to stand firm in God, believing and leaning completely on Him.

Verses 14-17 reveal to us the spiritual clothing we need to put on to walk in unity and victory within God's army. We read in verse 14, "Stand therefore [hold your ground], having tightened the belt of truth around your loins and having put on the breastplate of integrity and moral rectitude and right standing with God."

- *Stand therefore:* We must stop running and cowering from the enemy every time he launches an attack on us. More often than not, he uses our thoughts and emotions to attack our minds. Satan will work to cause upset in our circumstances, situations, and relationships in order to get into our inner lives. But God's Spirit empowers us to go *through* these hard things.
- *Hold your ground:* We need not waver, back off, or lose ground in our relationship with and trust in Christ. Don't fall for the set-up to become upset! Hang on to the Holy Spirit's inspiration and teachings for the enemy is trying to get you to quit. He wants you to doubt God's ability and provision, give up, and run. We must learn to stop, breathe, shut out the noise, and get quiet on the inside before we react.

- *Having tightened the belt of truth:* The belt of truth is the Word of God. In the physical realm, a belt is used to keep our clothes from falling off our bodies. In like manner, the belt of truth, or the Word of God, keeps our spiritual clothes from falling off our souls. Lastly, it is important to remember that truth is truth only when it coincides with the character of Christ.

**Remember that truth is truth only when
it coincides with the character of Christ.**

The word *"tightened"* indicates there is no room for slack in our spiritual clothing. The spiritual slack in our lives must go! Our "belt(s) of truth" will become looser and looser if we don't spend time with God every day. This slack makes room for the enemy and the ways of the world to come in and pull our spiritual garments away from us. Creating godly habits, such as reading and studying God's Word, praying and believing it, and speaking the Word into our situations, work to tighten up our belts of truth and hold us up in the day of trouble. Being clothed with His armor every day is our part of the preparation needed. Don't wait for a crisis to hit before you cry out to God.

- *Having put on the breastplate of integrity (righteousness*):* We must determine to remain in right standing with God through every encounter and situation we face. Our moral integrity must not waver but, consistently withstand the temptations of the flesh. If we slack off in this area, we find our belt loosened again. *Romans 13:13-14 testifies to this truth:*

  Let us live and conduct ourselves honorably and becomingly as in the [open light of] day, not in reveling (carousing) and drunkenness, not in immorality and debauchery (sensuality and licentiousness), not in quarrelling and jealousy. But clothe yourself with the Lord Jesus Christ (the Messiah), and make no provision for [indulging] the flesh [put a stop to thinking about the evil cravings of your physical nature] to [gratify its] desires (lusts).

As members of the body of Christ, we must concern ourselves with the spiritual clothing we choose to wear, for we are shining His light into a dark world. If we live slack and loose lives spiritually, we will be no match to stand against the wiles of the enemy. But God's grace is an empowering force – Jesus Himself – that enables us to overcome and defeat sin from ruling in our lives. Believe that God's grace is sufficient for you!

**God's grace is an empowering force – Jesus Himself – that enables
us to overcome and defeat sin from ruling in our lives.**

Proverbs 4:23-27 sums this up nicely. It says,

  Keep and guard your heart with all vigilance and above all that you guard, for out of it flow the springs of life. Put away from you false and dishonest speech, and willful and contrary talk put far from you. Let your eyes look right on [with fixed purpose], and let your gaze be straight before you.

Consider well the path of your feet, and let all your ways be established and ordered aright. Turn not aside to the right hand or to the left; remove your foot from evil.

Having right standing with God and knowing His truth are two of our greatest weapons. They keep us close to God and defeat the enemy of our souls.

Questions for Study
1. Why is it necessary to understand the wiles of the enemy?
2. Once we identify Satan's ways, what is necessary for every believer to do?
3. What does it mean to be a "F.I.T." Christian?
4. More often than not, where is the first place the enemy will wage his attack against us?
5. Do you believe that Satan is able to work his wiles through your circumstances, situations, and other people in order to upset you?
6. Why does Satan want to keep the fruit of the Spirit from being displayed within you?
7. What godly habits might you incorporate into your life in order to establish Ephesians 6:10-14 into your daily routine?
8. What is the empowering force that comes from God and enables us to overcome and defeat sin from ruling in our lives?

Personal Prayer
Lord, help me to identify the areas in my life which Satan is using to gain control over me. Thank You for giving me Your armor to place on myself so I can walk, live, and move about in this sin-filled world. First of all Lord, Your Word tells me that my union with You will empower me. It tells me to draw my strength from You, which Your boundless might provides (Ephesians 6:10-13). Lord, forgive me for trying to be strong on my own. I realize that spiritual warfare is real and that I am not wrestling against flesh and blood, but against the devil and his evil powers (Ephesians 6:10-13). Help me, Lord, to get into agreement with You, (Amos 3:3), knowing that apart from You I can do nothing (John 15:5). Thank You that You have given me power to trample on the enemy (Luke 10:19). I know I won't be able to do that if I am in agreement with him or unable to identify his methods. Thank You that I do not fight against him through my own power or might, but by Your Spirit (Zechariah 4:6) through Your empowering grace. Your Word says for me to live and conduct myself in an honorable and becoming way, not in immorality, quarrelling, and jealousy. It tells me I am to clothe myself with You, make no provision for indulging in my flesh, and to put a stop to thinking about evil cravings and gratifying their desires (Romans 13:13-14). I desire to live for righteousness through Your Holy Spirit. Thank You, God, for providing me with Your grace which empowers and enables me to overcome. Truly, Your grace is sufficient for me to meet all things head on (2 Corinthians 12:9).

Chapter 47

The Armor of God:
Part II

*I*n this chapter we will continue our study on the armor of God. We've already discussed the first four verses of this section in Ephesians 6. In this chapter we will focus on the next three, verses 15-18.

In Ephesians 6:15 we read about the Gospel of peace. It says, "And having shod your feet in preparation [to face the enemy with the *firm-footed stability,* the *promptness*, and the *readiness* produced by the good news] of the Gospel of peace."

- *"Having shod your feet in the preparation of the Gospel of peace:"* No army would enter a battle if they were not properly trained. Of course basic training is not fun. But it prepares soldiers for battle. It involves grueling and uncomfortable situations in which they must learn how to survive. They learn how to use certain equipment and how to protect and defend themselves. Most of all, when a soldier is trained, he or she learns how to stay on task, no matter what, for the safety and betterment of the whole group, even when they don't feel like it. Just as the text in Ephesians says, a soldier in training learns "firm-footed stability." God is looking for people willing to be trained in stability withstanding both difficult and good times in the same manner. Becoming stable is vital for "firm footedness."

Likewise, our feet must be suited with the gospel if we are to walk in peace in this world. The soldier of the Lord must learn to walk just as Jesus did, in peace. This means leaving our fleshly and selfish desires behind and submitting our stubbornness to God.

Colossians 3:15 tells us to

let the peace (soul harmony which comes) from Christ rule (act as umpire continually) in your hearts [deciding and settling with finality all questions that arise in your minds, in that peaceful state] to which as [members of

Christ's] one body you were also called [to live]. And be thankful (apprecia-tive), [giving praise to God always].

And in 1 Peter 3:11 we are told,

Let him turn away from wickedness and shun it, and let him do right. Let him search for peace (harmony; undisturbedness from fears, agitating pas-sions, and moral conflicts) and seek it eagerly. [Do not merely desire peaceful relations with God, with your fellowmen, and with yourself, but pursue, and go after them!]

When we spend time training by preparing our hearts with the gospel of peace, God's Spirit enables us to remain in the powerful position of trust and thanksgiving when life's storms hit.

As we move on to verse 16, we find the call to "Lift up over all the [covering] shield of saving faith, upon which you can quench all the flaming missiles of the wicked [one]."

- *"Lift up over all the covering shield of saving faith:"* God has given each one of us faith. It's not just faith *in* God, but it's the faith *of* God. Therefore, if our faith, confi-dence and belief in God's ability, efficiency, and might are stable, we are undefeatable and nothing the enemy throws our way will thwart us. Entrusting ourselves totally to God and believing He is in control extinguishes the enemy's flaming, lying mis-siles intended to harm us. God's grace empowers us to face anything and we need to believe that.

Psalm 91:1-6 gives witness to this account. It says,

He who dwells in the secret place of the Most High shall remain *stable* and *fixed* under the shadow of the Almighty [Whose power no foe can withstand]. I will say of the Lord, He is my Refuge and my Fortress, my God; on Him I lean and rely, and in Him I [confidently] trust! For [then] He will deliver you from the snare of the fowler and from the deadly pestilence. [Then] He will cover you with His pinions, and under His wings shall you trust and find refuge; His truth and His faithfulness are a shield and a buckler. You shall not be afraid of the terror of the night, nor of the arrow (the evil plots and slanders of the wicked) that flies by day, nor of the pestilence that stalks in the darkness, nor of the destruction and sudden death that surprise and lay waste at noonday.

Our belief in God will always defeat the fearful darts that Satan uses to stab us with. Again, I cannot stress enough the importance of learning to remain stable and fixed in Christ. The only way to do this is to partner with the Holy Spirit by feeding on God's Word, believing it, and receiving God's empowering grace. His grace enables us to go through anything we face with boldness, confidence, and unfailing trust in Him. Are you protected with God's shield of faith?

**Our belief in God will always defeat the fearful darts
that Satan uses to stab us with.**

Ephesians 6:17 tells us to, "take the helmet of salvation and the sword that the Spirit wields, which is the Word of God."

- *"Take the helmet of salvation:"* What is a helmet used for? Obviously, it is used to protect our head. Are you protecting your head with the saving Word of God? Or do you take in every thought the enemy throws your way?

God has rescued us from the sins and temptations that so easily entangle us, and He has brought us into right relationship with Himself. He has given us this salvation by grace through faith. God has bestowed the right to deliverance, forgiveness, preservation, wholeness, soundness, prosperity, rescue, and general well-being for every believer. We put on the helmet of salvation by obeying God, spending time renewing our minds with His word, and speaking it into our lives. If we are not willing to do this, our eyes, minds, ears, and mouths remain vulnerable to the lies and tricks of the enemy.

We would all agree that playing a game of football without a helmet would be crazy. No football player would do that—nor would he be allowed to. The same truth applies to us in the spiritual realm. If we don't understand what God has saved us from, we cannot stand firm when opposition comes our way. Why would any of us think that we can enter the "game" of life without a helmet and armor? We can't. If we do, we will be inclined to think and say things that oppose God's Word, which will open our souls to more of Satan's entanglement. Remember, God has already given us everything we will ever need pertaining to life and godliness. (See 2 Peter 3:1.) We just need to understand how to access it and work it out into the physical realm.

- *" . . . and the sword that the Spirit wields which is the Word of God:"* This sword, the Word of God, is our only offensive weapon. The Holy Spirit uses it to cut through the lies, attacks, and accusations of the enemy. This verse clearly describes God's intention for how we are to use our minds and mouths. They should be used for the purposes of redeeming, renewing, and restoring. We come against Satan not with our own works, words, and human efforts, but with God's empowering grace. Jesus gave us a great example of this when He faced Satan's temptations in the desert. He came against Satan by quoting Scriptures.

**We come against Satan with
God's Word, not our words!**

Consider how the helmet and the sword can work together in every situation of your life:

1. The enemy throws a fiery dart your way. It is filled with self criticism, resentment, grumbling, complaining, jealously, anger, doubt, and unforgiveness.
2. If you will get quiet inside, stay in peace, and remain stable, you will hear the Holy Spirit's voice place a verse or personal word from God into your heart.
3. Refuse to meditate on and repeat whatever your mind wants to say (such as, "I look ugly, or "he will never change," or "I wish I could do what she does," or "I'll never be able to kick this habit, or I'm done, I quit,"). Instead, recognize Satan's lies. Submit your will, thoughts, and words to the Holy Spirit and repeat the same verse He places in your heart. This requires watering and nurturing yourself with the Word.

Remember, the Holy Spirit cannot bring a verse to your memory if you haven't fed your mind the Word.

4. Your partnership with the Holy Spirit, along with God's empowering grace, *together,* make a three-fold strength that cuts through the ropes of entanglement and releases you (or the person we are praying for) from Satan's power.

5. Remain fixed, stable, and determined to do this as long as necessary. (This is so important).

Ephesians 6:18 gives testimony to these truths. It says, "Pray at all times (on every occasion, in every season), in the Spirit, with all [manner of] prayer and entreaty. To that end keep alert and watch with strong purpose and perseverance, interceding on behalf of all the saints (God's consecrated people)."

*   *"Pray at all times, on every occasion, in every season, in the Spirit:"* We are told to talk to God about everything at all times. It is necessary to talk to Him before we talk to anyone else. We would save ourselves so much grief if we ran to God with everything first, instead of consulting with our own opinions and friends. That is why the Spirit of the Living God lives inside each of us. We must stay tuned in to Him, live in His Presence and listen as He directs us. Sadly, for a lot of Christians, God is the last one we consult. Even then it's often out of desperation. Let's change this habit!

**We would save ourselves so much grief if
we ran to God with everything first, instead of
consulting with our own opinions and friends.**

Ephesians 6:18 is saying:

1. Come to Him first.
2. Get quiet inside and listen to what the Holy Spirit is saying to your spirit.
3. Tell God your requests based on His Word and His truth.
4. With that in mind, pay attention, and watch out for your spiritual brothers and sisters, mothers or fathers. Watch that the precious people in your life do not fall prey to the enemy's entanglements. Pray for them, using the Word that God places in your heart, in order that they might overcome. Do not give up praying for them no matter what!

Deuteronomy 30:14 says, "But the word is very near you, in your mouth and in your mind and in your heart, so that you can do it." Awesome! Yes, by God's grace we can do this!

When we persevere in prayer, we are spiritually clothing and preparing ourselves to become encouragers who strengthen each other's hearts. Through these spiritual clothes, we bring peace and empowerment to God's family. In this setting, God's grace abounds as we walk in unity and victory, not only for ourselves, but for the sake of all the brethren, our spouses, children, friends, and family. Unity among believers is a bond which the enemy can never sever if we will just take the time to become F.I.T. vessels (spirit, soul, and body), for God's army. The body of Christ is designed to rule and reign on this earth because we trust in and rely on the empowering, enabling grace of our Lord and Captain, Jesus Christ. (See Romans 5:17).

Questions for Study
1. Why is it so important to walk and be in peace at all times?
2. According to Colossians 3:15, peace is to act as an umpire in our lives. As far as it depends on you, are you at peace with others?
3. According to 1 Peter 3:11, what causes us to lose our peace?
4. Does your faith and belief in God cover you in all your circumstances and relationships? What quenches the fiery darts (attacks) that the enemy launches against us?
5. What is a helmet used for, and are you using your spiritual helmet?
6. How should the helmet of salvation and the sword of the Spirit work together in our lives?
7. Are you in the habit of talking to God first about all things? Ask Him to help you do this.

Personal Prayer

Lord, I take up the helmet of salvation, understanding who I am in You and what You died to give me (Ephesians 6:17). I realize that the salvation You offer is forgiveness, rescue, deliverance, wholeness, soundness, healing, prosperity, blessing, and general well-being. I thank You for that! I place the breastplate of righteousness and integrity over my heart to keep me in right standing with You (Ephesians 6:14). The belt of truth—Your Word—holds me together and keeps me clothed with Christ (Ephesians 6:14). I will walk with the shoes of peace, having prepared my steps with the gospel (Ephesians 6:15). I desire for peace to be the umpire in my life (Colossians 3:15). I turn away from wickedness and shun it and I choose to do what is right in all things. I will search for peace with others and seek it eagerly (1 Peter 3:11). Cover me with the shield of faith, my belief and confidence in You, which defeats and quenches all the fiery darts that the enemy throws at me (Ephesians 6:16). I will use the sword of the Spirit—Your Word—coming out of my mouth to cut through the darkness and defeat the enemy (Ephesians 6:17). Thank You, Lord, for Your protection; help me to put on this armor every day. Your Word promises me that if I live in the secret place of the Most High, I will remain stable and fixed on You, and no foe can withstand that. You are my refuge and my fortress, my God; on You I lean and rely and place my trust.

Chapter 48

The Past, Present,
and Future

---

*G*od has many good things planned for us. First, though, we must to choose to align our thoughts with His about our lives. We must be willing to exchange our thoughts, words, attitudes, and ways for His. Period. He wants to heal all of our past and present hurts. He desires that we live His abundant life, right now, regardless of our circumstances, and He wants to prepare us for the future. I hope this chapter will reveal to you how God wants you to view your past, the present, and your future.

The Past:

Unfortunately, many people struggle with moving forward in life. When we look backward instead of forward, however, the past only acts as a stumbling block. Every single person on earth has something in his or her past that needs overcoming. Perhaps it involves negative words that were spoken to you as a child or an abusive home life. Perhaps it includes undue criticism from family, peers, or teachers, or rejection, fear, shame, guilt, or even self-hatred—you name it. Here's good news: Jesus wants to heal the wounded, insecure child in all of us.

We cannot change our pasts, but we can change how we view them. For example, if you grew up in a negative and abusive environment as a child:

1. Realize it was not your fault—you were a helpless child and a victim.
2. Realize that as an adult, it is now your responsibility to take charge of your own actions and attitudes.

Most people continue in an abusive cycle, not because they want to, but because they don't understand how to break it. The truth is, without Jesus Christ's love and acceptance it would be impossible. In order for God to heal our wounds from the past we must confront the fear and dysfunction in our lives, instead of running from them. Many of us believe that once we escape the situation all will be well. Unfortunately, that is not entirely true. If we don't learn how to properly view all the "junk" from our past, it will stay with us and hinder our destiny.

In order for God to heal our wounds
from the past, we must confront the dysfunction
and fear in our lives instead of running from them.

Jesus came to release us from our bondages and to restore us to the Father, but we have to let go of all the negativity and guilt from our past in order to embrace God's plan. Chapter 61 of Isaiah talks about the Lord giving us beauty instead of ashes, the oil of joy instead of mourning, the garment of praise instead of a burdened and failing spirit. It speaks of rebuilding the ancient ruins, rising up what was formerly desolate, and restoring the ruined devastations of many generations. I implore you to partner with the Living God and let Him give you this kind of healing. Paul wrote to the Philippians in Chapter 3, verses 13-14, " . . . but one thing I do [it is my one aspiration]: forgetting what lies behind and straining forward to what lies ahead, I press on toward the goal to win the [supreme and heavenly] prize to which God in Christ Jesus is calling us upward."

Let's break these verses down and study what they reveal to us:

1. *"Forget what lies behind."* If we are to forget what lies behind, we have to walk through the process of forgiveness first. We cannot run from our "stuff," our past, or problems inside of us and pretend that we're forever okay. These things will come out of us in one way or another.

2. *"Strain forward to what lies ahead."* It is the enemy who desires to keep us entangled in our past. He will constantly remind us of where we came from, how unworthy we are and how bad we have been. He will convince us to believe that God couldn't forgive us of "that sin." Satan desires to cause despair by making us believe that things will never change. As long as we entertain those kinds of thoughts, things won't change because those thoughts do not agree with God's Word or His plan for our lives. These thoughts will eventually become strongholds in our lives if we don't destroy them with God's Word.

3. *"Press on toward the goal."* In order for us to press on, we will experience pressure. Our flesh doesn't like to do things that feel uncomfortable, and pressing on can be one of those things. We will always feel pressure when we begin to exchange our thoughts, words, actions, and attitudes for God's. Pressing on involves fighting our flesh's desire to remain the same or continue doing what "it" wants. We must keep staring at Jesus. By faith, God's empowering grace keeps us pressing on. Our goal is found in Isaiah 61:1-2, where it says that our broken hearts will be bound up and healed, that we will be set free to experience liberty in all realms of life—spiritually, mentally, emotionally, socially, and financially,—that our prisons will be flung open, and we will start living in the favor, blessing, and abundance of the Lord. If we exchange our ways for God's, the suffering we experience in our flesh will be turned into good.

4. *"Christ Jesus is calling us upward."* Jesus picks us up from out of our pits and calls us upward, but we need the ears to hear this call. Did you know that to hear means to *listen, receive, love, and obey?* This is how Jesus pulls us out of our pit! He is calling and we need to listen to Him. We need to receive His Word, obey Him, love Him with

our entire beings, and depend on Him totally. We must allow Jesus to walk us through every necessary step. Then we will be free from Satan's strongholds and lies, and from the negative things that have happened to us in our pasts. We most certainly do need "untangled" from "doing" life apart from Him.

Isaiah 61:7 says, "Instead of your [former] shame you shall have a twofold recompense, instead of dishonor and reproach [your people] shall rejoice in their portion. Therefore in their land they shall possess double [what they had forfeited]; everlasting joy shall be theirs," and Joel 2:25 says, "And I (the Lord)* will restore or replace for you the years that the locust has eaten . . ." Was your childhood stolen? Was your innocence exploited? God will heal and restore you if you let Him in. No matter what has occurred in our pasts, if we partner with the Holy Spirit He will bring us to the abundant living He originally intended for us to experience here on earth. We were not meant to do life apart from God. Life and God go hand in hand. The only way to escape the past is walking with God *through* it. We cannot ignore it or run from it, or it will remain a stumbling block to us. Allow the Lord to teach you what to sever, what to keep, and how to keep walking with Him.

**No matter what has occurred in our pasts, if we partner with
the Holy Spirit, He will bring us to the abundant living
He originally designed for us to experience here on earth.**

The Present:

Our lives today are the result of the choices we made yesterday. The only way to repay the devil back for all he has done to us is to determine to follow God and stick with His program, no matter what. Then God will use us to help untangle someone else and rebuild their ruins. Isaiah 61:8 says, "For I the Lord love justice; I hate robbery and wrong with violence or a burnt offering. And I will faithfully give them their recompense in truth, and I will make an everlasting covenant or league with them." We must understand that the only way to get different results is to start thinking differently. Then we will start doing differently. I've heard it said that the definition of insanity is to keep doing the same thing while expecting different results. The negative, destructive thought patterns, and old habits in our lives need uprooting, and the former things of old must go. The seeds of a new and different harvest must be planted in our thoughts first if we want a different tomorrow. The only true way to enjoy our future is to make wise, consistent, godly choices today.

**The only true way to enjoy our future is to make wise,
consistent, and godly choices today.**

First Corinthians 3:9 refers to us as gardens under construction. In order to start a garden we have to uproot what was previously there. We must turn over the soil first, and then plant today for the harvest that we want to receive tomorrow. What we believe, what we think about, what we talk about, and how we choose to act are all ways we plant for tomorrow. We must uproot the weeds in our lives and turn over the "soil" of our hearts. This might be in the form of bad attitudes, negative mindsets, destructive thought patterns, complaining, grumbling, and so on. It's time we're completely done with these things. Second, we must agree with what

God has to say in His Word about who we are and what He desires for us. We will reap what we sow! If we are constantly involved in strife and quarrelling, that is what we will reap. But if we start sowing mercy, hope, love, and kindness, we will reap accordingly. This process takes place within us. It takes much time, nurturing, plowing, weeding, and the watering of the Word to make us grow. As a farmer would go to a seed store to purchase the seeds he wants to plant, we too must go to the Source for the seeds we intend to plant: God's Word. As we exchange our beliefs, thoughts, words, attitudes, and actions to agree with God's, we will begin to reap His promises. Truly, what we think, say, and do today absolutely matters for our tomorrow—not only for ourselves, but for those around us as well.

**What we think, say and do today absolutely matters for our tomorrow,
not only for ourselves, but for those around us as well.**

If we will seek, speak, and surrender to God each day, He will:

- Heal us from our pasts.
- Prepare our hearts to receive His blessings.
- Prioritize our lives.
- Keep us in proper balance.
- Teach us to plant seeds for tomorrow that match His will for us.
- Create an unshakeable inner peace and joy, regardless of our circumstances.
- Rebuild what has been ruined.
- Raise up a generation—our offspring—who fears Him.

The Future:

Jeremiah 29:11 says, "For I know the thoughts and plans that I have for you, says the Lord, thoughts and plans for *welfare* and *peace* and *not for evil,* to *give you hope* in your final outcome." Wow, what an amazing promise! Once again, the only way we will see this promise come to pass in our lives is by choosing to live in agreement with God continually. A great truth about our future is that, "All things are *possible* with God." (See Matthew 19:26.) Yet these things are not probable without our constant belief, obedience, and submission to God. I believe God is ready and waiting to bless us, but He will not do so if we continue to walk in our own stubborn ways. Look at the promises in Isaiah 30:18,

> And therefore the Lord [earnestly] waits [expecting, looking, and longing] to
> be gracious to you; and therefore He lifts Himself up, that He may have mercy
> on you and show loving-kindness to you. For the Lord is a God of justice.
> Blessed (happy, fortunate, to be envied) are all those who [earnestly] wait
> for Him, who expect and look and long for Him for His victory, His favor,
> His love, His peace, His joy, and His matchless, unbroken companionship]!

That's an incredible verse . . . Pause and think about it!

We must decide to surrender our self-will to God and His leading *every single day of our lives.* We have the Holy Spirit's power living inside of us to help us, along with God's grace, favor, mercy, and loving kindness. He even provides us with the faith to believe. But if we are not surrendering to Him daily, He cannot lead and govern us totally. Remember, He's not forceful and will not make us follow Him; we have to want to.

God is ready and waiting to bless us. However, He will not do so if we continue to walk in our own stubborn ways.

We have the mind of Christ living inside of us (see 1 Corinthians 2:16)—are you activating His mind into your life? Or are you continuing to remain tuned into the mind of your flesh? Every time you choose to come into agreement with the mind of your flesh, you destroy your tomorrow. That's a really harsh and sobering thought. Beloved son or daughter of God, renew your mind daily with God's Word and live out by faith the fact that you can plow and plant the future He desires for you. 1 Corinthians 2:9 says,

> What eye has not seen and ear has not heard and has not entered into the heart of man, [all that] God has prepared (made and keeps ready) for those who love Him [who hold Him in affectionate reverence, promptly obeying Him and gratefully recognizing the benefits He has bestowed].

God wants us to set our hope in Him for a brighter tomorrow! Here is our part:

- Love Him with everything in you (heart, soul, mind, and strength).
- Reverence Him in all your ways (heart, soul, mind, and strength).
- Promptly obey Him at all times (heart, soul, mind, and strength).
- Be thankful at all times (heart, soul, mind, and strength).
- Recognize His benefits that He graciously bestows upon you (heart, soul, mind, and strength).

Isaiah 64:4 says, "For from of old no one has heard nor perceived by the ear, nor has the eye seen a God besides you, Who works and shows Himself active on behalf of him who [earnestly] *waits* for Him." I believe the reverse of this scripture is true as well. If we actively prepare for our futures without Him, He'll just wait until we decide to include Him. Are you planning for tomorrow, rushing before God to stay ahead of the game of life? Look at Isaiah 30:20-21. It says,

> And though the Lord gives you the bread of adversity and the water of afflic-tion, yet your Teacher will not hide himself any more, *but your eyes will constantly behold your Teacher.* And *your ears will hear a word* behind you, saying, This is the way; walk in it, when you turn to the right hand and when you turn to the left.

Indeed, as we stare at Jesus, our Teacher, our "eyes" see and our "ears" hear Him.

We can become so concerned about stockpiling our possessions that we forget to entrust ourselves to God's care each day. I'm not suggesting that we become irresponsible and live for the moment. I do believe, however, that if we entrust ourselves totally to God, He will direct our steps and cause us to stockpile that which He desires. (See Proverbs 3:5-7 and 16:3.) Look at these words that Paul wrote to the Philippians in chapter 4:11-13, 19,

I have learned how to be content (satisfied to the point where I am not disturbed or disquieted) whatever state I am. I know how to be abased and live humbly in straitened circumstances, and I know also how to enjoy plenty and live in abundance. I have learned in any and all circumstances the secret of facing every situation, whether well fed or going hungry, having sufficiency and enough to spare or going without and being in want. I have strength for all things in Christ Who empowers me; I am self-sufficient in Christ's sufficiency]. And my God will liberally supply (fill to the full) your every need according to His riches in glory in Christ Jesus.

Paul believed not only in God's care for him, but he also understood the power and importance of God's grace which enabled him to be "okay" no matter the circumstance or situation he found himself. His stability resulted in peace and joy because his confidence was not in his circumstances, relationships, or things, but in God Himself. Paul knew that God was behind the scenes, working things out for his own good (see Romans 8:28).

God desires us to believe these same things regarding our pasts, our presents and our futures. God's heart attitude toward us is filled with H.O.P.E. . . . . *H*ealth, *O*pportunities, *P*ossibilities and the *E*xpectation of a bright tomorrow! Believe!

Questions for Study

1. How do you view your past? Is it a stumbling block or a history lesson?
2. What must we be willing to do in order for God to heal us from our past?
3. Ask the Holy Spirit to reveal what you need to sever from your past in order to move forward.
4. What must we do in order to receive different results in our lives?
5. What do you want to reap in the future? Are you sowing those seeds today?
6. Are you seeking, speaking, and surrendering your entire life to God every day?
7. Like a garden, how do we make grow that which we sow?
8. What is your hope for the future? Write it out and determine the necessary steps to receive it.

Personal Prayer

Lord, help me to view my past as You want me to see it. I don't want to struggle with it any longer; I want to move forward. Therefore I choose to come into agreement with You regarding my past (Philippians 3:13-14). Help me to confront any dysfunction in my life that needs to be addressed and corrected. I realize that I do not need to face any situation without You and Your help. As Your Word says, You are my Shepherd and, true to Your Word, You help me become aware of any wrong choices and send me in the right direction. Even when the way goes through Death Valley, I will not be afraid, for You are by my side, making me feel secure. You serve me a six course dinner right in front of my enemies. You revive my drooping head; I am so blessed. Your beauty and love chase after me every day of my life. I'm back home in the house of God for the rest of my life! (Psalm 23). Thank You, Lord, that You promise to restore and replace the years the locust has eaten (Joel 2:25). I realize that I am a garden under construction, and I desire to make godly choices every day of my life (1 Corinthians 3:9). Help me to establish the discipline to do this and to plant the seeds that I would like to see as a harvest in my own life (Galatians 6:7). Uproot anything that hinders me, at this moment, from walking into the future that You have planned for me — a future planned for welfare and peace, not evil, but of hope in my final outcome (Jeremiah 29:11). Thank You, Lord for health, opportunities, possibilities, and the expectancy of a bright tomorrow!

Chapter 49

Living the Abundant Life
on Earth

hrist died and rose again from the grave in order to give us abundant life on earth. There
is new and abundant life in Jesus Christ and by His grace, through the gift of faith, we
can choose to enter into His abundant life! The same power that raised Jesus from the dead now
works in our hearts and transforms us into the image of Jesus Christ. We can do this as we learn
how to view and process our past, present, and future in accordance with God, His Word, and
the Holy Spirit's leading within our lives. I hope you are convinced by now that you and I are
not capable of living this abundant life alone and apart from the Holy Spirit. Consider everything
we have learned thus far about the soul, (our minds, wills, attitudes, and emotions) and now let's
connect each facet of our lives to living the abundant life that Christ came to give us.

In John 10:10, Jesus said, " . . . but I came that they may have and enjoy life, and have it
in abundance (to the full, till it overflows)." What an incredible promise! If we are to see this
promise fulfilled, we must exchange our thoughts about our past, present, and future for God's.

Here is what this looks like:

- We must understand who Jesus is and what He deposited on the inside of us at salvation when He came to live in our hearts. (See 1 Peter 1:2-5; 2 Peter 1:3-10.)
- We must center our faith and hope in God's Word. (See 1 Peter 1:21.)
- We must renew our minds daily by acknowledging all that God has placed inside of us pertaining to life, salvation, heath, blessings, godliness, and the fruit of the Spirit. (See Romans 12:2; 2 Peter 1:3-4; Romans 4:17.)
- We must constantly be renewed in the spirit of our minds, having a fresh mental and spiritual attitude about our circumstances. (See Ephesians 4:23.)
- We must believe what the Word says, obey it and speak it so it comes to pass in our lives (See 1 Corinthians 2:9-13; Romans 4:17.)
- We must choose our words wisely. Our words are powerful, and what we choose to say today will determine our tomorrows—for death or life. (See Proverbs 18:20-22.)

- We must keep our eyes focused and fixed on what God says in His Word. We must always be looking at Jesus' life as an example and be very careful of the things we place before our eyes. (See Psalm 15; 1 Corinthians 2:9.)
- We must keep our ears tuned in to God's Spirit, and tune out anything that would poison and keep our inner lives from holiness and purity. (See 1 Corinthians 2:9; Mark 4:22-24.)
- We must be givers seeking whom we can bless, especially fellow believers. (See Luke 6:38 and Galatians 6:10.)
- We must go about doing good and overcoming evil. (See Acts 10:38 and Romans 12:21.)

Truly, if we do these things we shall never be moved! Living the abundant life on earth requires us to become unglued and unabsorbed with ourselves. It forces us to be willing to focus solely on the life of Christ and His finished work on the cross in order to become like Him. Our joy is made complete when we embrace all that Christ has freely given to us by His grace. Receive what He gives and pass it on to others. Romans 14:17 says, " . . . the Kingdom of God (working within us)* is righteousness (that state which makes a person acceptable to God) and [heart] peace and joy in (partnership with)* the Holy Spirit."
Isaiah 43:18-19 says,

> Do not [earnestly] remember the former things; neither consider the things of old. Behold, I am doing a new thing! Now it springs forth; do you not perceive and know it and will you not give heed to it? I will even make a way in the wilderness and rivers in the desert!

God is at work doing a new thing in our lives, but we must stop thinking about the former things and open our eyes to the new. Indeed, we must change our focus. Many times we miss what God wants to do in our lives because we are focused on something other than Him. Remember, the enemy will try to convince us to look at everything but Jesus! Just like driving a car, we can't be driving forward and looking behind us at the same time... If we do, we will crash.

**Many times we miss what God wants to do in our lives
because we are focused on something other than Him.**

God wants us to pay attention to what He is doing in our lives and to give heed to that! Do you believe that He is making a way for you in the difficult circumstances and relationships that you may be experiencing? He is giving living water to the dry and deserted parts of our lives as we become more like Him. We will see it come to pass if we keep our eyes and hearts fixed on Him and obey His Word. (See John 11:40).
Jeremiah 33:3 says, "Call to Me and I will answer you and show you great and mighty things, fenced in and hidden which you do not know (do not distinguish and recognize, have knowledge of and understand)." We live the abundant life on earth through our rich partnership with Jesus Christ. It's that simple. He said, "Call to Me and I will answer you!" He promises to show us the things we didn't recognize before. I believe the first thing He wants to show us is that we need to change our mindset.

We live the abundant life on earth through our rich partnership with Jesus Christ.

Unfortunately, many believers think that living the abundant life consists of leisure, material riches, no problems, and total comfort. Such thinking reflects the views of the world. However, we live the abundant and rich life that Christ died to give us when our minds, mouths, eyes, ears, wills, attitudes, and emotions (spirit, soul, and body) are surrendered to and in tune with the Holy Spirit. We are no longer searching for gratification through our own means or self-effort. Instead, we are turning our focus solely on Jesus, our Provider. Then nothing can overcome us.

Once we allow the Holy Spirit to work on and heal our souls, we will find abundance in the physical realm as well. (See 1 Thessalonians 5:23-24.) Christ Himself will teach us how to manage our finances. We will learn how to own things while not allowing them to own us. He will show us what to do in our relationships and circumstances, who to pick for friends, what to devote our time to, and so forth. Then our lives will be so full of abundant joy, we won't be shaken by what's going on around us. At this stage, our minds will habitually be renewed, fixed, and set on God who is above all things.

Yes, Jesus said we will have trouble in this world. But He told us to be of good cheer (having and maintaining a positive attitude and hopeful expectations in God's ability, power, efficiency, and might), for He has overcome the world. (See John 16:33.) What a wonderful promise! Remember what Hebrews 10:35-36 says?

> Do not, therefore, fling away your fearless confidence, for it carries a great and glorious compensation of reward. For you have need of steadfast patience and endurance, so that you may perform and fully accomplish the will of God, and thus receive and carry away (and enjoy to the full) what is promised.

Consider this mindset when trouble comes your way:

1. God, how do you want to change me?
2. What is my responsibility?
3. This too shall pass and manifest Your glory.
4. No matter what's coming my way, You're bigger.
5. Help me.

I remember one time in my personal life when it seemed like several negative and over-bearing things were happening all at once. I felt overwhelmed and anxious. One morning in my time alone with the Lord, I heard the Holy Spirit speaking. He told me to write down these things that were bothering me. So I did. Then, He told me to put His Name in front of each problem and place the greater-than symbol pointing away from His Name.

It looked like this:

God > _____.
God > _____.
God > _____.

Every time I started thinking about the problems, I remembered the equation: God is greater than. . . . That is how I responded when the enemy tried to bring about worry, doubt, and confusion. God is greater than!

Friends, we have the mind of Christ and we are one with His Spirit. (See 1 Corinthians 2:16 and 4:17.) We must start incorporating His thoughts, His Words, and His ways into our everyday lives, situations, circumstances, relationships, problems, and so on. We need to do this if we are to live the promised abundant life He died to give us! We must stop living out of the mind of the flesh, and get in tune with the mind of the Spirit, who is the mind of Christ within us. If we will live by the Spirit, He will guide, counsel, instruct, and lead us to overcome by His power! (See Romans 8:5-14.) This happens as we live in and by His Word.

Perhaps you've heard these insights before. Think about this:

1. If you keep doing things the way you have always done them, you will keep getting the same results. (This also happens to be the definition of insanity!).
2. Real heart change comes when the pain of staying the same is greater than the pain of changing.

We can take action by:

1. Establishing godly habits now.
2. Sticking with them, no matter how difficult it may seem at first.
3. Asking the Holy Spirit to help us.
4. Waiting on His directions and timing.
5. Expecting the harvest of abundant life come to pass in our lives!

Questions for Study
1. How can we live the abundant life that Jesus died to give us, even today? Read over the lists from the first and second pages of this chapter. Are you doing them? Remember, complaining about your life won't change it; it will only make matters worse.
2. Is *joy* present in your life?
3. Look up Romans 14:17, and write it out. Ask the Holy Spirit what you need to do in order to obtain righteousness, peace, and joy in every area of your life.
4. What is the "new thing" that God is teaching you or doing in your life, and how does He want you to respond?
5. Are you living out Jeremiah 33:3?
6. After reading this chapter, how do you view the abundant life? Is your focus on the material or the eternal?
7. Write out the things that are troubling you right now. Then in front of each statement, write this: God > _____.

Personal Prayer

Lord, help me to live the abundant life that You died to give me (John 10:10)! I realize that the promises in Your Word come with obedience. Help me to be responsible for what I feed my soul. I know that I have to renew my mind daily (Romans 12:2), have a fresh mental and spiritual attitude (Ephesians 4:23), and that I must choose my words wisely (Proverbs 18:20-21). Help me to keep my mind and the eyes of my heart focused on You and to be careful of the things I place before myself (Psalm 15; 1 Corinthians 2:9). Help me to keep my ears tuned in to Your Spirit and to stay far from anything that would poison my inner life (1 Corinthians 2:9; Mark 4:22-24). I desire to be a giver, seeking whom I can bless, especially fellow believers (Luke 6:38; Galatians 6:10). Anoint me to go about doing good in the power of Your Spirit (Acts 10:38). I want to live the abundant life on earth in the richness of my partnership with You, despite any suffering or negative circumstances I may face. Thank You that You have overcome the world and help me to be of good cheer! (John 16:33). I realize that no matter what may come my way, You are bigger! Your grace is sufficient for me (2 Corinthians 12:9). Help me to lean and rely on You for my effectiveness rather than on my own efforts, energy, or talents. Help me not to be tempted to do Your work on my own, especially in the areas where You have gifted me. I admit that I am weak; now fill me with Your power and grace.

Chapter 50

Abiding in Christ
and Bearing Much Fruit

⁂

To abide in Christ means to live continuously in the presence of God. This is His will for our lives. Through our constant union, abiding, and communicating with the Father, our lives will begin to resemble Jesus Christ's. As we place our faith in God's grace and practice obedience, our lives will begin to resemble the character and power of Jesus more and more. As stated in Galatians 5:23, there is no law or rule that can bring a charge against such character. Abiding in constant union with the Father is the goal of every Christ-follower. Jesus was the perfect example of this for us.

Now we too are called to live out this life, empowered and governed by the Holy Spirit living within us, loving others, and going about overcoming evil with good. Every time we submit our ways to the Holy Spirit's leading, we are cutting off the old nature and stopping it from having dominion over us. When we live in the Shadow of the Most High, our lives will become emotionally stable. Our wills conform to Christ's. Our minds are renewed daily with the Word of God, and we understand the importance of exercising our faith in Christ. This strengthens our unity with Jesus through the Holy Spirit and allows us to reach out to others who are in need of His touch.

As we allow the Holy Spirit to take us through the process of soul cleansing, healing, and purification, we begin to bear fruit even as He continues His work of pruning in us. This is what it means to become an equipped and F.I.T. Christian here on earth.

Abiding in Christ looks like this:

1. We focus our attention on Jesus and walk in His love. This will be revealed by how we respect God, ourselves, and other people. Remember, we will become what we constantly stare at. Stare at Jesus and His work on the cross for you, not on your flaws or sins.

2. We become free of confusion. We let go of our cares and entrust ourselves to Him. We no longer try and reason situations out with our natural mind, but we choose instead

to live by the Holy Spirit's direction within our hearts. Once we abandon our "fleshly" reasoning and follow the Holy Spirit's direction, what previously seemed illogical, at first, begins to make perfect "God sense."

3. We live responsibly before Him in all aspects of our lives. He causes us to embrace lives of simplicity, following His priorities both individually and corporately as a body. When we do this, we become like well-oiled machines, full of love, compassion, and peace, empowered by God Himself.

4. We interpret Scripture as the Holy Spirit has designed it to be interpreted, aligning our character with His. The focus is no longer on rules, roles, or pleasing people. Rather, we focus on letting the fruit of the Spirit grow within us, uplifting and encouraging others and equipping people to become just like Christ. In this way, we become bodies of people working together, endowed with His gifts, and going about doing what He did—teaching, preaching, healing people, and casting out demons: freeing people from oppression. In this manner, we make His will known on earth as it is in heaven. Jesus Himself lives on earth through our bodies in the form of the Holy Spirit. God's Word is spirit and life. We use it for instruction, reproof, conviction of sin, correcting those in error, discipline in obedience, and for training in righteousness (in holy living), and in conformity to God's will in thought, purpose, and action. (See 2 Timothy 3:16-17.) When the inner man dwells and remains in Christ, the Word and the Spirit equip us for every good work.

5. Christ uses us to draw others to Himself. In John 15:1-2, Jesus says that He is the true vine, and His Father is the vinedresser. Jesus cleanses us and repeatedly prunes us so that we continue to bear much excellent fruit! (Please understand that this passage is not about salvation, but about what we do with the salvation we've been given. The purpose of our Christian lives is to bear much fruit through our constant union and faith in Him).

We learn from these verses that:

- Jesus is the Vine in whom we are to remain. This is a command for every Christ-follower.
- We are the branches. The job of a branch is to cling to the Vine and bear fruit.
- The Holy Spirit is the life-giving sap that flows from the Vine into the branch. He connects us to the Life-Giver.

Therefore, God cuts off every branch, or areas of our lives that do not bear or show forth the fruit of the Spirit. This means the Holy Spirit will cleanse the areas of our lives that continue to resemble the old nature, by cutting off our old ways as we willingly submit ourselves to His direction and care. For example, every time we become selfish, prideful, envious, jealous, resentful and unforgiving, the Holy Spirit will convict us, prune us, and cleanse us of it. He does this because we cannot exhibit Christ's character and power through those dead selfish-induced behaviors.

If we remain in partnership with the Holy Spirit, we will no doubt have times where we feel like we have been cut back to nubs. Our flesh, (what we want, think, and feel), will hurt because of it. But after the pruning and cleansing, new life will begin to grow up out of these nubs and the riches of Christ-like character and grace will fill our lives with the fruit of the Spirit in greater measure than before!

John 15:4 tells us that we cannot bear fruit without living permanently in vital union with Him. However, many times we run around without this connection to the Vine. To be connected to the Vine means:

- He is involved in all areas of our lives.
- He is the first Person we run to in all situations and relationships.
- He is the first Person we call when we need help.
- He is the first Person we praise at all times because He is good and His ways are right.
- He is the first Person in whom we place our hope, trust, and dreams.

Many times we try running around and doing "good things" in the name of Christ, without being in constant union with His Holy Spirit. Friends, those efforts are in vain. They come from immature and fleshly motives. Such a Christian might be busy, but he is not necessarily fruitful. If we are too busy to spend time with God because we are doing things for Him, we do not understand what it means to be like Christ. I think, at one time or another, we've all been guilty of this.

Please hear this: We cannot possibly do His will if we do not spend time in relationship with God renewing our minds through reading the Word and prayer. The Holy Spirit uses this relationship with Christ to teach us how to become like Him. It's how He shows us the areas of our lives that need adjusting. Jesus says in John 15:5 that apart from Him we can do nothing. We cannot and will not accomplish His will on earth by coming up with and tacking on our own appropriate behaviors, methods, programs, or forms of entertainment to capture people. Jesus asks us instead to become like Him through an intimate, ongoing relationship. He longs to make us healthy and whole individuals who are completely devoted and attached to Him. Then we can sacrificially give ourselves to others out of the supernatural empowerment He gives us.

On the other hand, if the branch (believer) has been separated from the Vine (Jesus), it is sick, and the fruit is unhealthy. The branch needs to remain, relax, and draw life from the Vine (Jesus), through the life-giving sap (the Holy Spirit) in order to resemble the Person (Jesus Christ). Verse six tells us, "If a person does not dwell in Me, he is thrown out like a [broken-off] branch, and withers." Verse 7 goes on to say, "If you live in Me [abide vitally united to Me] and My words remain in you and continue to live in your hearts, ask whatever you will, and it shall be done for you." Unfortunately, many times we want the promises without the conditions. Visiting with God occasionally, spending time alone with Him once a week for five minutes before bedtime, or going to church twice a week does not qualify us for the promise in verse seven. We remain vitally connected to Him through His Word and His Holy Spirit. If we have not submitted our will to Him and His Word, we will never live the life Christ died to give us. His promises will not be fulfilled in our lives. However, if we allow the Word and the Spirit to grow within us, through our union with the Holy Spirit, our lives will bear the kind of fruit that glorifies the Father. The Word of God will be made obvious in our lives for others to see. The Father is glorified when the fruit of the Spirit is expressed naturally through our daily lives in all that we think, say and do. (See verse eight.)

Jesus tells us to live in His love and to continue in the process of His love matures us and make us like Him. As we remain in Him, we become more like Him, a transformation that takes a lifetime. In verse ten, we read how to live in this love. Keep His commandments. Obey Him promptly. Be motivated by agape, sacrificial, love in all things. Then His joy and delight will be in us, and our joy and gladness will become mature, complete and overflowing.

Jesus states in verse 12, "This is My commandment: that you love one another [just] as I have loved you." And He says it again in verse 17, "This is what I command you: that you love one another."

Remember, the world often persecutes conservative and biblical beliefs causing Christians to suffer. This is the type of suffering that we all must endure for the sake of Christ. The enemy is constantly trying to work through people to remove the ways of Christ from society. But we are not alone. The Holy Spirit is with us. He empowers us to endure and as we do so we are comforted, helped, and strengthened by our union with Him. Thus we have unspeakable joy, for in our heart of hearts we are standing up and doing the right thing in the sight of God—the only One to whom we will answer to in the end.

Through our union with Christ, the Holy Spirit causes us to become spiritually F.I.T. This means:

1. We grow in *Faith*—our confidence in Christ.
2. Our souls are *Free* from the enemy's entanglements. We live with minds that have been renewed by the Word of God, wills that have conformed to God's, and emotions and feelings that no longer control or lead us. We are stable and led by the Holy Spirit regardless of the situation at hand. Our reactions and responses will become like Christ's.
3. This cause us to bear much *Fruit*—the fruit of the Spirit coming from within our lives, exposing the character, power, and ways of Christ to a dark and perishing world.
4. We will continue our journey *In* the *Transformation* process of becoming more like Christ Himself in all we think, say, and do.

There truly is *Freedom In Transformation!*

My prayer for all believers is that:

- We learn to let go of the cares of the world and the cares of our past, present, and future.
- We make it our purpose to remain connected to the Vine.
- We stop trying to "do" things for God, and instead return our hearts to prayer, praising, and seeking Him as our lifeline.
- We wait for Him to change us and to take action only when He sees fit.
- We focus our attention on walking in love.
- We show others what the Father in Heaven is like by the fruit of the Spirit, revealed in our attitudes, actions, and behaviors.
- We draw others to Him through our powerful, life-giving, and unbroken fellowship with our Lord and Savior Jesus Christ.

God bless you on your journey this side of Heaven! You can do whatever God asks you to do when you stay connected to Him! His grace, love, efficiency, power, and might will flow through your entire being, passing on more life to those around you! This is the legacy of love that we are called to leave to those who come after us.

Questions for Study

1. What does it mean to abide in Christ? Are you doing this daily and in every area of your life?
2. If you are not abiding, do you realize you are choosing to live in sin?
3. What does John 15:1-2 mean to you? Are you doing this in your daily life?
4. What are some areas of your life that need to be pruned?
5. What is the only way to be severed from our old ways and nature?
6. What happens after we are pruned and cleansed? Is this an ongoing process?
7. What is the one new commandment Jesus gives us? Do you love Him? Do you obey Him? Do you love yourself? Do you love others? Remember, you cannot love others properly until you have a healthy Christ-like love for yourself.
8. What does it mean to be spiritually F.I.T.?

Personal Prayer

Lord, help me to live in You and bear much fruit (John 15). I desire to have constant union and communion with You (Ephesians 6:10). Please help me through the ongoing process of soul cleansing, healing, and purification. I desire to become a vessel fit for your service. Thank You that the Holy Spirit within me is Jesus Himself living through my body. Your Word is Spirit and life, used for instruction, reproof, conviction of sin, correcting those in error, discipline in obedience, training in righteousness—holy living and conformity to Your will in thought, purpose, word, and action (2 Timothy 3:16-17). Thank You for the riches found in Your Word, brought forth by Your Spirit. I know that You are the Vine, Your Father is the Vinedresser, and I am the branch. Cleanse me and prune me so that I may yet bear more excellent fruit (John 15:2). As a branch bears fruit through its connection to the vine, so let my life bear fruit because I dwell in You and You dwell in me. Fill me with the knowledge of Your will in all spiritual wisdom and understanding, so that I will walk in a manner worthy of You. Help me to please You in all respects, bearing fruit in every good work and increasing in the knowledge of You. I pray that I will be strengthened with all power, according to Your glorious might, for the attaining of all steadfastness and patience, joyously giving thanks to the Father, who has qualified me to share in the inheritance of the saints (Colossians 1:9-12). Lord, I do not fear the unseen forces of darkness, because I have been transferred from darkness to light, from the slavery of keeping rules, pleasing people and the system of the world to being led by the Holy Spirit. From the bondage of selfishness to freedom, from pride to love, from guilt to forgiveness, from death to life (Colossians 1:13-14), help me, Lord, to grow in this faith. Help me become free of any entanglements and to bear much fruit in this process of transformation. Thank you for making me F.I.T.!

APPENDIX

Prayer of Repentance

Lord Jesus, I come to You, recognizing the sin in my life and the need to turn from my sin and turn toward You. Lord, forgive me, for sinning against You, a holy and righteous God. Thank You for the work that You did on the cross for me. You gave up Your life and You shed Your blood so that I can be cleansed, once and for all, from all of my sins. Thank You for giving me right-standing with God. I realize this is a free gift that You are giving to me. I can't earn it, nor do I deserve it, so I'll just say, "Thank You" for it. Thank You, for being my Savior, Deliverer, Healer, Provider, and Protector. I believe in my heart and I confess with my mouth that You are Lord. (See Romans 10:9.) Now I'm asking You to be the director of my life. Please fill me and empower me with Your Holy Spirit to help me live a life that is dead to sin and alive to You and Your ways. Thank You for loving me so much. Please help me to receive that love and love You in return. Please put a desire in my heart to study Your Word and allow the Holy Spirit to teach me and live through me. Let Your Kingdom be established in me drawing others to You.

ACKNOWLEDGMENTS

I'm always amazed at the grace and patience that God is so willing to give to me. He has brought me through so much inner turmoil, deception, and hardship to the place of rest in His perfect love and peace. I am grateful to my Savior, Jesus Christ. He continues to show me the love and value that He has for me and all people. This is where I choose to "make camp," in the security of His love for me. It's good to be able to look in the mirror and see myself as He sees me. To love and enjoy myself in a healthy and balanced way without guilt and condemnation is nothing short of God's mighty strength and healing power continuously at work in me. Indeed, life has plenty of challenges, but He has already given me everything I need to be more than a conqueror through His Spirit living in me. May He use this book for His glory. It is only because of Him that I can put on paper my continual experience of transformation. And thankfully, He's not finished with me yet!

To my Mom, I am truly grateful for the countless hours that you poured into reading this material and helping me with "round one." Mom, I could not have done this book without your help.

To my dear sister, Liana, thank you for designing my book cover. You nailed it!

To Pastor Steve Kern, thank you for your willingness to read this material and meet with me regularly to help this project move along.

To Warren Dick, thank you for being that special encouraging friend and mentor who is always honest with me.

To Bria Wasson, thank you for all of your help in the editing process. I am forever grateful.

To the many people who have read and studied this book and given me feedback, I appreciate your input and encouraging words.

To my wonderful husband, Ray, you are the most supportive husband ever. You are "one in a million!" Thank you for all you have done and continue to do to make this book possible.

I appreciate your willingness to help me see this project through to completion, no matter what! Thank you for being the stable force that you are. Thank you for truly showing me what real love and sacrifice looks like—Jesus style. As you always say, "It just keeps getting better every year!" I love you, Ray. You absolutely have what it takes – for all things! It's an honor to spend my life with you.

Jacob and Jordan, my "at-home-editors", thank you so much for spending hours and hours of your time combing through this project with me. You two bring such joy and happiness to my life! I thank God so much for you and for the privilege of being your mom. I love our hang-out times in the living room, watching movies, playing cards, walks in the woods, taking adventurous vacations, playing sports together, and watching you two play sports! I love the fun we get to have! Please, please, please, keep Christ at the center of your lives, and He will make everything else work out for your good—no matter what! God has great plans for you, never forget that. You are both so precious to me and your dad. I love you both so much! Thanks for everything and for all of your help.

ENDNOTES

Chapter One

1. Don Fleming, *World's Bible Dictionary,* Student Edition (Iowa Falls, IA: World Bible Publishers, Inc., 1990), 407.

Chapter Three

1. Jack W. Hayford, *The Hayford Bible Handbook,* (Nashville, Tennessee, Thomas Nelson, Inc., 1995), 811.
2. Ibid, 788.
3. Ibid, 788.
4. Ibid, 788.

Chapter Four

1. Jack W. Hayford, *The Hayford Bible Handbook,* (Nashville, Tennessee, Thomas Nelson, Inc., 1995), 811.

Chapter Six

1. W.E. Vine, Merril F. Unger, William White Jr., *Vine's Complete Expository Dictionary of Old and New Testament Words,* (Nashville, Tennessee, Thomas Nelson, Inc., 1996), 230.
2. Ibid, 229-230.
3. Joyce Meyer, "Straight Talk," (New York, NY: Warner Faith, 2004), 108.

Chapter Eight

1. Don Fleming, *World's Bible Dictionary,* Student Edition (Iowa Falls, IA: World Bible Publishers, Inc., 1990), 367.
2. Ibid, 368.
3. Ibid, 369.

Chapter Nine

1. Don Fleming, *World's Bible Dictionary,* Student Edition (Iowa Falls: World Bible Publishers, Inc., 1990), 77.

2. W.E. Vine, Merril F.Unger, William White Jr., *Vine's Complete Expository Dictionary of Old and New Testament Words,* (Nashville, Tennessee, Thomas Nelson, Inc., 1996), 400.

Chapter Ten

1. W.E. Vine, Merril F. Unger, William White Jr., *Vine's Complete Expository Dictionary of Old and New Testament Words,* (Nashville, Tennessee, Thomas Nelson, Inc., 1996), 346-347.

Chapter 12

1. W.E. Vine, Merril F. Unger, William White Jr., *Vine's Complete Expository Dictionary of Old and New Testament Words,* (Nashville, Tennessee, Thomas Nelson, Inc., 1996), 558.
2. Jack W. Hayford, *The Hayford Bible Handbook,* (Nashville, Tennessee, Thomas Nelson, Inc., 1995), 773.
3. James Strong, LLD., S.T.D., *Strong's Complete Word Study Concordance,* Expanded Edition #7291 (Chattanooga, TN AMG Publishers, 2004), 1967.
4. *Webster's New World Dictionary of the American Language; Second College Edition,* (The World Publishing Company, 1970), 1188.

Chapter 13

1. *Webster's New World Dictionary of the American Language; Second College Edition,* (The World Publishing Company, 1970), 78.
2. Jack W. Hayford, *The Hayford Bible Handbook,* (Nashville, Tennessee, Thomas Nelson, Inc., 1995), 661.
3. Ibid, 713.

Chapter 14

1. Jack W. Hayford, *The Hayford Bible Handbook* (Nashville, Tennessee, Thomas Nelson, Inc., 1995), 812.
2. Ibid, 737.

Chapter 15

1. *Webster's New World Dictionary of the American Language; Second College Edition,* (The World Publishing Company, 1970), 1526.
2. Don Fleming, *World's Bible Dictionary,* Student Edition (Iowa Falls, IA: World Bible Publishers, Inc., 1990), 176.
3. W.E. Vine, Merril F. Unger, William White Jr., *Vine's Complete Expository Dictionary of Old and New Testament Words,* (Nashville, Tennessee, Thomas Nelson, Inc., 1996), 233.
4. Zodhiates Spiros, *The Complete Word Study Old Testament, Bringing the Original Text to Life,* King James Version #6960 (Chattanooga, TN: AMG Publishers), 2360.

Chapter 16

1. Jack W. Hayford, *The Hayford Bible Handbook* (Nashville, Tennessee, Thomas Nelson, Inc., 1995), 588-589.

Chapter 18

1. W.E. Vine, Merril F. Unger, William White Jr., *Vine's Complete Expository Dictionary of Old and New Testament Words,* (Nashville, Tennessee, Thomas Nelson, Inc., 1996), 110.

2. Ibid, 132.
3. Ibid, 301.
4. Ibid, 330.
5. Ibid, 110
6. Ibid, 603.
7. *Webster's New World Dictionary of the American Language; Second College Edition,* (The World Publishing Company, 1970), 1387.
8. W.E. Vine, Merril F. Unger, William White Jr., *Vine's Complete Expository Dictionary of Old and New Testament Words,* (Nashville, Tennessee, Thomas Nelson, Inc., 1996), 553.
9. Ibid, 478-479,
10. Zodhiates Spiros, *The Complete Word Study New Testament with Parallel Greek King James Version,* #1904, 1909 (Chattanooga, TN: AMG Publishers), 30.

Chapter 32
1. *Webster's New World Dictionary of the American Language; Second College Edition,* (The World Publishing Company, 1970), 458.

Chapter 36
1. Zodhiates Spiros, *The Complete World Study New Testament with Parallel Greek King James Version,* #5215 (Chattanooga, TN: AMG Publishers), 942.
2. Ibid, #5215, 942.
3. Ibid, #4152, #5603, 931, 947.
4. Ibid, #2168, 906.

Chapter 38
1. W.E. Vine, Merril F. Unger, William White Jr., *Vine's Complete Expository Dictionary of Old and New Testament Words,* (Nashville, Tennessee, Thomas Nelson, Inc., 1996), 481.

Chapter 41
1. W.E. Vine, Merril F. Unger, William White Jr., *Vine's Complete Expository Dictionary of Old and New Testament Words,* (Nashville, Tennessee, Thomas Nelson, Inc., 1996), 307.
2. Ibid, 498.

Chapter 50
1. W.E. Vine, Merril F. Unger, William White Jr., *Vine's Complete Expository Dictionary of Old and New Testament Words,* (Nashville, Tennessee, Thomas Nelson, Inc., 1996), 1-2